JEWS AND CHRISTIANS IN CONVERSATION

Crossing Cultures
and Generations

Edited by

E. Kessler, J. T. Pawlikowski, and J. Banki

First published in 2002 by Orchard Academic, 16 Orchard Street, Cambridge, CB1 1JT

Typeset and designed by Jane Doyle

©the authors

ISBN 1903283094 (paper)
ISBN 1903283108 (cloth)

To Cardinal Joseph Bernardin for making Catholic-Jewish relations a central part of his episcopal ministry

In appreciation of Paul Banki and Susan, for their support and understanding, and to the memory of Rabbi Marc H. Tanenbaum, a pioneer, scholar and activist on behalf of interreligious understanding and cooperation.

To Shoshana, Asher and Eliana, a source of joy and of hope for the next generation.

CONTENTS

CONVERSATION SEVEN
The Road Ahead: The Next Generation Speaks

ACKNOWLEDGEMENTS

This book emerged from a consultation in March, 2001 in Cambridge, England, conceived, organized and co-sponsored by The Joseph Cardinal Bernardin Center at the Catholic Theological Union, Chicago; the Tanenbaum Center for Interreligious Understanding, New York; and The Centre for Jewish-Christian Relations, Cambridge. We express our grateful thanks to these organisations for their support.

We would also like to thank the Sir Halley Stewart Trust and the Fourth World Foundation. In addition, we are grateful for the assistance of Nicholas James Stirk who helped prepare the manuscript and for the encouragement of Justin Meggitt of Orchard Academic.

Publisher's Note

The editors of this volume have retained the referencing style adopted by each contributor.

CONTRIBUTORS

James Aitken
University of Reading and Centre for Jewish-Christian Relations
Barbara Bowe, R.S.C.J.
Catholic Theological Union, Chicago
Marcus Braybrooke
World Congress of Faiths, Oxford
Judith Hershcopf Banki
Tanenbaum Center for Interreligious Understanding, New York
Martin Forward
Centre for Faith and Action, Aurora University
Helen Fry
London
Konstanty Gebert
Midrasz, Warsaw
Edward Kessler
Centre for Jewish-Christian Relations and Cambridge University
Clifford Longley
The Tablet, London
Jürgen Manemann
Institut für Fundamentaltheologie, Münster
John T. Pawlikowski, O.S.M.
Catholic Theological Union, Chicago
Richard L. Rubenstein
University of Bridgeport, Connecticut
David Fox Sandmel
Chicago
Marc Saperstein
George Washington University, Washington
Michael A. Signer
University of Notre Dame, Indiana
Liam Tracey, O.S.M.
Servite Priory, Dublin
Melanie J. Wright
Centre for Jewish-Christian Relations and Cambridge University

Introduction

The transformation in the relationship between Judaism and Christianity is a recent development – indeed, for some, it is still within living memory. This book brings together those who have been involved in the transformation, have set the agenda of dialogue since World War II with those who are beginning to make their voices heard – in other words, with the next generation. The editors decided to ask the pioneers of the Jewish-Christian dialogue from the USA, Europe and Israel to meet with its younger leaders in Cambridge in March 2001. The meeting allowed the pioneers to listen and respond to the views of a new generation of scholars, teachers and activists who are raising and exploring questions of their own. This collection of papers is therefore the outcome of a meeting between generations and cultures.

The book addresses not only to what extent views vary between the generations but also highlights the diversity of issues which concern Americans and Europeans. Indeed, the reader may notice a greater difference between the latter than the former. The post-World War II pioneers of Jewish-Christian dialogue share many of the same views as the next generation. However, there is a striking difference between North American concerns and those in Europe. To a certain extent, American optimism and hope contrast with European scepticism and uncertainty.

The significance of the international and cross-generational aspects of Jewish-Christian dialogue is particularly important because of increasing globalisation. In the words of Martin Luther King, "we are caught in an inescapable network of mutuality. Whatever affects one directly affects all indirectly". Greater awareness of globalisation and of the resulting massive historical shift has implications for Jewish-Christian relations. As our society, economy, politics and so on, are moving global, so must Jewish-Christian dialogue.

In sum, this book tackles three significant topics in the present day Jewish-Christian dialogue:

Cross generational concerns
Inter continental differences
Issues associated with globalisation

*****

The word "dialogue" has often been both misconstrued and ill-defined. A casual conversation between Jews and Christians that may add up to no more than a loose restatement of entrenched theological positions is sometimes claimed as dialogue. Any communication between persons of two differing religious points of view that does not involve a genuine hearing of the other is all too easily claimed as dialogue. In addition, dialogue is used in a haphazard way as almost an umbrella term to cover a whole host of related word activities that are good in themselves, some of them even providing an essential framework for dialogue, but are not the equivalent to dialogue. For example, some adopt the term Jewish-Christian relations as synonymous with dialogue. You can after all have good or bad relations. However, the term 'relations' is not the equivalent of dialogue; nor does dialogue consist of the comparative study of religions.

In reality, dialogue consists of a direct meeting of people and involves a reciprocal exposing of the full religious consciousness of the one with the "Other". Dialogue speaks to the Other with a full respect of what the Other is and has to say. This is never less than personal but can develop in such a way as to be extended to a group and even to communities. However, it begins with the individual and not with the community. This book is an outcome of personal encounters which took place in Cambridge and describes the dialogue between individuals – a dialogue which contains lessons for the wider community.

That such an encounter occurred at all illustrates the great transformation which has taken place. Indeed, the changes in Jewish-Christian relations are one of the few pieces of good news that can be reported in today's world. The dramatic change in understanding and respect between Christianity and Judaism has occurred first, as a result of the Shoah (Holocaust), and an awareness of the Christian contribution to antisemitism; second, as a result of the establishment of the State of

Israel; third, as a result of the Statements issued by religious institutions, initially by the Christian partners in dialogue and most recently by the Jewish side.

The Shoah resulted in a general awareness of the immensity of the burden of guilt which the Church carried not only for failing to speak out publicly, with some noble exceptions during 1933-45, but also because of the 'teaching of contempt' towards Jews and Judaism which it carried on for so many centuries. As Jules Isaac showed immediately after the war, it was this that sowed the seeds of hatred and made it so easy for Hitler to use antisemitism as a political weapon. Although no one would deny that Nazism was opposed to Christianity, it is well-known that Hitler often justified his antisemitism with reference to the Church and Christian attitudes towards Judaism.

As a result of the soul searching which took place after 1945, many Christians began the painful process of re-examining the sources of the teaching of contempt and repudiating them. This process is often mentioned in the forewords and introductions of modern Christian writings on Jews and Judaism, many of which begin with a personal reflection on this reality. Christianity has shifted from what was, for the most part, an inherent need to condemn Judaism to one of a condemnation of Christian anti-Judaism. This has not led to a separation from all things Jewish but in fact, to a closer relationship with "the elder brother".

The Shoah not only caused Christianity to reassess its relationship with Judaism but also stirred greater Jewish interest in Christianity. Jonathan Sacks spoke for many when he stated that, "today we meet and talk together because we must; because we have considered the alternative and seen where it ends and we are shocked to the core by what we have seen". On the Jewish side there was a need to overcome an infantile understanding of Christianity and most significantly, to confront the mark that anti-semitism has left on the Jewish psyche.

The need to tackle the Shoah in Jewish-Christian dialogue is self-evident but there are dangers if it is not conducted in perspective. Fackenheim's proclamation that the Shoah resulted in a new commandment, the 614th, which stressed that it was incumbent upon Jews to survive as Jews, is a case in point. According to Fackenheim one remained a Jew so as not to provide Hitler a posthumous victory. However, for some, Jewish identity has become Shoah centred as has Jewish-Christian dialogue. The danger is that by focusing solely on the Holocaust Jews and Christians will gain a distorted view. For example, a young Jew will construct a negative Jewish identity, which without the positive side of Judaism, will not be a value to be handed down over the generations. A young Christian will come away with an exclusive picture of the Jew as victim, without an awareness of the positive aspects of Jewish culture.

Whilst reaction to the Shoah is clearly important, dialogue can not be built solely on responses to antisemitism and Christian feelings of guilt. Indeed, no healthy and enduring relationship between people is built on guilt. If recent Christian soul-searching in the aftermath of the destruction of European Jewry leads to a new approach and a revision of traditional anti-Jewish teaching so much the better. However, a strong relationship cannot be built on the foundations of guilt. The sense of guilt of is transient and does not pass to the next generation; moreover, it is unstable, inherently prone to sudden and drastic reversal.

If Jewish-Christian dialogue can no longer be based exclusively on the Shoah and antisemitism, one might consider the second cause for the transformation in relations as an alternative - the establishment of the State of Israel. There is little doubt that whilst the Church has for some years been grappling with issues related to Christian antisemitism, attitudes towards the Land and State of Israel have, from the theological perspective, proved more difficult to tackle. Simply put, it has been easier for Christians to condemn antisemitism as a misunderstanding of Christian teaching than to come to terms with the re-establishment of the Jewish State. Nevertheless, it is clear that a dramatic shift in Christian thinking is taking place and that there is greater understanding than ever before among many but not all Christians of the significance to Jews of the Land and State of Israel. This is illustrated by the 1994 Vatican recognition of the State as well as the Papal visit in 2000. Christians are now called to accept Israel as a focus of Jewish faith and a culmination of age-old longing.

However, a number of tensions still exist such as those which arise out of Christian sympathy with Israel and concern for the Palestinians, some of whom are Christians. In addition, most of the Christian holy places are now in Israel or in Israeli controlled territory. This means that the entire Christian world takes a close interest in the developments, which has led to strong reactions - both of a favourable and unfavourable nature. The very existence of this spotlight shining so strongly on Israel, and especially on Jerusalem, gives particular importance to any attempt at mutual understanding between Christian and Jew, inside Israel. The ongoing conflict in Israel and Palestine (and the tensions in the Middle East in general) indicates the importance of developing relations with the other great monotheistic faith, Islam. Perhaps most difficult of all in their discussions together, Jews, Christians and Muslims have to reckon with a situation in Israel and the Middle East that is constantly changing.

Like the Shoah, there are a number of dangers with basing Jewish-Christian dialogue primarily on Israel. For example, it is extremely problematic to argue that what was once an interpretation about the nature of the biblical word and promise is now in the situation of Israel concretised in a contemporary event. The challenge to Jewish-Christian dialogue as a result of an emphasis on fulfilment of biblical prophecy can be seen in the writings of some evangelical Christians as well as fundamentalist Jews. What happened a hundred years ago to the Jews outside of Israel is considered by some as historically remote compared to biblical events, which are viewed as almost contemporary.

The dangers of basing Jewish-Christian dialogue primarily on Israel are also illustrated by those who, in the name of dialogue, move from a position of commitment for the well being of Israel to one of almost Israel can do no wrong. This is not conducive to dialogue for it is not an honest and sober conversation firmly related to present realities.

Although both Israel and the Shoah and Christian antisemitism have contributed significantly to the dramatic changes in the relationship between Judaism and Christianity in recent years, neither is the basis for the relationship today. The opening chapters by Bowe, Braybrooke and Rubenstein illustrate this important point as they chart the course of Jewish–Christian relations these last 40 years. Barbara Bowe, from Catholic Theological Union in Chicago, discusses the changes through the lens of teaching courses on New Testament. Team teaching the Gospel of John with a Jewish partner has made her more aware of the anti-Judaism in the Gospel and has also helped develop the tools with which to tackle it. In her view, the consequences of Christianity's re-awakening to its Jewish origins is still in the process of being implemented in New Testament studies. As an example she analyses the approach of Christian feminist scholars whose sharp critique of patriarchy has resulted in a new form of anti-Judaism in New Testament scholarship.

Marcus Braybrooke, an Anglican Minister from Oxford, has pioneered Jewish-Christian relations in the UK and under his direction the Council of Christians and Jews grew significantly. Looking back on its development he suggests that Christians should not be tempted to conclude that they have repented sufficiently of the past and put things right with the Jews. He suggests that Jewish-Christian dialogue still has an extremely important role to play in the multi-faith world of dialogue and that there are insights that Christians can only learn from an encounter with Judaism.

In the last of the three opening chapters, Richard Rubenstein offers a personal account of his experience in Jewish-Christian relations and tackles the age-old question of exclusive claims of each religion. In this chapter Rubenstein, a major force in Jewish-Christian relations during the last forty years, offers a personal (and therefore unique) critique of his own life and writings. He takes as his starting point the Shoah and discusses the problem of the 'absolute other' – in other words, the Jew – in some recent theological interpretations.

These three chapters set the scene for the meeting between generations. Each of the following chapters begins with the views of a younger scholar, which are followed by the response of an elder scholar. Edward Kessler, from the Cambridge Centre for Jewish-Christian Relations, considers the institutional statements on Jewish-Christian relations and charts their development. He points out that although open and direct consultations have taken place, formal declarations and guidelines have been issued, something is missing – the implementation of these statements in communal life. He calls for the implementation of the guidelines at regional levels. Although no-one can doubt that the Church today has a far more constructive and benevolent attitude to Jews and Judaism than ever before, he asks how long will it take for the new teachings to percolate down from the Vatican to the pew. A similar question can be asked about the teaching of faiths in the synagogue.

John Pawlikowski, from the Catholic Theological Union, in response, agrees that the documents remain marginal to the majority of Jews and Christians because they have not been properly digested. He argues that whenever self-identity is discussed, the Jewish-Christian encounter should be mentioned. This is not presently the case, from the Christian perspective, in the fields of christology and liturgy. He also believes that Christian tackling of the Shoah the Church has yet to come to terms with the fact that many Christians espoused antisemitic views because that is what they honestly believed the church was telling them to believe.

The next chapter, by David Sandmel, from Chicago, offers a detailed analysis of *Dabru Emet*, issued in September 2000, which is the first detailed modern cross-denominational Jewish statement and which reflects on what Judaism can now say about Christianity. The significance of *Dabru Emet* is highlighted by the lack of other official Jewish statements about the Jewish understanding of Christianity. Although it is understandable that some Jews looked upon dialogue with an element of mistrust, perhaps viewing it as a veiled attempt at Christian conversion, Christian partners in dialogue were beginning to say, 'we have made many changes and offered new thinking, isn't it your turn now, to respond?' *Dabru Emet*, marks the response and, like *Nostra Aetate* is a milestone in the Jewish-Christian relationship. For the first time in the modern era, Jewish thinkers have not only begun to face the world of contemporary Christian ideas but also to develop a Jewish theology of Christianity.

Jürgen Manemann, from Münster, challenges the temptation to reject tradition in order to better society. In his view religions based on tradition, institution and community have an important role to play for they enable us to become human. A society without these features will enable us to march forward into inhumanity – this is the contemporary lesson of the Holocaust for Jews and Christians. What is required is not overcoming tradition but the return to a state of challenging and being challenged by tradition – in other words, allowing each generation to change and be changed by tradition.

Michael Signer, from the University of Notre Dame, continues this discussion in his response to Manemann and places modernism and tradition side by side. He applies the Jewish canon as a lens for interpreting tradition and suggests that each section of the Hebrew Bible – the Torah, Prophets and Writings – provides meaning in the search for the place of tradition in Jewish-Christian dialogue. The Torah informs both the 'what must I do' with the 'why must I do it'. The Prophets bring out societal responsibilities and the Writings allow us to develop the identity of the individual and the community.

The relationship of Scripture to Tradition is reminiscent of a story concerning a conversation between Hillel and a prospective convert to Judaism who had informed Hillel that he was prepared to accept the Written Torah but not the Oral Torah i.e., only the text itself, not the rabbinic interpretations. Whereupon Hillel proceeded to instruct him in the meaning of the letters differently that he had done previously i.e., yesterday's letter *aleph* became today's *bet* and vice versa. When the prospective candidate protested that previously Hillel had taught the opposite, Hillel replied, 'You see, no text speaks for itself. You cannot make sense of a text without recourse to some tradition as to how a text should be read'. (Shabbat 31a) Thus scriptural texts do not speak by themselves but need to be interpreted and historically Jews and Christians have based their interpretations on their traditions.

The dramatic changes in Jewish-Christian relations are matched by the changes in European political boundaries. 1989 marked a significant turning point in European history as communist governments in Central and Eastern Europe began to collapse. The media played a key role in these changes and became the conduit through which democracy and prosperity were promised. Today the euphoria has vanished and the promises have yet to be redeemed but the role of the media remains as important as ever. The next section considers how the media has become both a forum within which Jewish-Christian dialogue is presented as well as a stimulus for further dialogue. Konstanty Gebert, a Polish journalist, makes it clear that although superficially, the problems in central and eastern Europe are economic they cannot be isolated from social, political and moral ones. He takes as an example the recent discovery of the 1941 wartime massacre of 1500 Jews in Jedwabne by their Polish Catholic neighbours and discusses its implications for Jewish-Christian relations in Poland. His contribution points to the possibility of a more constructive relationship and implies – albeit in a tantalising way – that Christian-Jewish relations may lie at the heart of the transformation of Europe.

Get it right, and we can entertain a rosy vision of the new Europe, one in which ethnic and religious diversity are the foundation for a cohesive social life within which Jews and Christians can flourish. Get it wrong, and that very same ethnic and religious diversity will destroy society and frustrate economic progress, as we have seen already in the former Yugoslavia.

Clifford Longley, UK journalist, examines the dangers of over-simplification in the media. He takes as an example the phrase 'Polish-Jewish relations'. The term "Pole" seems to be used almost as an everyday synonym for Catholic and in Poland does not seem to be claimed by or applied to the Jews. Yet from the outside, the Polish national community both in 1941 and now consisted and consists of both Catholics and Jews. Are not Polish Jews Poles? Is there no real identification of the Jewish community as part of the Polish nation? Longley writes as someone who regards himself as fully Catholic and fully English, who would not dream of suggesting, and would be deeply shocked to hear it suggested by others, that Jews cannot be just as English as he is. Longley concludes by comparing the situation in Poland to Northern Ireland where Poles were the Protestants (the 'civilised' majority), and the Jews were the Catholics (the 'looked-down-upon' minority).

The role of liturgy, like tradition, is often played down in contemporary Jewish-Christian dialogue. Liam Tracey, from Maynooth, near Dublin, considers the Christian understanding of worship and liturgy in the present day. He challenges the accepted opinion of the existence of a common Christian experience of worship. In his view, the relationship between liturgy and cultures still has to be worked out. Tracey's argument is considered by Marc Saperstein, from the George Washington University, and applied to the American Reform Jewish experience. He questions, for example, how Jews can claim a special relationship with God in prayer (for example, "You have chosen us from among all peoples...") and at the same time include the whole human family as part of God's people. The tension arises between including the family in prayer – in other words, the Jewish people – and including all of humanity.

This tension provides the context for the next section on the relations between Judaism, Christianity and other faiths and deals with the issue of what might be described as "particularities of faith"- in other words, those points which Christians and Jews claim a universal significance and finality. From a Jewish perspective they include, for example, an emphasis on Torah, the conviction that Israel's covenant with God remains and that the Jewish attachment to the Land of Israel has divine sanction. From the Christian perspective, they include the Christian conviction that in the life, death and resurrection of Jesus God acted decisively for all humanity and that Christ is Lord of all and the Saviour of all. These claims apply not only to the Jewish-Christian dialogue but also to the dialogue with other faiths.

James Aitken, from Reading University and the Cambridge Centre for Jewish-Christian Relations, cites Gadamer's 'fusions of horizons' as a way forward. He calls for an appreciation of the worth of other faiths without simply judging them from our own standards. He points out that the values in religions allow for transition between different stages such as movement between minority and majority status in different places and at different times. Aitken's paper shows that dialogue cannot simply be limited to the areas of common ground, though these will always provide a bridge.

Genuine dialogue will not be prevented by the acknowledgement of the particularities of faith and the assumption of each partner in dialogue that the ultimate and deepest insight into God's purpose lie on its side. Dialogue must also take into account the ever changing identity of each group in society.

In response, Judith Banki, from the Tanenbaum Center for Interreligious Understanding in New York, agrees that the lessons of the Jewish-Christian dialogue need to be applied to the wider interfaith dialogue(s), but that there remains an important place for the Jewish-Christian dialogue. She notes the tension between the universal (in other words, multi-faith dialogue) and the particular (in other words, the Jewish-Christian dialogue) and warns against applying too many particular questions to universal themes. She argues that many questions are relevant only to the Jewish-Christian relationship and require a Jewish-Christian response, citing the Christian roots of antisemitism as one example.

The book concludes with three papers from younger scholars, who raise questions about the future direction of Jewish-Christian dialogue. Melanie Wright, from the Cambridge Centre for Jewish-Christian Relations, points out that dialogue is an activity to be experienced and lived as much as talked about, lectured on, analysed and appraised. She warns of the danger of conflating between the activist who is actually involved in dialogue and the academic who studies the dialogue. There is presently, she argues, a confusion of terminology. She calls for the creation of a new field of study, that of Jewish–Christian relations, which needs to keep pace with developments in other academic fields. Such a field will use the tools and insights from a range of different disciplines. In her view it is essential to separate the two although an individual can adopt both activist and academic roles. It will take a new degree of maturity to let them co-exist without pretending that they are identical. She also emphasises the importance of bringing into the discussion people, whose voices remain unheard, marginalized or ignored.

Helen Fry, from London, identifies three areas in need of particular attention. Firstly, there is a need for Jewish-Christian dialogue to take into account women's voices. On the one hand, she points to women's story-telling as a positive way of 'dialoguing' but on the other hand, she highlights the dangers of stereotyping the status of women in Judaism,. Secondly, she discusses the issue of Christology and the associated topic, mission. She calls for a shift in Christian understanding of salvation in relation to Jews. Thirdly, Fry points to problems which remain outstanding in Christian liturgy and preaching and suggests that the encounter with *the Other* must result in changes.

In the final chapter, Martin Forward, Director of the Center for Faith and Action in Aurora, Illinois, picks out a number of themes from the previous chapters, which he suggests may provide the basis for future conversations. He points out that dialogue is not simply about respect and tolerance but also about revealing clear differences and considering the difficult issues. Too often a 'safe' subject is chosen for discussion and whilst Jewish-Christian dialogue has achieved a great deal in recent years – Forward offers an intriguing list of what Jewish-Christian dialogue has achieved and what it can offer to others involved in inter-religious dialogue – it should not avoid attempting to tackle the challenging, and even dangerous, questions.

Conversation One

The Road We Have Taken: Forty Years
of Christian-Jewish Dialogue

From Guarded Turf to Common Ground: biblical terrain and contemporary dialogue among Jews and Christians

Barbara E. Bowe

In the past Fall Quarter at Catholic Theological Union in Chicago I had the wonderful experience of team teaching a graduate course on the Gospel of John with Professor Sarah Tanzer of McCormick Theological Seminary, the Presbyterian seminary in Chicago. For years Sarah and I had looked for an opportunity to teach John together since we are good friends and had been graduate students at the same time in the mid-80s at Harvard University; in fact we had studied the Gospel of John together. Sarah is a Jewish scholar, who like myself has earned a doctorate in New Testament studies. With a class of thirty-five students (half Roman Catholic, half Presbyterian), we set about to explore this multi-faceted and difficult text and to alert our Christian students to the minefield of Jewish-Christian issues it contains. In dialogue with Sarah, I found each class to be a mutual learning experience and a modelling of what we hoped our students might learn: mutual respect and appreciation for the intertwining of our Jewish and Christian traditions, a sharper awareness of the anti-Judaism that saturates this "gospel of love," and a commitment to teach and preach this text differently in Christian assemblies. Together we could explore, not just the ancient text itself, but its impact on generations of Jews and Christians before us and up to our own time. Ours was both a serious and sometimes a playful exchange, for example when Sarah would delight in irreverently demystifying the character of the Beloved Disciple in John by referring to him as "Mr. Goodie Two-Shoes." In a more serious vein, our exchanges wrestled with the perennial problem of how to translate and, more importantly, how to understand John's repeated, and often hostile reference to the *ho Ioudaioi* (the Jews?, the Jewish authorities?, the Judeans?) throughout the gospel, or how to explain and contextualize the bitterly caustic remarks in John 8 that culminate with Jesus' accusation to his Jewish audience: "You are of your father the Devil" (John 8:44). Texts like these had to be dissected and disarmed. Without a Jewish interpretive voice, such an agenda limps on one-legged limbs. But together — our two voices could explore, disagree and dialogue in a most helpful fashion. I hope never to have to teach John again without it.

This recent experience has enriched both my scholarship and my teaching. But more than that, it reminds me that I have benefited — at both a personal and an institutional level — from a different climate of cooperation and dialogue between Jew and Christian than many of my predecessors enjoyed. To describe this present climate, and to trace the contours of its scope in the field of biblical studies, I want to address briefly four distinct areas under the following headings: 1) Players in the Field, 2) At last, a Jewish Jesus, 3) the Ethics of Feminism in a Jewish Key, and 4) Siblings All.

Players in the Field

On December 27, 1961 the then President of the Society of Biblical Literature delivered his Presidential Address to the annual meeting of the Society. The President's name was Samuel Sandmel, the distinguished Jewish professor of New Testament at Hebrew Union College and the Jewish Institute of Religion. Sandmel concluded his presidential remarks with the following observation:

> Two hundred years ago Christians and Jews and Roman Catholics and Protestants seldom read each other's books, and almost never met together to exchange views and opinions on academic matters related to religious documents. Even a hundred years ago such cross-fertilization or meeting was rare. In our ninety-seventh meeting we take it as a norm for us to read each other's writings and to meet together, debate with each other, and agree or disagree with each other in small or large matters of scholarship. The legacy from past centuries, of misunderstanding and even animosity, has all but been dissolved in the framework of our organization. Would that humanity at large could achieve what has been achieved in our Society.[1]

It is now forty years since Professor Sandmel's address and in the interim his words have become all the more true. The players in the field of biblical study, and in particular those who study the Christian writings, now include for every facet of early Christian experience essential Jewish voices without which no serious scholar can claim credibility. For example, who would think of speaking or writing on the apostle Paul today without engaging Alan Segal's, *Paul the Convert?* Who could explore the Galilean setting of Jesus' day without the insights of Shaye Cohen? Who would study early Christian prayer without learning from the work of Reuven Kimelman on the *Amidah?* Is there a commentary on Matthew's gospel that fails to dialogue with the astute critique of Amy Jill Levine, or does anyone write on the gospel of John without attending to the voice of Adele Reinhartz? No portrait of the Pharisees in the Second Testament could be drawn without Ellis Rivkin's brilliant analysis. This list could, no doubt, be expanded a hundredfold, but the point is clear. Sandmel's words from 1961 have indeed now become the rule, and we can be grateful for such a state of affairs.

At Last, a Jewish Jesus

A second indicator of the state of affairs in Jewish – Christian dialogue in the world of Second Testament studies is illustrated by the titles of two recent books, one by the distinguished Jewish, Oxford scholar Geza Vermes entitled *Jesus the Jew: A Historian's Reading of the Gospels*[2], published in 1981and the other by an American Roman Catholic, John Meier, entitled *A Marginal Jew. Rethinking the Historical Jesus*,[3] with two volumes already in print (1991 & 1994), a third volume in press and a final volume still in the author's pen. No matter what the on-going and often contentious Christian "Third Quest" for the historical Jesus will finally yield, for the great majority of scholars, some form of a thoroughly Jewish Jesus is here to stay.

But *what kind of* Judaism and *what kind of* Jewish Jesus do these, and a myriad other historical studies provide? The answer, of course, is not one but many. In Vermes for example, we encounter Jesus as a Galilean, charismatic holy man no different from his counterparts, Hannina ben Dosa or Honi the Circle-Drawer. In Meier, we find an emerging (but still unfinished) portrait of an eschatological prophet, an apprentice to John the Baptist, a Jewish reformer who took up the mantle of Elijah and announced the good news of God's imminent and future coming. Both these portraits stand in stark contrast to the wandering Cynic preacher of Burton Mack[4] or even to the wandering Jewish Cynic of John Dominic Crossan.[5]

Crucial issues are at stake here for both Christian and Jew. How do we characterize the rich diversity of Palestinian Judaism in the 1st century C.E., and where exactly does Jesus fit in that picture? In an insightful essay on the Jewishness of Jesus for a volume of the same name edited by James Charlesworth, Dan Harrington identifies a second key method-ological issue at stake in the question of Jesus the Jew[6], namely, how to assess the sources themselves. On the Jewish side, sources for Jesus are scant. In Harrington's words, "the few talmudic passages and the *Toledot Jeshu* tradition are fascinating examples of religious parody and polemic but tell us practically nothing of any value for understanding Jesus in the first century C. E."[7] The references to Jesus in Josephus (*Ant* 18.3.3 §63–64) are most likely interpolation. And so we are left with the four gospels of the Second Testament.

Reclaiming a Jewish Jesus in these texts, however, demands that we jettison the former well-used criterion of "dissimilarity or discontinuity" which stated that a saying or deed of Jesus could be claimed as more authentic if it were unique and could not be explained by the language or practice of either Judaism or the early Church. To hold to such a criterion is to envision a Jesus so unique as to transcend his own culture entirely.[8] And yet, a different but related problem arises if one accepts the opposite premise using a criterion of similarity and continuity. By that token, Jesus is a loyal and observant Jew and "whatever differs from Judaism is dismissed as uninteresting or unimportant or simply mistaken."[9] Or, in the words of Claude G. Montefiore: "His teaching, where good, was not original, and where original was not Jewish or good."[10]

A claim for the Jewishness of Jesus in our day invites Christian and Jew to continue the dialogue that will, one hopes, lead to a more nuanced position, midway between either of these extremes of absolute dissimilarity or complete similarity.

The Ethics of Feminism in a Jewish Key

In thinking of the many ways that scriptural scholarship has changed in the last several decades because of the renewed commitment to Jewish-Christian dialogue, I could not overlook the intense and sometimes heated debates among Jewish and Christian feminists that have changed the landscape of feminist biblical studies. As the second wave of Christian feminist biblical scholars gathered steam in the late 70's and 80's, their sharp critique both of patriarchy and of the exclusion of women from the mainstream of Christian leadership and ministry took a sometimes unconscious, but not-so innocent, turn. In the words of Judith Plaskow, "The impulse to vindicate Christianity by laying its patriarchal elements at the feet of Judaism seems to have emerged along with Christian feminist interpretation. . . ."[11]   This brand of anti-Judaism has taken multiple forms in Christian feminist writing. Katharina von Kellenbach has schematized these forms as: 1) a dualistic pairing of the negative (Jewish) and positive (Christian) through the rubric of the biblical language of "letter and spirit, works versus faith, particularism versus universalism," 2) the persistent scape-goating or blame placed at the feet of Jews for the death of Jesus, and 3) the rule of formation as *prologue* identifies Judaism with the religion of the so-called "Old Testament" and thus with Christian pre-history. Each of these perspectives merely undergirds a pernicious form of supersessionism in a feminist key.[12] Playing the name game with references like "late Judaism" only serves to underscore the claim that everything before Christ was prelude and prehistory.

The anti-Judaism of feminist writings was particularly evident in their portraits of Jesus, sketched largely by means of Judaism as a foil. So, as the argument went, where Judaism in Jesus' day restricted women to the private sphere and forbade men to speak to women in public, Jesus interacted freely with the woman of Samaria, counted among his regular company wealthy Jewish women, and reached out to women with healing and forgiveness. Likewise, Jesus transgressed the Jewish purity restrictions by healing the woman with the flow of blood and by extending forgiveness to the woman taken in adultery. With respect to divorce, Jesus is said to have protected women from the harsh Jewish custom of cavalier divorce initiated solely by male prerogative. Those that make the case are fond of caricaturing Hillel's casual ruling that a woman could be divorced if she cooked a poor meal. The problem with this line of argument, of course, as Jewish feminists were quick to point out, is that it is guilty of simplistic and selective use of the Rabbinic sources where texts are selected to support an already established thesis. This is no doubt "proof texting" in a different key.

The same game has been played with Paul so that Robin Scroggs, for example, draws a sharp contrast between the "Jewish Paul" and the "Christian Paul" with respect to his ambivalent position regarding women, with the Jewish Paul antiquated and oppressive and the Christian Paul open to new notions of egalitarian relationships.[13] Where it can be proved by feminist writers that Paul betrayed certain negative Jewish attitudes supporting women's subordination, then these can be rejected as no longer applicable in the new [and implicitly better] "Christian dispensation."

Together with women of color and women of the developing countries, Jewish feminists are challenging white, western feminists to greater honesty and rigor in their approach to texts and traditions about women stemming from first-century Palestine. Plaskow suggests four strategies "toward a more critical feminist hermeneutic": 1) raising consciousness that anti-Judaism persists in feminist writings, 2) making the problem of traditional Christian anti-Judaism a regular dimension of the feminist consciousness and agenda by explicit discussion, teaching and preaching, 3) engaging in serious research in Jewish women's history which, for example, would dispel the exaggerated and inaccurate notion that, in every case, only the male partner could initiate divorce, 4) by retrieving a *Jewish* Jesus who expressed openness to and respect for women which leads to the obvious conclusion that *Judaism* itself was more diverse and multi-faceted on the question of women than we had admitted, and 5) overcoming the "institutional isolation" that exists between Jewish and Christian feminists and both their common, as well as their distinct, agendas.[14] The fruits of the implementation of these strategies remain to be seen in the future.

Siblings All

The final issue I would like to call attention to is the on-going search for a "new paradigm" for the Christian-Jewish relationship. If, as Mary Boys has so eloquently written, the medieval imagery of Synagoga and Ecclesia must be reconceived, if the last vestiges of supersessionism must be abandoned and eradicated, how shall we speak today of the relationship of Jew and Christian and how shall we claim both our common and distinct traditions? This is, of course, first and foremost a deeply biblical question whether we focus on the language of covenant, of blessing, of promise/

fulfilment, or of revelation itself. In the Bernardin Center series of "conversations," of which I was a part, Rabbi Michael Signer proposed that on this question we should listen to the wisdom of Psalm 62:12 - "God has spoken once, we have heard it twice" as a sort of koan pointing toward both our unity and difference at one and the same time.[15] Perhaps leaving the mystery unsolved is the only way. Signer opts for a single covenant language as the best paradigm for ourselves. The other partner in that conversation, John Pawlikowski, maintains that the double covenant terminology "more faithfully represents the reality of the Christian-Jewish relationship both historically and theologically."[16] Nevertheless, one thing is clear, "old and new," whether applied to the covenant language or to the testaments, will no longer do.

To speak of a distinction between "Jew" and "Christian" in the first century of the Common Era is, as we all know, an anachronism. Moreover, if Daniel Boyarin is correct, the boundary between Judaism and emerging Christianity remains entirely porous through the first three centuries and into the fourth. He writes, "The crucial end-point of the emergence of Christianity out of Judaism and thus of Rabbinic Judaism as Judaism *simpliciter* consists of Christianity's establishment as the official religion of the Roman State under Theodosius; i.e., Christian orthodoxy's emergence as a separate socio-cultural entity, a religion, is tied to that juridical event."[17]

In my classes, I have found myself resorting at times to the biological image learned long ago in my biology lab – that of cell division. Mitosis, the creation of two separate entities from one single cell, with the gradual process of nuclear material migrating along lines or spindles, until each entity is a separate living being, seems to suggest both the unity in origin and the gradual distinctness that emerges. Rabbi Perelmuter's fondness for the paradigm of "siblings" also speaks to the dual claim of similarity and difference. The same might be said for Mary Boys' "fraternal twins" model. Each of these stress the 'common origins' dimension of Jewish-Christian relations, but in the words of John Pawlikowski, they fail "to safeguard the unique contribution for Christians of the revelation in Christ. Christianity has something distinctive to offer to the covenantal partnership with Jews."[18] We need to discover new and more adequate paradigms with which both to understand and to speak of our mutual identity. A cross-generational conversation is one step toward our common goal of fruitful dialogue and mutual respect.

Notes

1   Samuel Sandmel, "Parallelomania," *JBL* 81 (1962) 13.
2   Geza Vermes, *Jesus the Jew: A Historian's Reading of the Gospels* (rev. ed. Philadelphia: Fortress, 1981).
3   John P. Meier, *A Marginal Jew. Rethinking the Historical Jesus.* Two Volumes (New York: Doubleday, 1991, 1994). See also in this vein, E. P. Sanders, *Jesus and Judaism* (Philadelphia: Fortress, 1985) and Bart D. Ehrman, *Jesus. Apocalyptic Prophet of the New Millennium* (Oxford: Oxford University Press, 1999).
4   Burton Mack, *The Lost Gospel: The Book of Q and Christian Origins* (San Francisco: Harper Collins, 1993).
5   John Dominic Crossan, *The Historical Jesus. The Life of a Mediterranean Peasant* (San Francisco: Harper Collins, 1991).
6   Daniel J. Harrington, S.J., "The Jewishness of Jesus: Facing Some Problems," in James H. Charlesworth, ed. *Jesus' Jewishness. Exploring the Place of Jesus in Early Judaism* (New York: Crossroad; The American Interfaith Institute, 1991) 123-136.
7   Harrington, "Facing Some Problems," 131.
8   Harrington, "Facing Some Problems," 133.
9   Harrington, "Facing Some Problems," 133.
10 C. G. Montefiore, "Jewish Conceptions of Christianity," *Hibbert Journal* 28 (1929–30) 249; quoted in Harrington, "Facing Some Problems," 133.
11 Judith Plaskow, "Anti-Judaism in Feminist Christian Interpretation," in Elisabeth Schüssler Fiorenza, ed., *Searching the Scriptures.* Vol. 1: A Feminist Introduction (New York: Crossroad, 1993) 117.
12 Katharina von Kellenbach, "Anti-Judaism in Christian-Rooted Feminist Writing: An Analysis of Major U. S. American and West German Feminist Theologians" (Dissertation, Temple University Graduate School, 1990) 57, quoted in Plaskow, "Anti-Judaism,"118.
13 Robin Scroggs, "Paul and the Eschatological Woman,' *JAAR* 40 (1972) 290.

[14] Plaskow, "Anti-Judaism," 124-127.

[15] Michael A. Signer, "One Covenant or Two: Can We Sing a New Song?," in John T. Pawlikowski, O. S. M. and Hayim Goren Perelmuter, editors, *Reinterpreting Revelation and Tradition. Jews and Christians in Conversation* (Franklin, WI: Sheed & Ward, 2000) 3-23.

[16] John T. Pawlikowski, O. S. M., "The Search for a New Paradigm for the Christian-Jewish Relationship: A Response to Michael Signer," in John T. Pawlikowski, O. S. M. and Hayim Goren Perelmuter, editors, *Reinterpreting Revelation and Tradition. Jews and Christians in Conversation* (Franklin, WI: Sheed & Ward, 2000) 41.

[17] Daniel Boyarin, "The Dialogue of Justin Martyr and the Mishna," unpublished paper, Catholic Theological Union, January 26, 2000, 3.

[18] John T. Pawlikowski, O. S. M., "The Search for a New Paradigm for the Christian-Jewish Relationship: A Response to Michael Signer," 41.

Christian-Jewish and Wider Interfaith Dialogue

Marcus Braybrooke

When I became Director of the British Council of Christians and Jews in the early 1980s, I probably knew more about Hinduism than Judaism. Kosher was easy after learning about Brahminical dietary rules!

My interest in wider interfaith dialogue dates back to the nineteen sixties, when I spent a year trying to learn about Hinduism at Madras Christian College and Madras University. On my return I joined the World Congress of Faiths and got to know some Jews who were active in that wider dialogue. I also joined the Council of Christians and Jews (CCJ) and found several of the same Jews and Christians were active in that organisation.

When I became Director of the British CCJ in 1984 I remember receiving a letter from Dr Stanley Samartha, the distinguished Indian Christian theologian, who was then Director of the World Council of Churches Sub-Unit on Dialogue with People of Other Faiths. He said that he hoped I could help to bring the wider dialogue and the Christian-Jewish dialogue together. They seemed often to be separate worlds and I quickly discovered that there were Christians who were keen to affirm that the covenant with Israel was still valid but who had no wish to acknowledge God's presence in other faith traditions.

Indeed it is still a question whether there is a particular bond or whether we locate Judaism with other religions. There is a significant difference between the Vatican and the World Council of Churches. In 1966 Pope Paul VI approved the creation of an office for Catholic-Jewish Relations, which was placed within the Secretariat for promoting Christian Unity. At the World Council of Churches, however, Christian-Jewish Relations were subsumed under the Sub-Unit on Dialogue with People of Living Faiths, although related to this was a special body know as The Consultation on Church and the Jewish People (CCJP).[1]

In my view there is a special relationship - Christians cannot understand their faith without some understanding of its Jewish matrix. This is why I think the suggestion sometimes made in India to replace in the Christian liturgy readings from the Hebrew Bible with readings from the Vedas is wrong. They may be valuable in addition but not instead of the Hebrew Bible. Equally it is right for Christians to recognise that God's covenant with the Jews has never been revoked, but my sympathy is with Rosemary Ruether when she suggests that instead of arguing about how many covenants there are, we should recognise God's presence in every faith community. This, she says, would solve the dilemma of Christian competitive negation of Judaism and other religions by moving to a consistent universalism which would allow every human culture, and its quest for truth and justice, to have its own validity[2]. This implies that we can recognise the special ties that bind Jews and Christians together without suggesting that in some way our two religions are more important to God than other religions. Sikhs, I know, dislike Jews, Christians and Muslims describing themselves as belonging to the three monotheistic faiths. Even Hindus often resent the implication that they are polytheistic.

Yet if as Christians and Jews we do not wish to appear in a privileged position, does this mean we always have to talk to everyone? In a family, it is good on occasion to be all together, but sometimes you want to speak to your wife or husband by yourselves without your children or the in-laws listening. As early as the mid 1980s discussion was underway as to whether the CCJ should become the Council of Christians, Jews and Muslims. In part, the CCJ was seen as a gateway to the establishment, so it was understandable that Muslims also wanted to be involved. However, the British CCJ has rejected that option, so besides CCJ we have the Three Faiths Forum as well as several multi-faith bodies, such as the Inter Faith Network of the UK and the World Congress of Faiths. Theologically there continues to be a special agenda for Christians and Jews and this may get lost in trilateral and multi-lateral organisations. There is in my view a place for bilateral dialogue, trilateral and multi-lateral dialogue. Each has its own dynamic.

In terms of wider interfaith dialogue the last decade has seen significant advances. The 1993 Parliament of Religions at Chicago was a turning point. The process of eradicating prejudice and getting to know the other (although it still is needed) was replaced by the desire to tell the world that religions, instead of causing extremism and conflict, could be a power for peace. Agreement on basic moral values were articulated in the Declaration

"Toward A Global Ethic". This consensus was reaffirmed at the 1999 Parliament of World Religions in Cape Town, which issued *Call to the Guiding Institutions*. This recognised that the moral insights of the world religions will only be applied if people of faith engage in dialogue with politicians, leaders of business, members of the media and with others who shape the future of our planet. This is being recognised by some members of those disciplines. Through the World Faith Development Dialogue, The World Bank now engages in dialogue with thinkers of different faiths. UNESCO has been giving increasing attention to inter-religious dialogue. Then in August 2000, the Secretary General of the United Nations invited one thousand spiritual and religious leaders to a Millennium Peace Summit, which met in the General Assembly Hall of the United Nations. Indeed, one columnist of the New York Times complained of the low level pollution being caused by the reiteration of religious pleas for peace and protection of the environment, as well as by the expensive cars in which religious leaders were driven the few blocks from the UN to the Waldorf Hotel. The emphasis on shared moral values is a significant development and is matched by the willingness of the UN and of some political and economic leaders to take seriously the moral dimension of the enormous problems that face our world society.

Further since 1993, we have seen the creation of the International Peace Council and also the growth of the United Religions Initiative as well as the increasing influence of the World Conference on Religion and Peace. There is also a steady development of local interfaith work. In addition, a growing number of people of different faiths are taking action together in defence of human rights and in helping to heal conflict. The International Peace Council, for example, brought the witness of the religions to the campaign to banish land mines. In a similar way, there are some Jews, Christians and Muslims in Israel/Palestine who continue to work for reconciliation and to speak together for human rights.

Do Jews and Christians have something particular that they can bring together to the search for shared moral values? Is there a Judaeo-Christian ethical tradition? Certainly both religions hold that each individual is made in the divine image and this gives a biblical basis for statements about human rights. Belief in a Creator God and hope for the coming of God's Kingdom also unite Jews and Christians. When I was in India recently, several conversations also made me realise that my non-belief in karma and reincarnation gave me a significantly different perspective to that of

Hindu friends. But even if Jews and Christians do have a perspective which has much in common, I think the search for shared values and for a religious under-pinning of human rights now has to be on a multi-faith basis and indeed in many national societies the search for shared values has to be multi-religious. Interfaith can no longer be an alliance of Catholics, Protestants and Jews.

The importance of multi-faith dialogue, however, does not do away with the continuing importance of Christian-Jewish dialogue. Christians are tempted too quickly to think they have repented for the past and put things right with the Jews. Many people in the churches still have not faced the bitter legacy of anti-Jewish teaching and the penitence that is required. Maybe the annual Holocaust Remembrance Day in the UK will encourage the churches to devote more attention to this, although in Britain the worthy desire to remember all victims of genocide and to condemn all forms of prejudice may mask the specific challenge of the Shoah to Christians. Many Christians are still not aware of the centuries of anti-Jewish teaching by the churches and of attempts to rethink the Christian relationship to Judaism and the Jewish people. Further, Christians dare not forget that bad theology and false teaching are dangerous. This is perhaps a warning that interfaith dialogue cannot be vacuous agreement with all points of view that call themselves religious. There is a danger that truth questions may be avoided in the search for inter-religious harmony, especially with the emphasis in wider interfaith work on the need for practical co-operation for peace, justice and human welfare.

When I became Director of CCJ, theological dialogue was *verboten*. This was because the Orthodox Jewish view was that theological dialogue was improper. Lord Coggan, as Chairman, recognised that CCJ could not be inhibited in this way. Certainly, for Christians a new appreciation of Judaism demands rethinking of many traditional Christian doctrines. For example, to recognise that God's covenant with the Jews is still valid calls in question organised attempts to convert Jews. The emerging picture of the gradual parting of the ways between Church and Synagogue means that Jesus ministry and the development of Christological beliefs have to be seen in a new light. In my recent book[3] I try to contribute to this rethinking and to respond to Shaye J D Cohen's challenge to work out a theology of the other. In his response, which is the final chapter of my book, Rabbi Tony Bayfield indicates that there is also rethinking to be done by Jews.

But there is also need for theological dialogue between Jews and Christians if our relationship is to develop. This was what a small group of liberally minded Rabbis and Clergy tried to do in the Manor House Group. The book *Dialogue with a Difference*[1] is a reflection on that experience. We met two or three times a year for a couple of days each time over a period of nearly ten years. It was a closed group so that relationships could deepen and friendships grow. The trust established allowed each of us to be really honest and to share our wrestling with our own faith tradition. We talked together how we understood the place of scripture and about in what way it was still possible to believe in God after the Shoah. We explored our varying understandings of the meaning and possibility of forgiveness.

I think all of us who were members of that group would acknowledge its lasting influence upon us. When the time came to part, some of us have sought to continue a similar dialogue in a trilateral group of Jews, Christians and Muslims.[5] It soon became clear that this new grouping had its own agenda and had to discover its own way of working. We quickly found that references back to the previous group were unhelpful. Muslims do not engage in the critical study of the Quran in a way which is common to liberal Jews and Christians. In one of the groups to which I belong I think there has slowly developed a similar level of trust and friendship and we have shared our struggle with our traditions, but only slowly and partly through the study of texts are we entering deeper theological dialogue. There has been a more practical emphasis to much of our discussion, for example in talking about the role of religion in modern secular society and in attempting to understand more about fundamentalism and extremism. In the other such group, the discussion has been more academic and we have to some extent hidden behind the papers that we have read.

The deeper dialogue that is so enriching is to begin to discover the spiritual experience that lies beneath the other's tradition of faith. Too seldom do we articulate and share our deepest spiritual convictions. Perhaps we only sense these as we wait together in the presence of the Divine.

For me deeper dialogue is a spiritual and truth-seeking quest. I know that this is unfashionable in these post-modernist days; the emphasis on ethical and practical co-operation has also made quite a lot of interfaith activists impatient with this time-consuming dialogue. I learned in India that the deepest meeting is in the cave of the heart. There we discover the

Spiritual Reality in whom we are one. This means that our growth in spiritual understanding can be nourished by all the great traditions of faith. My hope, while continuing to be a disciple of Christ, is that I might also begin to become a follower of the Buddha, learn from God's word in the Quran and the Torah and sense the oneness taught long ago by the *rishis* of India. Whilst it was India that taught me this approach, it has been in Christian-Jewish dialogue that I have discovered its rich potential and I think there are lessons, which may be relevant to wider interfaith dialogue.[6]

One is how we deal with the evil of the past. Jewish-Christian dialogue has had to confront the horrors of the Shoah. Christians have had to face the painful knowledge of their share in and responsibility for Jewish suffering. A sense of the pain caused and real penitence for it has been an essential step towards a new relationship. This has opened up deep discussion of the meaning of forgiveness and reconciliation. Some of what has been learned is very relevant to the attempt to move on from the conflicts in, say, South Africa and Northern Ireland. The International Interfaith Centre has been involved in discussions in both countries about how religions together can help people move on from a painful past. But religious communities have still much to do in putting right their own relationships. As an outsider, I do not see much evidence that Muslims and Hindus and Sikhs have really grappled with their inheritance of conflict. Until they do, they will be used to foment communalism and strife rather than be agents of healing and reconciliation. There have been some attempts of Japanese religious groups, especially *Rissh Kosei Kai*, to say sorry and to heal the deep wounds caused to their neighbours and to prisoners during the Second World War.

We need the courage to discuss our difference without causing offence. I have listened to several explanations of the law of karma and re-incarnation, but only seldom have I really had the chance to ask a Hindu what this means to him or her personally in his or her view of life. Some of the conversations with Buddhists allow a real discussion of the meaning of the word 'god' and of the existence or non-existence of such a being.

This is to move, however, from a discussion of belief to a sharing of experience. What is it in our personal and spiritual journey that a belief says to us? This points to what I call spiritual dialogue trying to enter into the spiritual experience of the other and allowing the other to enter into ours. In part this means being present at each other's times of prayer and meditation, in part it means giving time to be together in the presence of the Eternal. It was this dimension that I found lacking at the first International Council of Christians and Jews Colloquium that I attended. When I mentioned this, others agreed and so the practise of times of spiritual sharing developed.

Dialogue often seems so full of words, but the deepest meeting in the cave of the heart takes us beyond words into a shared experience of the Divine Mystery, the *Ein Sof* (Without End). That can happen wherever we are fully open to the other – to be the other a Jew, a Christian, a Hindu, a Muslim or a Buddhist. Each relationship has its own dynamic, but each can remind us that we all are made in the image of the one God.

Notes

1   *Dominus Iesus*, however, failed to affirm that Judaism is in a special relationship with Christianity.
2   Rosemary Ruether in *The Holocaust Now*, ed. Steven Jacobs, Cummings and Hathaway 1996, pp. 346-347.
3   Marcus Braybrooke, *Christian-Jewish Dialogue: The Next Steps Forward*, SCM Press 2000.
4   *Dialogue With A Difference*, ed. Tony Bayfield and Marcus Braybrooke, SCM Press 1992.
5   Marcus Braybrooke, *Faith and Interfaith in a Global Age*, CoNexus and Braybrooke Press 1998
6   Alan Race's recent book *Interfaith Encounter*, SCM Press 2001, has a chapter on the relation of Christian-Jewish Dialogue to wider interfaith dialogue.

Forty Years of Jewish-Christian Relations: a personal testimony

Richard L. Rubenstein

From 1970 to the present I have neither followed nor been a participant in the activities of the mainstream American Jewish community save for my synagogue memberships in Tallahassee, Florida and Fairfield, Connecticut. I have, however, been actively involved in dialogue and encounter between Jewish, Christian and Muslim scholars in my own country, Eastern and Western Europe, Asia and the Middle East. I will briefly discuss some aspects of those encounters as well as how I became involved in the theologian's vocation.

I was born in the city of New York in January 1924. My parents were assimilated Jews and my mother was a university graduate, a relatively infrequent occurrence for a woman in those days. My forebears had come to the United States from Vilna, Lithuania in the eighteen-eighties and nineties. My parents were secular Jews who had no interest in the Jewish labor, socialist, or Zionist movements. In the late 1920s and early 1930s my mother spent much time in psychoanalysis and regarded traditional Jewish ritual practices, mistakenly I believe, as irrational and easily dispensable. Hence, I had neither Hebrew training nor a Bar Mitzvah.

I was, however, cognizant of the bitterly intensifying anti-Semitism of the 1930s. We lived in Manhattan's Upper East Side and I was keenly aware of the rise of National Socialism on the European continent and the strong presence of the Nazi German-American Bund in nearby Yorkville. My closest high school friend was an Irish-American youth, Bob Abbott. His mother, a widow, ran a rooming house on East 86th Street in the heart of Yorkville above one of the many German beer halls that were found on that street, all of them profusely decorated with swastikas. I was also aware of a strong current of Irish Catholic anti-Semitism fostered and encouraged by Father Charles E. Coughlin, a famous radio preacher, who was strongly pro-Hitler and who had organized a nation-wide, anti-Semitic movement, the Christian Front. The organization's weekly journal was hawked on street corners throughout New York.

A crucial event in my adolescence occurred one evening when I was set upon and beaten up rather badly by three young Irish hoodlums who had no interest in robbing me but great pleasure in beating up, as they put it, "a God-damn dirty Jew." When I made my way home, my parents called the police. The call was answered by two Irish detectives who demanded to know why I was out so late. I was then about 16 and was returning from a high school event. Their only interest was to find a reason to blame me for the unfortunate affair. As a result of the beating and the detectives' response, I must confess that I developed a hatred of the Irish, save for Bob and his mother, that took years to dispel. Make no mistake about it. Hatred can be a two-way street although, as Friedrich Nietzsche understood, the hatred of the powerless must, of necessity, take covert forms. The incident proved explosive for my personal development. I equated Judaism with powerlessness and, given my non-religious family, saw nothing about it worth preserving. In my ignorance I was under the illusion that Jewish identity was a matter of free choice.

When I was 12 years, old my paternal grandmother, also an assimilated Jew, gave me some money to buy books for my small but growing library. I chose *The Basic Writings of Sigmund Freud* and a two volume edition of Gibbon's *Decline and Fall of the Roman Empire*. I was especially interested in Gibbon's description of the rise of Christianity and spent much time on his discussion of the controversies concerning how Christ was to be understood. At an early age, I was hooked on theology and at 16 I determined to seek out and join a Christian movement with which I could affiliate with minimal intellectual discomfort. Not surprisingly, that turned out to be Unitarianism.

Bob Abbott was just as interested in divesting himself of his Catholic background as I was of my Jewish background. Together we met with Elizabeth Reid, the Youth Minister, of the very upscale All Souls Church, Unitarian, at 80th Street and Lexington Avenue, not far from where I lived. All Souls was not a happy-feeling, liberal Unitarian church such as were to be found in and after the 1960's in the United States. The Church structure is one of the finest, lofty single spire Georgian colonial churches in America, ultimately inspired by London's St. Martin's in the Fields. There was definitely a strong Harvard and Boston connection. In 1936 our minister, Minot Simons, a graduate of Harvard and Harvard Divinity School, was given the singular honor of offering both the opening and the closing prayer at the international ceremonies commemorating Harvard's 300th anniversary. It was very much an establishment church.

Within a short time Bob and I became members and were active in the Youth Group. I also joined the church choir and sang as a member every Sunday. Given my strong interest in religion and my equally strong interest in escaping from Judaism to the imagined safety of Christianity, I decided to become a minister.

When people in the church and in the denomination realized that I was serious, I began to get mixed signals. With a keen sense of social reality, Minot Simons asked me why I had not considered Reform Judaism, given the relatively similar ideas about God in classical Reform Judaism and Unitarianism. I let him know politely but emphatically that I was determined to become a minister. He assured me that he would help me in any way that he could. I have no doubt that he would have.

My network of friends and acquaintances in the Unitarian movement grew rapidly. One of my new acquaintances was Lewis C. Dexter, a professor of sociology whose father was a senior official in the American Unitarian Association. In one of his letters, Dexter, out of a genuine desire to be helpful, wrote that it would be a good idea were I to change my name to one that was less Jewish, preferably Anglo-Saxon, because there was still "residual anti-Semitism" in some Unitarian churches. Dexter's letter was as crucial in my development as was the beating incident. Within 24 hours, I decided that I could not change my name. I had no desire to spend the rest of my life fearing that my true identity might be found out. At a deeper level, I realized that I could not run away from who I was or as I put it "rat on my background."

I stress this incident because it has been the key to my lifelong understanding of my relationship to Judaism. *Judaism is for me a matter of identity, not belief.* It was the way I had been thrust into the world. Had I been thrust into the world as an Irishman, a Pole or a Spaniard I undoubtedly would have seen Roman Catholicism as a crucial aspect of my identity. This sudden and graphic insight was a recognition of my historical and cultural roots, not Jewish nationalism. I was neither ashamed nor proud of being Jewish. It was possible for me to be proud of what I had achieved but not of something to which I had made no active contribution, such as having been born into a particular community. It was also the reason why, as an informed adult, I have never seen greater "truth" in Judaism than any other religion and vice versa.

Through the good offices of friends and with the *hutzpah* that only the totally ignorant could possess, I met with Rabbi Nathan Perilman of Manhattan's Temple Emanu-el, the "cathedral" sanctuary of Reform Judaism, and announced that I wanted to become a Reform Rabbi. He encouraged me and saw to it that I became a member of the Junior Society of Temple Emanu-el. The meeting took place in the late 1930s while I was still a high school student.

The United States entered World War II in December 1941. Fearful that the reform movement would lack rabbis, the faculty of the Hebrew Union College enrolled an unusually large entering class in September 1942. I was one of the new students. I have from time to time thought of the difference between the comfortable life I led during the war and how the war affected millions of European Jews. Under normal circumstances the faculty would have counselled me to delay entrance and spend several years in preparation, but those were not normal times.

When I recollect my years at the Hebrew Union College (1942-1945), I am especially grateful for the training I received from the refugee professors who had held posts at Heidelberg, Marburg, Giessen and other German universities before finding sanctuary at the Hebrew Union College. Like the thousands of other so-called "non-Aryan" and anti-Nazi professors in America's colleges, universities and seminaries, they were responsible for nothing less than a veritable and enduring intellectual and cultural revolution. I am especially indebted to Professors Abraham Joshua Heschel and Professor Samuel Atlas. Both men were the product of the finest in East European and German training.

I did not complete my studies at the Hebrew Union College. The faculty was largely mired in a hopelessly optimistic understanding of religion and man's place in the order of things that had been radically disconfirmed by the Red Army's discovery of the Nazi death camps in 1944. Moreover, most were opposed to the establishment of the State of Israel. Fortunately, the students were more attuned to the needs of the time. My initial reaction was simplistically to regard Germans as a race of monsters but also to recognize in my hatred the seeds of a destructiveness within me that had to be forcefully kept in check. With the demise of my own liberal optimism,

I began a spiritual journey that was to include a year at Brooklyn's Mesivta Chaim Berlin, a transplanted Lithuanian Yeshiva, in preparation for study at the Rabbinical School of the Jewish Theological Seminary in New York. I was encouraged to leave the Hebrew Union College by Abraham Joshua Heschel who himself left the Hebrew Union College to become a professor at the Jewish Theological Seminary.

One of the more interesting programs sponsored by the Seminary was a series of dinner meetings for a small group of JTS students and students from neighboring Union Theological Seminary. The meetings were addressed by a professor from each Seminary. On one occasion the speakers were Paul Johannes Tillich and Mordecai M. Kaplan, founder of the Reconstructionist movement in Judaism and one of the seminary's most influential professors. I was shocked. It was obvious to me that Tillich, a German and a Christian, possessed far greater depth, insight, and sophistication than our favorite professor. Later on, as a graduate student at Harvard, I attended Tillich's lectures on "Classical German Philosophy." They were to become a profound intellectual and theological influence upon me.

I began graduate studies at Harvard immediately upon my ordination and graduation from the seminary in 1952. Although I had been a student at Jewish institutions for eight of the ten years between 1942 and 1952, at no time had I been exposed to a course on Christianity, save for a research paper I had written on Kierkegaard for a Heschel seminar. Living in a fundamentally Christian world, I regarded that omission as a fundamental deficit in my training. I was accepted as a student at Harvard Divinity School. At the time I believe I was the only Jewish student. To support myself and my family, I accepted a position as rabbi of a small congregation in suburban Boston.

My wife at the time and mother of my children, Ellen van der Veen, was born in the Netherlands and was almost the exact same age as Anne Frank. When the Germans invaded Holland on May 10, 1940 her father simply said, "They aim to kill us!" Fortunately, he succeeded in getting his wife and three children on a British minesweeper in the harbor at Ijmuiden that took a shipload of Dutch refugees to safety in the UK.

Ours was not a trouble-free marriage. To save it, both of us undertook psychoanalytic psychotherapy. In the pursuit of personal insight and self-knowledge, I came to understand many things about myself and my role as rabbi. For example, I became aware of a deep and pervasive anti-

Christian hostility on my part in spite of being a student at Harvard Divinity School and maintaining superficially cordial relations with the faculty. Given the Holocaust and the pervasiveness of anti-Semitism, such feelings were hardly surprising. Nevertheless, they were distinctly unhelpful in a free society and were wholly unrelated to the way I was treated at Harvard.

I also learned about some of the things that were *emotionally* at stake in the encounter between Jews and Christians. I have attempted to spell out my views on that subject in *The Religious Imagination*, originally my doctoral dissertation, and *My Brother Paul*, a study of Paul of Tarsus.[1] We cannot go into detail on this occasion, but the Freudian myth of the Primal Crime offered me a clue. Before my encounter with depth psychology, I regarded Christians as the community that believed the Messiah had at least made his initial earthly visit and Jews as the community that either actually or metaphorically looked forward to his coming. Afterwards, I came to realize that the problems were by no means that simple, that issues of profundity and depth were involved in the convergences and separation between the Akedah and the Crucifixion, the Paschal Lamb and the Mystical Lamb, Circumcision and Baptism, the Passover Seder and the Eucharist.

I was especially intrigued by the way Paul of Tarsus explained to the Church at Corinth why most Jews, especially his former colleagues among the Pharisees, could not understand that Jesus is the end and fulfilment of Judaism:

> We do not act as Moses did, who put a veil over his face (so that the people of Israel could not perceive the ultimate significance of that which was to be abolished). But their minds became hardened (and that is why) the same veil remains drawn, even today (in spite of everything) at the reading of the Old Covenant. But until today, every time that Moses is read, a veil lies over their minds. It cannot be removed because it is only through Christ that it is abolished.[2]

When, later on, I became president of a university, there were many occasions when I attended a Christian funeral service for a trustee, faculty member, civic leader, or the close relative of someone with whom I had come into contact. One sentence in the funeral ritual taken from the Fourth Gospel left the deepest impression: *I am the way, the truth, and the life. No man cometh unto the Father but by me.*[3] Given the utter solemnity of the occasion, as well as the mourner's fears and hopes, that single sentence did infinitely more to fix in the minds and hearts of those present the Church's claim to have superseded Judaism than anything in Cardinal Ratzinger's letter of September 16, 2000, *"Dominus Iesus."* Nor do I believe that there is any way that the Christian Church can abandon its message that Jesus Christ has a unique and indispensable role in the salvation of humanity. In this respect, the relationship between Christianity and Judaism is asymmetrical. Judaism asserts that whatever salvation awaits non-Jews is dependent solely upon keeping the seven commandments to Noah, essentially, the moral law. By contrast, Christianity must assert that Christ is indispensable to the salvation of humanity. Nor is symmetry restored if one asserts that Christ bestows his salvation on good people who do not comprehend his nature as do Christians. There is generosity of spirit in such an extension, but it is one that few, if any, non-Christians will regard as anything other than a "kindler, gentler" version of supersessionism. In my own view, except for recent converts, Christianity is, like all other religions, an inheritance and, as such, an indispensable aspect of the believer's identity, not a tradition that is either more or less valid than mine. At the same time, I recognize that none of the great religious traditions can possibly abandon their claims to religious exclusivity.

In the summer of 1960, I visited Europe for the first time with Ellen van der Veen and our very young children. It was the first time she returned to the Amsterdam that she had left so suddenly 20 years earlier. During that summer I made the first of many trips to Germany. While there I came into contact with officials of the *Bundespresseamt,* the Press and Information Office of the German Federal Republic, who invited me to return to Germany the following summer. The date set for the return was Sunday, August 13, 1961.

August 13th was also the day the Berlin wall was suddenly erected. I passed most of the summer of 1961 in the Netherlands. When I learned of the crisis, I delayed entering Germany until Tuesday August 15th. At the urging of the *Bundespresseamt,* I then proceeded immediately to newly-divided Berlin where I had one of the most memorable Jewish-Christian encounters of my entire career, my meeting with Probst Heinrich Grüber, at the time Dean of the Evangelical Church in East and West Berlin and the only German to testify at the trial of Adolf Eichmann that took place in Jerusalem from April to December 1961. Having often written about that meeting, I need not repeat the details. The crucial moment came when Probst Grüber expressed the conviction that, like Nebuchadnezzar,

Hitler was yet another instrument of God's wrath in punishing the Jews at Auschwitz.[4] The dramatic circumstances surrounding that meeting undoubtedly intensified my response which was to define the *Shoah* and the reconstitution of the State of Israel as the fundamental theological problems of our time.

My response was radical and in the mid-nineteen-sixties, I came to be associated with the movement known as "death of God" theology. In October 1965, I was invited to lecture in Warsaw, Lublin and Krakow, Poland under the auspices of the ZNAK group, a Polish Catholic intellectual and religious organization. While in Krakow, I visited Auschwitz, which had yet to become a tourist attraction, for the first time. One month later, in November 1965, I was invited to respond to the paper entitled "Theology and the Contemporary Sensibility" that Professor Thomas J. J. Altizer presented at the conference on America and the Future of Theology at Emory University. Both he and Professor William Hamilton were exploring the meaning of the "death of God" in Christianity. By that time I was attempting a somewhat similar enterprise in Judaism. There were and still are certain parallels between Altizer's thought and mine.[5] Both of us have been profoundly influenced by Paul Johannes Tillich, dialectic mysticism, and one of its most important philosophical expressions, Hegelian philosophy.

Nevertheless, there is much in Altizer's thought that I have never been able to share. For example, I do not share his belief that *Christ is now present in the concrete actuality of our history.* For me the so-called "death," so to speak, of the biblical God of history, covenant and election is a cultural rather than an ontological event. In both the first and second editions of *After Auschwitz*, I made this explicit. Indeed, the final chapter of the second chapter has the title, "God after the Death of God."[6]

To the best of my knowledge, in the nineteen-sixties Altizer did not relate his idea of Christ as present "in the concrete actuality of our history" to the Holocaust. Nor at the time did either William Hamilton or my good friend Harvey Cox address themselves to the Holocaust as a theological issue. On the contrary, Hamilton wrote that "a certain kind of God-rejection with a certain kind of world-affirmation is the point where I join the death-of-God movement."[7] Deeply sensitive both to the unfolding technological civilization and to popular culture, Hamilton asserted that "The death of tragedy is due to the death of the Christian God."[8] In the aftermath of the Holocaust, I was unable to detect the death of tragedy. There was also in both Hamilton and Cox an optimism about technological civilization, identified as "technopolis" by Cox, that I could not possibly share.[9] The Holocaust was simply not an issue for them.

As noted above, my encounter with Altizer came shortly after my first visit to Auschwitz and the Warsaw Ghetto. Moreover, on October 23, 1965 shortly after visiting the ruins of the Warsaw Ghetto, I learned of the death of Paul Johannes Tillich the day before.[10] The day that Tillich died was the very day I first visited Auschwitz. Less than a month later, I was to respond to Altizer in Atlanta for the first time. After Auschwitz and my visit to the ruins of the Warsaw Ghetto, I could not share Altizer's theological mood of celebration. Then as now, I saw Auschwitz as an intrinsic expression of technological civilization.

Nevertheless, I suspect that Auschwitz was implicit in Altizer's thought even then. He is simply too sophisticated a thinker not to have seen the connection between his own version of *Heilsgeschichte* and Auschwitz. Could he have been holding his fire? As a highly controversial, young radical theologian, he had enough on his plate with his proclamation of the "good news" of the "death of God" without adding a polarizing interpretation of the Holocaust shortly after Vatican II with its attempt to restore a measure of healing to Jewish-Christian relations.

By the nineteen-nineties Altizer saw no reason to withhold his distinctive interpretation of the Holocaust. Altizer made the connection fully explicit in the essay, "God as Holy Nothingness" that he contributed to the *Festschrift* presented to me on the occasion of my seventieth birthday.[11] In the essay, Altizer credits me with having grasped "the deep logic of Nazism" as "deicide," the primal human wish to murder God in order to be free of all impediments to unrestrained instinctual gratification.[12] He sees the Germans as motivated by that wish in the Holocaust. According to Altizer, deicide, the murder of God, is the deep ground and logic of the Holocaust, a logic demanding that "the primal victim be the Chosen People of God."[13] Acknowledging that this may be "an insane logic," Altizer nevertheless observes that the logic has become "historically actual in our time, which is truly the time of the death of God.[14]

In his interpretation of the Holocaust, Altizer sees the theme of deicide as related to that of the Divine Infanticide. In deicide the sons seek to murder the Supreme Father; in Divine infanticide, the Father murders the sons. Altizer holds that both are intrinsic to the Holocaust. Regarding the

Nazis as motivated by a deicidal will to power at Auschwitz, Altizer also argues dialectically that the *universal human will to deicide is actually an image of the Creator God's will to self-annihilation and the restoration of the original divine Urgrund.* Thus, the same Godhead is also present as Divine Infanticide at Auschwitz and in his relations with his human progeny. In this connection, Altizer cites my argument in *My Brother Paul,* "that if, as both Paul and the rabbis held, "the wages of sin are death," then God, though he be righteous and just, is the Divine Infanticide."[15]

Altizer takes up this theme and makes it his own, arguing that my conception of the Divine Infanticide is "a naming of that God who is present in the Holocaust, that God who submitted His Chosen People to the most horrible death in history and did so precisely as an expression of his love, for God slays those to whom he gives life."[16] This is a radical Christian view to which I could not possibly give assent. Nevertheless, "insane" though his logic may be, it does possess a certain consistency. If one accepts the view that there was providential divine involvement in the Holocaust, it is difficult to avoid a conclusion somewhat similar to Altizer's. That is why I have consistently rejected the idea of such involvement throughout my entire career.

In his interpretation of the Holocaust, Altizer finds an important place for the concept of *tsimtsum,* the kabbalistic idea of the voluntary self-diminution of Divinity. As noted, he holds that the Creator God, the transcendent God of biblical monotheism, can best be understood as the result of the self-diminution of the original Divine *Urgrund.* In true Gnostic fashion he further suggests that the diminished Godhead is "uniquely the God of Israel" and, as such, the God of the Holocaust. He sees this correlation as the unstated but nevertheless implicit expression of my thinking. Moreover, he claims that *only* if the God of Israel is the God of the Holocaust can one "draw forth" a uniquely Jewish identity whose "pure act" is manifest in the Holocaust as an act of infanticide. It is important to note the double sense in which Altizer uses the term infanticide. He means both the action of the Creator God in slaughtering His Chosen People through the agency of Adolf Hitler and the National Socialist state and the act by which the Creator God eliminated Himself, so to speak, in a reversal of the original *tsimtsum,* thereby making way for an end to both history and the cosmos so that God may be all in all and, as such, the Primordial Nothingness.

Altizer also connects the Creator God and the Holocaust to Israel's original rejection of ancient paganism. That fateful rejection resulted in Israel's coming to know the Creator God, the "God who is God and only God," that is the God of both Scripture and the Holocaust as distinct from the original Divine *Urgrund*. According to Altizer, the God of Israel is present in the Holocaust as an "ultimate and absolute iconoclasm." Just as Israel came to know its God through an initial radical iconoclasm that brought to an end the reign of ancient paganism, a latter-day iconoclasm is inherent in the Holocaust, namely, the self-annihilating iconoclasm of the Creator. In the Holocaust, the presence of the self-annihilating Creator obliterates every memory of Divinity. As a result, "for the first time the silence of God is both absolute and literal." The godless void of the Holocaust thus establishes the "possibility" of a new paganism that only the Jewish people can know. That is because only the Jewish people, whom Altizer characterizes as "the absolute Other" and those non-Jews who were in some way associated with their "otherness" have known the Holocaust. Moreover, only in the deathly silence of the Holocaust could the new paganism have arisen.

With some justice Altizer sees my thought as an expression of the new Jewish paganism, although in recent years I have preferred to emphasize the parallels between my thought and Mahayanna Buddhism rather than nature paganism, as well as my earlier affinities with Lurianic Kabbalism.[17] According to Altizer, I am alleged to have "heard the silence" as the Divine Nothingness that is fully coincident with mysticism's Primordial Nothingness. Altizer argues that the new Jewish paganism, of which I may be one of the very few self-conscious exemplars, is uniquely Jewish in that "it is grounded in the Creator alone," in the sense that it arises out of a Holocaust-motivated rejection of the biblical God of Covenant which, as noted, is simultaneously the self-annihilating movement of the same God. Nevertheless, Altizer argues that the Infanticide of God in the Holocaust is not the Crucifixion of God or Deicide as Christianity has known it. In the Holocaust, the biological sons and daughters are murdered. In the Crucifixion the victim is the "eternally generated Son." According to Altizer, God was present as Death in the Holocaust whereas Christianity has known that same Death as the Crucifixion of God which, as we know, is followed by Resurrection. Altizer further holds that post-exilic Israel has known this Death as its own "eternally repeated death," consummated both in the Holocaust and over and over again in Israel's history. Altizer contends that with the self-inflicted death of Israel's Creator God in the

Holocaust, Israel's history may be coming to an end, making way for the new paganism, even as history itself comes to an end.

When the editors of my *Festschrift* first received Altizer's essay, they questioned its suitability for inclusion in a volume celebrating my life's work. When I learned that I was to be honored with a *Festschrift*, I was asked whether Altizer's essay ought to be included. I encouraged the editors to publish it. In a very important sense, the essay continues the dialogue between us that began at Emory in 1965. We did not agree about important issues then and there was little likelihood that we would now, but I felt strongly that the dialogue should continue.

There is much in Altizer's interpretation of the Holocaust that most Jews would find offensive. Moreover, in characterizing the Jew as the "absolute Other," Altizer comes close to Gnosticism, if he does not actively embrace it. How could the Jew be the "absolute Other" if, as the historic Christian mainstream has maintained, Christians are the "New Israel" and Christ the "end (*teleos*) of the Law" in the double sense of fulfillment and completion? Nevertheless, I have no reason to believe that Altizer writes to offend. In interpreting the Holocaust, he remains what he has been throughout his adult career, a serious and thoroughly radical Christian theologian, arguably one of the most radical Christian theologians of all time. As such, Altizer exhibits a characteristic common to *all* radical theologians. They take religious belief with the utmost seriousness and they do not pretend that the "scandal" of belief can be made less offensive by liberal reinterpretation. In that sense, I remain one of their number.

Given his religious and theological commitments, Altizer must interpret the Holocaust in Christian terms. No matter how sophisticated his apocalyptic, mystical theology may be, he cannot abandon the idea of Israel as the Chosen People, a "witness people" whose continuing travail confirms the truth of Christ's Church. Using the potent intellectual tools at his command, including the history of religion, dialectic theology and the western philosophic tradition, he argues, as did Probst Grüber, for the *providential* character of the slaughter of perhaps 6 million Jewish men, women and children. Yes, even the children, many of whom were subject to the most unspeakable cruelties as the Germans killed them. True to the classical theological tradition that regarded Nebuchadnezzar and Caesar as unwitting agents of the Lord in their respective destruction of Jerusalem, Altizer offers a comparable identification of Adolf Hitler. Here again, Altizer's fundamental purpose appears to be neither malice nor the wish to offend but to carry the logic of his Christian version of biblical religion to its ultimate conclusion. Nor is Altizer lacking in Jewish counterparts. There are many Orthodox Jewish messianists who regard the Holocaust as "the birthpangs of the Messiah," the terrible travail through which Israel must pass on the road to final redemption.

Let me clarify my meaning when I employ the term "providential." I do not refer to a felicitous outcome in or beyond history for any individual or group of individuals. I refer to outcomes that satisfy the conviction that the entire course of history, no matter how blighted or horrible, up to and including the dissolution of all finite entities in the Divine Urgrund, is as it should have been. Perhaps no thinker has expressed this sense of the providential as well as Hegel whose thought on this issue is not unlike Altizer's. Contemplating the course of world history, with its record of crime, suffering and slaughter, Hegel was able to write in utter calm and philosophical detachment:

> In order to justify the course of history, we must try to understand the role of evil in the light of the absolute sovereignty of reason. We are dealing here with the category of the negative….and we cannot fail to notice how all that is finest and noblest in history is immolated on his altar. Reason cannot stop to consider the injuries sustained by single individuals, for particular ends are submerged in universal ends.[18]

For Hegel individual injury is overcome in a universal end. However, Hegel never faced a situation of universal injury such as the Holocaust or the threat of universal extinction in a nuclear holocaust. There is a profound difference between a situation in which some persons suffer and perish unjustly but the group survives and one in which an entire group or even all of humanity perishes. If I read Altizer's apocalyptic correctly, such a universal injury would not be inconsistent with the attainment of the New Jerusalem which for Altizer is the Christian eschatological fulfilment.[19]

There is, of course, no way that Altizer or his Jewish counterparts can be refuted.

They are engaged in the classical theological project of *dissonance reduction.* More than any other modern event, the Holocaust is one that neither Jewish nor Christian thinkers can ignore. By seeing that event as in some sense the deserved fate of the people that rejected Christ, even as Altizer does without resorting to the category of divine punishment, the

Holocaust can serve as a most powerful source of confirmation for Christianity. And, Altizer is by no means alone. By interpreting the event as an apocalyptic prelude to the eschatological Redemption of Israel, Orthodox Jewish messianists find confirmation for their distinctive views. Since neither Altizer nor the Jewish messianists can abandon their respective theologies, the horrors of the Holocaust must be shown to be somehow congruent with their fundamental beliefs. Unfortunately, such theological systems cannot be rendered intelligible across cultural boundaries as can, for example, mathematics, the physical sciences, some of the social sciences and music. That is why they must claim a superordinate source of legitimation for their views in some form of revelation. Put differently, their views lack universality. What, for example, can Altizer's statement, "Christ is now present in the concrete actuality of our history" possibly mean to a Muslim, a Hindu or a Jew? Undoubtedly, a Buddhist, Muslim or Hindu thinker could find a meaning for the idea of Christ in their respective religious systems but it would not be one that knowledgeable Christians could accept. Much as I respect Karl Barth as a theologian, I am at a loss to find in his writings anything fundamental addressed to non-Christians, save perhaps the implicit invitation to non-believers to abandon their darkness and enter the magic circle of belief. I have a somewhat similar experience reading Altizer albeit without detecting a comparable invitation to join. Nor would I be surprised were Christian thinkers to tell me that they fail to find any symmetry between the world of everyday human activity and the claim of Jewish messianists that the Holocaust can best be understood as the birthpangs of the Messiah.

Theological ideas can and do have profound consequences in the real world. During World War II, the view of the Jew as the "absolute Other" was widely shared by those who were convinced that European civilization would never be whole as long as it was polluted by the presence of emancipated Jews capable of influencing that civilization from within. Unlike Altizer the thinker, many of those people had the decision-making power necessary to eliminate the "absolute Other." And so they did, as long as they were able. Let us not forget that within Christianity the "absolute Other" of Christ is either the Devil or the Anti-Christ and that Hitler was by no means alone in considering the Jews to be the "absolute Other" whose elimination was unconditionally necessary in order restore the cultural and spiritual health not only to Germany but to the European civilization the Germans claimed they were defending. Let me make myself absolutely clear. I am not even remotely suggesting that Altizer is in any way motivated by sympathy for the National Socialist project. I simply want to point out that ideas have a life of their own that often escape their author's intentions. I suspect that is why in the aftermath of the Holocaust many thinkers refrain from interpreting Jews and Judaism in the manner that had been customary in their religious tradition. Nevertheless, there is a certain kind of theological consistency in Altizer's interpretation of the Holocaust. Moreover, he makes it abundantly clear in almost every sentence that he regards the pain endured by the victims as terrible in the extreme. That, however, does not and cannot alter his judgment that the catastrophe was both providential and inevitable.

In May 1993 I visited wartime Serbia and Croatia, meeting with both Metropolitan Pavlos, the Primate of the Serbian Orthodox Church, and Franjo Cardinal Kuharic, the Primate of the Roman Catholic Church in Croatia. What I witnessed there was a triangular Holy War -- not in the sense that an attempt was being made to enforce religious belief, such as was the case in the Inquisition -- but to expel or exterminate those who do not share the cultural identity that flows from a shared religious inheritance. That experience deepened my understanding of the Holocaust. I came to see the Holocaust as including elements of a Holy War whose fundamental objective was the elimination of Jews as a demographic and cultural presence in European Christendom.[20] I must confess that I did not see this clearly for a very long time because of the strongly anti-Christian elements in National Socialist Ideology.

If one seeks a theological motive for the *Shoah*, one need look no further than Altizer's definition of the Jew as the "*absolute* Other." No other characterization so clearly or so totally defines the Jew as a malignant, demonic presence whose presence in any form could no longer be tolerated within European Christendom, especially after the Bolshevik Revolution that was widely interpreted as a Jewish assault on European Christendom. Insofar as the Gnostic perception of absolute Jewish otherness was and is widespread, it is confined solely to Christianity for no other religion identifies Jews as deicides. Moreover, Jews have no comparable sense of absolute Christian otherness because they do not regard Christians as uniquely murderers of God.

Why bring up Altizer's theology? It can rightly be dismissed as an heretical aberration wholly outside of the Christian mainstream that has sought, at least since Vatican II, to foster better Jewish-Christian understanding and dialogue. By definition, there can be no dialogue with the "absolute other." Indeed, the Gnostic elements in Altizer have historically been rejected by the Christian mainstream as heretical in extreme. Nevertheless, his thinking cannot be dismissed as inconsequential. Born in 1927, with bachelor's, master's and doctor's degrees from the academically elite University of Chicago, Altizer is no unsophisticated fundamentalist. His theology of the Holocaust and his characterization of the Jew as the "absolute other" were formulated precisely in the years that the Christian mainstream was seeking ways of diminishing the harshness of traditional anti-Jewish rhetoric within Christianity and to seek ever expanding paths to Jewish-Christian dialogue and understanding. If nothing else, Altizer's thinking points to the fragility of our attempts to foster Christian-Jewish dialogue and understanding.

Indeed, ours efforts on behalf of Jewish-Christian understanding can be compared to a Sisyphian endeavor, but no less worthwhile on that account. The leadership of the churches, both Catholic and mainstream Protestant have made impressive gains in fostering inter-religious good will in recent decades and their leadership has influenced lay attitudes. Nevertheless, in times of radical stress, there have been times when lay and leadership behavior moved in opposite directions. The dangerous latent emotions embedded in religious differences cannot always be suppressed. They remind us of Albert Camus' characterization of Dr. Rieux's response to the plague in its latent stage as depicted at the end of his novel, *The Plague*:

> As Rieux listened to the cries of joy rising from the town, he remembered that such joy could always be imperiled. He knew what those jubilant crowds did not know but could have learnt from books: that the plague bacillus never dies nor disappears for good; that it can lie dormant for years and years in furniture and linen chests; that it bides its time in bedrooms, cellars, trunks, and bookshelves; and that perhaps the day would come when it would rouse up its rats again, and send them forth to die in a happy city.[21]

Notes

1 Richard L. Rubenstein, *The Religious Imagination* (Indianapolis: Bobbs Merrill, 1968) and *My Brother Paul* (New York: Harper & Row, 1972).
2 II Cor., 3:13-15.
3 John 14:6.
4 See Richard L. Rubenstein, *After Auschwitz*, 2nd ed. (Baltimore: Johns Hopkins University Press, 1992), pp. 9-12.
5 On this issue see Klaus Rohmann, *Vollendung im Nichts? Eine Dokumentation der Amerikanischen Gott-ist-Tot-Theologie*, (Cologne and Zurich: Benziger Verlag, 1977).
6 See Richard L. Rubenstein, *After Auschwitz*, 2nd ed. (Baltimore: Johns Hopkins University Press, 1992), pp. 293-306.
7 William Hamilton, "The Death-of-God Theology" in William Robert Miller, ed., *The New Christianity: An Anthology of the Rise of Modern Religious Thought* (New York: Delacorte Press, 1967), p. 335.
8 William Hamilton, "The New Optimism-from Prufrock to Ringo," in William Hamilton and Thomas J. J. Altizer, *Radical Theology and the Death of God* (New York: Bobbs-Merrill, 1966), pp. 164-68.
9 See Richard L. Rubenstein, "Cox's Vision of the Secular City," in Daniel Callahan, ed., *The Secular City Debate* (New York: Macmillan, 1960), pp. 129-44.
10 See Richard L. Rubenstein, *Power Struggle* (New York: Charles Scribners Sons, 1974), pp. 149-69
11 Thomas J. J. Altizer, "God as Holy Nothingness," in Betty Rogers Rubenstein and Michael Berenbaum, *op. cit.*, pp. 347-57.
12 See Richard L. Rubenstein, *After Auschwitz*, 2nd ed. (Baltimore: Johns Hopkins University Press, 1992), p. 37.
13 Altizer, *op. cit.*, p. 348.
14 Altizer, *op. cit.*, p. 348.
15 Richard L. Rubenstein, *My Brother Paul* (New York: Harper & Row, 1972), pp. 15-16.
16 Altizer, *op. cit.*, p. 351.
17 *After Auschwitz*, 2nd ed., pp. 293-306

[18] G. W. F. Hegel, "Introduction: Reason in History," in G. W. F. Hegel, *Lectures on the Philosophy of World History*, ed. Johannes Hoffmeister, trans. H. B. Nisbet (Cambridge: Cambridge University Press, 1975), p. 43.

[19] See Thomas J. J. Altizer, *The Descent into Hell: A Study of the Radical Reversal of the Christian Consciousness* (Philadelphia: Lippincott, 1970).

[20] I explore this issue in greater detail in Rubenstein, "Holocaust and Holy War" in *The Annals of the American Academy of Politics and Social Science*, 548, November 1996.

[21] Albert Camus, *The Plague* (trans. S. Gilbert, Hamish Hamilton: London, 1948) p 284-5.

Conversation Two

Jewish-Christian Relations in the Global Society: What the Institutional Documents Have and Have Not Been Telling Us

Working Towards an Appreciation of Common Purpose

Edward Kessler

Introduction

In the last 50 years or so, we have witnessed a massive change in Jewish-Christian relations. This has, for the most part, been so far-reaching that the time has now come to consider new directions in the Jewish-Christian relationship. If we Jews and Christians really are standing at the threshold of a new age how do we proceed?

The purpose of this paper is to outline the development of institutional statements in recent years and to point out the gaps and to suggest that (to adapt imagery from Isaiah 29:17), while the land may have been ploughed and seeds may have been planted, a fruitful field has yet to develop. I will suggest that 3 themes can be noted from Christian documents published in recent times, each of which has resulted in a Jewish response. From the Christian perspective, the documents illustrate what might be called *the principle of the 3 'R's*.

> **Realisation** that Christians and Christianity have made a significant contribution to Jewish Suffering.
> **Re-awakening** to the Jewishness of Christianity.
> And most recently…
> **Recognition** that the formation of Christian identity today is dependent upon a right relationship with Judaism.

The Jewish responses, which might be described as *the response of the 3 'D's*, have been as follows:

In light of point one – **Distrust** of Christian overtures.

In light of point two – **Defensive** involvement in dialogue (in other words, involvement for the sake of combating Christian anti-semitism).

In light of point three – **Developing** awareness of a commonality with Christianity as well as an appreciation of a common purpose.

My paper will outline each of these stages, as expressed by the documents, and whilst we need to be vigilant about points one and two I will suggest that point three provides the basis for relations today.

One final point in this introduction – why the reference to the global society? The adjective 'global' is put in front of many a noun today. As any glance of the burgeoning literature on globalisation indicates, little consensus exists on the precise character of globalisation. A new vocab--ulary has developed but there is disagreement on the nature, extent and direction of the change caused by globalisation.

Globalisation is probably as big a historical shift as was industrialisation. I shall suggest that we need to contemplate the scale of the challenge of globalisation and apply our conclusions to Jewish–Christian relations. It is wrong to see globalisation as either wholly positive or wholly negative. However, humankind can use it for good and also for evil. It therefore represents an opportunity, as well as a threat.

Christian contribution to Jewish Suffering: the legacy of the *adversus iudaeos* tradition and Christian antisemitism

The first theme deals with the awareness among Christians of the Christian contribution to Jewish suffering. We begin in 1948 when the WCC held its first meeting in the city of Anne Frank - Amsterdam. In the introduction to its *Report on the Christian Approach to the Jews* it made reference to the fact that the conference was taking place "within 5 years of the extermination of 6 million Jews".

The report marked a new stage in the attitude of the Protestant churches towards antisemitism as it disassociated itself from previously held views. These either denied the existence of religious antisemitism or, alternatively, blamed it on Jews. Typical of these views was this statement in 1931:

Judaism, when practised by observant Jews, certainly appears to the non-Jew a religion apart from the ordinary world. Within the quite limited meaning of the word 'religious intolerance', there is some basis for its existence, but the creating word, *the determining factor, is not to be cast up to the gentile but to the Jewish side of the ledger* [my emphasis][1].

In other words antisemitism is the fault of the Jews!

The WCC not only acknowledged the existence of religious anti-semitism but also accepted Christian involvement in it. This was a very important step. The report openly accepted that "the churches in the past have helped to foster an image of the Jews as the sole enemies of Christ, which has contributed to antisemitism in the secular world".[2] It called upon "all churches we represent to denounce antisemitism". Thus, Christian awareness of the Christian contribution to antisemitism was placed firmly on the agenda of Christian-Jewish relations. The WCC report marked an admission not only that Christian history was linked to the history of antisemitism, but also that it was one of the causes.

The magnitude of the step taken by WCC can be seen more clearly when compared with the failure of the Anglican Lambeth conference of 1948 even to mention antisemitism. The nearest the Lambeth conference came to confronting prejudice in terms of relations between Christians and Jews, can be found in a section entitled, *Palestine* which stated that the conference "greatly appreciates the efforts made to restore peace, and expresses its sympathy with all of every race, and particularly Christians of every Church, who are suffering".[3]

During the 40 years before the subject of Christian-Jewish relations appeared on the Lambeth Conference agenda, a large number of Protestant churches tackled the problems arising out of the legacy of the *Adversus Iudaeos* Tradition – not however the WCC General Assembly which has failed to produce a document on the Christian-Jewish relationship. The WCC encompasses over 300 non-Catholic Churches and any statement has to undergo a complicated process of decision-making, due to the many different attitudes prevailing among its Member Churches.

The WCC encounter with Judaism has only ever been an issue within the broader discussions by the delegates on inter-religious affairs. At this (lower) level, a number of documents have been issued such as the 1988 Sigtuna statement which affirmed that the Jewish people have not been rejected by God but remain the continuation of the biblical Israel. On antisemitism it stated:

> We deeply regret that, contrary to the spirit of Christ, many Christians have used the claims of faith as weapons against the Jewish people, culminating in the Shoah, and we confess sins of words and deeds against Jews in all centuries. Although not all Christians in all times and all lands have been guilty of persecution of Jews, we recognize that in the Christian tradition and its use of Scripture and liturgy there are still ideas towards Jews and Judaism that consciously or unconsciously, translate into prejudice and discrimination against Jews.

Yet neither this nor other documents were promulgated at the top level of the WCC because they would not be passed by the Central Committee. And here lies the key to the problem. The World Council of Churches is not only divided but is deeply involved in the struggle of the Liberation Groups in the Third World. This involved them in support for the PLO in its early years. The strongly pro-Palestinian Middle East Council of Churches is a constituent body of the WCC and has influenced its attitudes beyond the political issues of the Middle East. And the WCC Assembly, held every seven years, has regularly endorsed anti-Israel statements. The hostile attitude to Israel underwent a certain thaw during the Peace Process but more recently has reverted to the critical.

Fortunately, this is not typical of Jewish-Protestant relations elsewhere. For example, the *Adversus Iudaeos* teachings of Martin Luther were repudiated by the Lutheran World Federation who rejected "Luther's violent invective against the Jews and express deep and abiding sorrow over its tragic effects on subsequent generations". In particular, it deplored the appropriation of Luther's words by modern antisemites and called for increasing Lutheran-Jewish cooperation.

We now turn to the Roman Catholic Church and the Second Vatican Council. It is worth noting that during the preparatory work, which lasted three and a half years, the 1961 WCC assembly took place in Delhi. Although the Catholic Church took no part in the WCC, the pre-conciliar climate and the Assembly undoubtedly influenced each other. For example, the Holy See sent observers to the Delhi Assembly.

The significance of the Second Vatican Council for Jewish–Christian relations began to be recognised when shortly before Easter in the same year, John XXIII changed the Good Friday liturgy during which Catholics said, "Let us pray also for the perfidious Jews". A year later, the Pope received wide attention for publicly greeting Jewish visitors with the words, "I am Joseph your brother".

Nostra Aetate marked the beginnings of a fresh approach to Judaism when the Roman Catholic Church 'came in from out of the cold'. According to Edward Flannery, it "terminated in a stroke a millennial teaching of contempt of Jews and Judaism and unequivocally asserted the Church's debt to its Jewish heritage."[4]

Thirty years on, the short passage does not betray signs of the tensions in which it was born and *Nostra Aetate* provided no new general Christian thinking omitting, for example, any mention of the Shoah or the State of Israel: however, it did condemn antisemitismalthough some commentators have suggested that the languagecould have been more forceful. Most importantly of all, it ushered in a new era, fresh attitudes, a new language of discourse never previously heard in the Catholic Church concerning Jews. The concept of a dialogue now entered the relationship.

There were a number of questions raised which the Secretariat decided not to resolve formally in a conciliar document and to leave until a future time. One of these concerned the issue of Christian antisemitism. The document stated that nothing was to be taught or preached that was "out of harmony with the truth of the Gospel".[5] Yet, it was still too soon to consider why the texts of Matthew and John tended to excuse the disciples but accuse more and more Jews by excluding more and more Romans.

I agree with the opinion of Dr Norman Solomon, that what *Nostra Aetate* achieved most of all was "possibilities". In its wake came a rich growth of Catholic-Jewish dialogue. The "possibilities" can be seen in such phrases as "God holds the Jews most dear" and "mutual understanding and respect". However, the document's possibilities were one thing. Its success another and the latter was dependent upon "things still to be worked out".[6]

How did Jews respond? For the most part, Jews responded to Christian recognition of the legacy of the *Adversus Iudaeos* writings with distrust - a legacy of the consequences of the 'teaching of contempt'. There was, amongst the Jewish community, no general desire to engage in dialogue with Christians and Christianity.

It is true that Jewish leaders, such as Marc Tannenbaum, Nahum Goldmann and Gerhart Riegner, established an international Jewish dialogue body the International Jewish Committee for Interreligious

Consultations (IJCIC) - with the participation of the Synagogue Council of America, the American Jewish Committee, the B'nai B'rith and Jewish organisations such as ther World Jewish Congress, but the desire among the majority of Jews was lacking.

This was the result not only of suspicion of Christian motives but also because of the mark, which the *Adversus Iudaeos* tradition had left on the Jewish psyche. Most Jews did not trust Christian motives. But there was also another reason for Jewish distrust. Judaism reciprocated the Christian *Adversus Iudaeos* tradition and although there is little evidence of an *Adversus Christianos*, Christianity was dismissed as a religion practiced by morally and culturally inferior gentiles, based on unbelievable claims, which had degenerated into idolatry.

The 1988 Lambeth debate on the Christian attitude towards Judaism was a significant step forward. The discussion shared some of the features of Vatican II - for instance, the prepared document was significantly altered during the conference. The guidelines, which were presented for approval, were called *Jewish-Christian Guidelines for the Anglican Communion*. By the end they had been renamed *Jews, Christians, Muslims: the Way of Dialogue*. Clearly, the conference felt that Christian-Jewish relations could not be commented upon without reference to Christian-Muslim relations. We should also not forget the influence of the crisis in Lebanon and the concern over the hostages, one of whom, was Terry Waite. In addition, a separate document on Christian-Muslim relations was due to have been published but the draft for discussion had not been completed in time for the conference. Consequently, there was a danger that nothing would be published. However, as a result of intensive discussions as well as the support of bishops such as Richard Harries a compromise was reached.

The final document delivered a scathing denunciation of antisemitism and of the Christian teaching of contempt.

> Through catechism, teaching of school children, and Christian preaching, the Jewish people have been misrepresented and caricatured...In order to combat centuries of anti-Jewish teaching and practice, Christians must develop programmes of teaching, preaching, and common social action which eradicate prejudice and promote dialogue and sharing among biblical peoples.[7]

No document had so explicitly argued that there should be a fundamental change in Christian approach to Judaism. It pointed the way forward and it is now common for statements from Protestant churches and the Roman Catholic Church to acknowledge the legacy of the *Adversus Iudaeos* tradition and Christian antisemitism. The most recent document I have seen is the shortly to be published *Church and Israel* by the Leuenberg Church Fellowship (consisting of the Reformation Churches in Europe) which explicitly acknowledges the Christian contribution to Jewish suffering.

This survey of the Christian awareness of the Christian contribution to antisemitism shows that, over 50 years, significant changes have taken place. We can see that many of the churches have considered the problem, not only of antisemitism, but also of Christian antisemitism.

Unfortunately, the same is not true of the encounter with the Orthodox churches. The changes that have taken place in what may be described as the Western churches find few parallels in the East. The remarkably rapid growth of understanding and trust between Jews and Christians of the Latin tradition, particularly since the 1960s, contrasts with the very slow rate of progress in dialogue between Jews and Christians of the Orthodox tradition.

A few formal meetings of academics and leading figures on both sides have taken place since 1974, initially involving Greek theologians but since the 1990s including Christians from the Communist world and the Middle East. In Russia itself, a small number of gatherings have taken place including one in St Petersburg in January 1997 on 'Theology after Auschwitz and the Gulag'. Most recently (October 2000), a conference entitled 'Spiritual Culture Dialogue – Facing Each Other' took place in Moscow. It was addressed by the Patriarch of Moscow and All Russia Alexej II who stated that, "our Church is open to inter-religious dialogue and is interested in its continuation, as it testifies to the ability of believers to make society more healthy and consolidate it".

Despite these meetings however, and despite some helpful pronouncements by Orthodox leaders, there is simply no comparison with the current state of play in the Roman Catholic and Protestant churches. To some extent the uneasy relationship of the Orthodox churches with Judaism echoes the state of their involvement in the ecumenical movement too, and it is foolish to expect Orthodox Christians to be more forward in seeking reconciliation with the Jews than with their own Christian brethren.

Much has to be done before Orthodox Christianity abandons its repository of anti-Jewish polemic.

So where does that leave us? Do we concur with James Parkes, a life-long student of antisemitism who was once asked how long he thought it would last. "300 years," he replied. Or should we believe that we are in the last stages of a millennial malady. Should we agree or disagree with the central character of *The Plague*, by Albert Camus, quoted so poignantly by Richard Rubenstein earlier in this book.

I am rather more optimistic. The institutional statements of the Protestant Churches and Roman Catholic Church have taken and continue to take a strong stand against antisemitism as well as Christian antisemitism. John Paul II has firmly condemned it as a sin and called on the faithful to do *teshuva* for misdeeds against Jews. This is illustrated by their tackling of the Shoah.

Christian contribution to Jewish Suffering: the Shoah

While rounding condemning antisemitism, the Vatican until recently largely avoided the question of the Shoah. In 1987 in the wake of Jewish ire over the Pope's reception of Austrian President, Kurt Waldheim, who had been an active Nazi, the Vatican promised to issue such a document and this was affirmed by the Pope at a meeting with Jewish leaders.

The Vatican statement *We Remember: Reflections on the Shoah* was published in 1998. You know it well. It stresses the evils of antisemitism, concluding "we wish to turn awareness of past sins into a firm resolve to build a new future in which there will be no more anti-Judaism among Christians or anti-Christian sentiment among Jews but rather a shared mutual respect." It incorporates much of Pope John Paul II's forceful criticism of antisemitism. But its treatment of the Shoah had many disappointing aspects for some Jews, especially those who were over-expectant.

They had unrealistically hoped for a formal apology, on the lines of that issued by the French bishops who stated that "it is important to admit the primary role played by the consistently repeated anti-Jewish stereotypes wrongly perpetuated by the Christians in the historical process that led to the Holocaust". *We Remember* speaks of those Christians who helped the Jews and those who failed to do so but implies a balanced picture. It fails to give a plain statement on the role of Christian teachings and stereotypes in motivating those who behaved negatively.

Yet it is a highly significant document and should be recognised as such. It must be remembered that this document is directed to a Christian public and is primarily, a sincere call for the renunciation of antisemitism. Statements such as *We Remember* and Protestant statements which are equally significant reach not only Christians in Western Europe and North America, where dialogue has progressed, but also Christians in regions such as Eastern Europe, Africa, Asia and Latin America where many have never encountered a Jew in their lives and know little of them except from the New Testament accounts.

Thus, as far as the Christian contribution to Jewish suffering is concerned, the Protestant Churches and the Roman Catholic Church instead of being part of the problem have now become part of the solution. Yet, we must notice a danger in these documents on the Shoah. Notice the following 1996 Methodist statement, *Building Bridges of Hope*, which states

> Especially crucial for Christians in our quest for understanding has been the struggle to recognize the horror of the Holocaust as the catastrophic culmination of a long history of anti-Jewish attitudes and actions in which Christians, and sometimes the Church itself, have been deeply implicated. Dialogues with Jewish partners have been central for Christians in our process of learning of the scope of the Holocaust atrocities, acknowledgment of complicity and responsibility, repentance, and commitment to work against antisemitism in all its forms in the future.

The Leuenberg document, after having acknowledged Christian contribution to the Shoah states that

> Irrespective of the particular responsibility of Germany and the Christians in Germany related to the National Socialist period – all the Christian churches in Europe share in the special history of European guilt towards Israel [the Jewish people], wherever they failed clearly to contradict antisemitism or even promoted it directly or indirectly.

The great danger is of building a relationship on guilt, a danger faced by both Jews and Christians. This perhaps lies behind the following statement in *Dabru Emet* which in opposition to the distrust felt by many Jews states,

> Nazism was not a Christian phenomenon. Without the long history of Christian anti-Judaism and Christian violence against Jews, Nazi ideology could not have taken hold nor could it have been carried out... But Nazism itself was not an inevitable outcome of Christianity... We encourage the continuation of recent efforts in Christian theology to repudiate unequivocally contempt of Judaism and the Jewish people. We applaud those Christians who reject this teaching of contempt, and we do not blame them for the sins committed by their ancestors.

Whilst reaction to the Christian contribution to Jewish suffering is an important driving force, Jewish-Christian relations can not be built solely on responses to antisemitism and Christian feelings of guilt.

We need to move onto a more positive basis for relations and the institutional documents do exactly that.

The Jewish Origins of Christianity and the Mission of and Mission to Israel

As well as acknowledging the Christian contribution to Jewish suffering, institutional statements illustrate a second revolution in Roman Catholic and Protestant attitudes towards Jews and Judaism. They are reawakening to the Jewish origins of Christianity and are reconsidering the meaning of the mission of and the mission to Israel.

They have renounced many of the triumphalist doctrines, most significantly the renunciation of the teaching of the divine rejection of the Jewish people since the time of Jesus – in other words, the divine covenant with the Jewish people is now no longer viewed as having been annulled. According to the 1980 Evangelical Church of the Rhineland statement,

> We believe the permanent election of the Jewish people as the people of God and realize that through Jesus Christ the church is into the covenant of God with his people.

For its part, *Nostra Aetate* taught Christians that 'the Jews remain most dear to God' who 'does not repent of the gifts He makes nor of the calls He issues'. John Paul II spelled it out in the early years of his pontificate as follows: God's covenant with the Jewish people had never been broken, retains eternal validity; God does not renege on his promises (cf. Romans 11:29). If the Jews were not rejected, then Judaism was not a fossilized faith, as had been taught previously, but a living, authentic religion.

The ramifications were manifold. Christians were now told that Jesus, his family and his followers were Jewish and the Jewish background to Christianity was now stressed. Stated first in recent times by the 1947 Seelisburg document, Christians are commended to "remember that Jesus was born of a Jewish mother of the seed of David and the people of Israel, and that His everlasting love and forgiveness embraces His own people and the whole world" and to "remember that the first disciples, the apostles and the first martyrs were Jews".

The rediscovery of the Jewishness of the origins of Christianity led to Christians being taught about the richness of the Jewish context as well as to the perils of relying on the literal text of the New Testament. New subjects for consideration were also broached which included the closeness of the relationship between Jesus and the Pharisees. Previously, this subject was limited to the consideration of scholars such as George Foot Moore and Travers Hereford. Now, however Catholics, for example, learnt (from the 1985 Vatican *Notes*) that Jesus "had very close relations" with the Pharisees to whom "he was very near".

In addition, Christian ordinands were being taught that the final text of the Gospels was edited long after the events described and, for example, that the authors were concerned with denigrating those Jews who did not follow Jesus. At the same time they were concerned with vindicating the Romans, whose goodwill they were seeking. This was courageously admitted by the Vatican's 1985 document on the teaching of Judaism, which stated forthrightly:

> It cannot be ruled out that some references hostile or less than favorable to the Jews have their historical context in conflicts between the nascent Church and the Jewish community. Certain controversies reflect Christian-Jewish relations long after the time of Jesus. To establish this is of capital importance if we wish to bring out the meaning of certain Gospel texts for the Christians of today.

There was a realisation that too often Christians have pictured Torah as a burden rather than as a delight. Christians were reminded that Jesus was a faithful Jew and 'that from the Jewish people sprang the apostles', the foundation stones and pillars of the Church who 'draw sustenance from the root of that good olive tree onto which have been grafted the wild olive branches of the Gentiles'.

Christian re-acquaintance with Judaism resulted primarily from an increased awareness of the Jewish origins of Christianity. That Jesus was born lived and died a Jew; that the first Christians were Jews; that the New Testament is, for the most part, a Jewish work. From the Jewish side individuals such as Martin Buber and Claude Montefiore reminded Jews that Jesus was a fellow Jew (their 'great brother' as Martin Buber described him). But this is rarely stated in Jewish documents. Witness what *Dabru Emet* says and does not say about Jesus. It fails to mention the Jewishness of Jesus but simply states that "Christians know and serve God through Jesus Christ and the Christian tradition".

It is true that *Dabru Emet* recognises that questions such as the purpose behind the creation of Christianity need to be considered. However, the document does not address the question whether the fact that Jesus was a Jew has any implications for Jews. It is well known that Jews are very proud of the Albert Einsteins, the Heinrich Heines and the Sigmund Freuds; yet, Israel's most famous Jew is generally ignored. Now, in a freer climate as far as Jewish–Christian relations are concerned, is it not time that there was a greater Jewish interest in the Jew, Jesus? I suggest that *Dabru Emet* missed an opportunity in this respect.

For Christians, the tackling of Christian triumphalism illustrates not just a shift from what was, for the most part, an inherent need to condemn Judaism to one of a condemnation of Christian anti-Judaism. It has led to a closer relationship with "the elder brother" and not, as some have feared from the time of Marcion onwards to a separation from all things Jewish (who called for a total separation from the Hebrew Bible and much of the Gospel writings).

This shift can be illustrated with a brief discussion of mission, which in many ways is a far more complicated subject than antisemitism. It is easier for Christians to condemn Christian antisemitism as a misunderstanding of the Christian teaching. Mission, however, has been, and still is, central to the Christian faith. This is illustrated by the legacy of the command found in the Gospels of Matthew to "go therefore and make disciples of all nations".[8]

In 1948, the WCC did not only condemn antisemitism but also, perhaps incredibly when viewed in hindsight, called for a redoubling of effort at the conversion of Jews. The report recommended that the churches should "seek to recover the universality of our Lord's commission by including the Jewish people in their evangelistic work". The conclusion of the WCC was that, in light of the Shoah, an even greater effort should be made to convert Jews. The report stated that "because of the unique inheritance of the Jewish people, the churches should make provisions for the education of ministers specially fitted to this task. Provision should also be made for Christian literature to interpret the Gospel to Jewish people."[9]

It is interesting that the 1948 assembly linked the two issues: the condemnation of antisemitism with an exhortation to preach the gospel to the Jews - on the one hand, a call "to denounce antisemitism"; on the other, a call for the conversion of Jews.[10] At this time, Jews throughout the world were trying to recover from the Shoah. Their view of this report - if they knew it existed - could only have been: the Nazis wanted Jewish bodies, the churches wanted Jewish souls.

As far as the Roman Catholic Church was concerned, I mentioned earlier that there were a number of questions raised which the Secretariat decided not resolve formally in a conciliar document but to leave until a future time - one concerns mission. Thomas Stransky explains the dilemma for Catholics - indeed for all Christians - and puts into context the reasons why the subject has, until recently, been avoided. He argues that Christians in their witness should always avoid proselytism (in the pejorative sense); they should shun all conversionary attitudes and practices which do *not* conform to the ways a free God draws free people to Himself in response to His calls to serve Him in spirit and in truth.

> In the case of the Jewish people, what is Christian proselytism in practice? And what is "evangelization" - the Church's everlasting proclamation of Jesus Christ, "the Way, the Truth and the Life"? Is open dialogue a betrayal of Christian mission? Or is mission a betrayal of dialogue?[11]

Interestingly, he also asks the reverse question i.e., what is the continuing mission of the synagogue to the church? What is the *common* mission of the synagogue and church?

The 1985 *Notes* illustrate Stransky's point: on the one hand, "the Church must preach Jesus Christ to the world"; on the other, it must "spread their Christian faith while maintaining the strictest respect for religious liberty".

Such a tension is disturbing to many Jews. For example, the belief that salvation can only come through Jesus (or through the Church) relegates not only Judaism but all other faiths to a position of inferiority. Have the changes in doctrine starting with Vatican II robbed this belief of its former triumphalism? Some Jewish participants in the dialogue remain unconvinced and the publication of *Dominus Iesus* serves only to confuse rather than clarify.

However, we must remember that traditional Jewish eschatology, while not foreseeing the conversion of all to Judaism does anticipate that all nations will acknowledge the superiority and sovereignty of the God of Israel. Jews and Christians remain adherents of very, different faiths and we must recognize that there are beliefs in all religions that characterize that faith and are too fundamental to compromise. This is acknowledged by *Dabru Emet* as follows:

> The humanly irreconcilable difference between Jews and Christians will not be settled until God redeems the entire world as promised in Scripture…Jews can respect Christians' faithfulness to their revelation just as we expect Christians to respect our faithfulness to our revelation. Neither Jew nor Christian should be pressed into affirming the teaching of the other community.

The 1988 Lambeth Conference confronted the issue of mission to Israel and represents the first occasion when the subject of mission has been tackled by institutional documents. Although, the first time Christian-Jewish relations appeared on the Lambeth Conference agenda was as late as 1988, a report entitled *Witness of the Church to the Jews in London* was produced in 1949. The report stated that the church must first denounce all forms of antisemitism. "The first step in presenting the gospel to them [Jews] is the removal of those barriers which pre-dispose them against accepting it…Very little advance can be made in the matter of proclaiming the Christian gospel unless antisemitism is first attacked." It advised its readers to convert Jews by "making friendly contact"; it recommended them to "invite Jewish neighbours into Christian homes" with the hope that, eventually, Jews would convert.[12]

The report was especially critical of the recent establishment of the Council of Christians and Jews in 1942. Firstly for creating the impression that the majority of Christians have no other than a humanitarian message for the non-Christian and non-Gentile community. Secondly, for stating that the few in the Church who are missionary-minded towards the Jews are irresponsible and isolated individuals. Thirdly, for suggesting to Christians that in fraternising with their Jewish neighbours they have discharged their Christian duty towards them.

The 1988 conference took a totally different position. Unlike the other conferences or official documents we have discussed, Lambeth 1988 emphasised, rather than minimised, the importance of missionary activity for Christian-Jewish relations. It re-examined the understanding of the Christian mission, which was seen not in terms of the conversion of Jews, but rather of a *common mission*. In the light of Christian-Jewish and Christian-Muslim relations, proselytism was to be rejected and the conference called for "mutual witness to God between equal partners". It stated that although:

> there are a variety of attitudes towards Judaism within Christianity today...All these approaches, however, share a common concern to be sensitive to Judaism, to reject all proselytising, that is, aggressive and manipulative attempts to convert, and of course, any hint of antisemitism. Further, Jews, Muslims and Christians have a common mission. They share a mission to the world that God's name may be honoured.[13]

This is not to imply that there are no missionary problems today. However, there has been a dramatic downscaling of Christian mission to Jews. For many Christian churches a distinction has been drawn between "mission" and "witness".

Instances of missionary problems come mainly from some evangelical churches (including those "messianic" movements such as Jews for Jesus). Relations with the Evangelical Protestants are especially complex. First of all, they often do not dialogue - even with other Christians. Their fundamentalist views are not to be discussed with others (similar to fundamentalist Jews) and mission is ingrained - as was again exemplified by the recent decision of the Southern Baptist convention, one of the largest groupings in the United States, to intensify mission to the Jews in a resolution "to direct our energies and resources toward the proclamation of the gospel to the Jewish people".

Nevertheless, the institutional statements illustrate a significant shift in the Christian understanding of the mission of and the mission to Israel.

They have not only revised the traditional negative assessment of Judaism but have explained Israel's role in positive terms. This has had a major impact and has resulted in an emphasis on partnership and a common mission rather than the mission of one in contradistinction to the other.

The formation of Christian identity and the Issue of Commonality

The biggest challenge raised by the institutional statements for Christian-Jewish relations today, (far bigger challenging than is appreciated), is illustrated by the following statement of the 1974 Guidelines, "Christians must strive to learn by what essential traits the Jews define themselves in the light of their own religious experience".[14] I do not think the Church knew at that time, nor knows today) how difficult it might be to abide by that principle.

This view is similarly expressed in Protestant churches as, for example, expressed by Leuenberg document which states that "the relationship with Israel is therefore for Christians and for the churches an indispensable part of the foundation of their faith". Similarly, the latest statement of the WCC, 'Christian–Jewish dialogue beyond Canberra 1991', adopted in 1992 by the Central Committee states that the WCC "will assist the churches to understand the theological significance of living Judaism, to examine contemporary theological affirmations vis-à-vis Judaism [...] and to foster implementation of the churches' recommendations in Christian teaching, mission and liturgical life".

How are these changes in thinking going to be implemented? How are they going to be brought down to grass roots level? We have seen that Christian theology on Jews and Judaism has been revised drastically.

It is clear that the documents have reached a stage where many of the main divisive issues have been either eliminated or taken to the furthest point at which agreement is possible. The efforts of Catholics and Protestants towards respect of Judaism are reflected in these documents, which project attitudes that would have been unthinkable a few decades ago. Christian theology has been profoundly revised at the official level - all Churches are committed to the fight against antisemitism; to teaching about the Jewishness of Christianity and the problem of mission to Jews has declined significantly.

There is of course an important agenda for top-level dialogue and consultations but the emphasis should now shift to filtering to regional and local levels. It is possible today to respond effectively to regional requirements in the new global reality. Consciousness of the changes have been largely been confined to the elite (although in certain regions, such as the United States, it has been more widely disseminated). The object now is to get these changes into the everyday understanding of all the faithful and the fields to be addressed are churches and synagogues, seminaries and yeshivahs, schools and universities as well as informal education, including the media.

This is where the effects of globalisation enter our discussion.

Examples of global phenomena abound in today's world e.g., e-mail and McDonalds are global in that they can extend anywhere on the planet at the same time; BBC broadcasts and Credit Cards are not restricted by distances or borders; global conditions can surface simultaneously at any point on earth that is equipped to host them e.g., an internet connection; global phenomena move almost instantaneously across any distance on the planet e.g., telephone calls. Air travel, telecommunications, computer networks and electronic mass media allow us to collect and disseminate information more or less instantaneously between any locations on earth. Technology is crucial since developments in communications and information processing have supplied the infrastructure for global connections.

Yet, the extents of the shifts should not be exaggerated. We inhabit a globalising, rather than a completely globalised world. While this process is taking place and resulting in a massive historical shift we must consider the implications for Jewish–Christian relations and set in place new arrangements to help manage this process. Managing globalisation means strengthening key international institutions. If our society, economy, politics and so on, are moving global, then Jewish–Christian relations must be global too. And for that we need an effective international system.

We must ensure that the positive developments achieved, particularly the themes identified by this paper, are properly applied at the regional level. This means attention to education and information (including the media) to ensure that the new teachings are disseminated at grass-roots levels. It involves dealing with the fight against antisemitism in regions such as Russia, certainly to combat any manifestations within a religious context.

Most importantly educational guidelines are required – designed for each region. This requirement is equally true of Jews as well as Christians. History has understandably moulded negative Christian stereotypes among Jews and we must now teach the Jewish community about the contemporary changes of attitudes by the churches. The beginnings can be seen in *Dabru Emet* but this is simply the first step. Claude Montefiore's call for a Jewish theology of Christianity over 75 years ago still waits to be answered.

Yet there is a curious paradox at the heart of globalisation. While peoples are being drawn ever more closely together, some forces seek refuge in narrow nationalism and isolation. The demands of nationalist identification have been clearly conveyed in the recent upsurge in nationalism in Central Europe. For instance, witness the following comments by the Croatian writer Slavenka Drakulic

> Along with millions of other Croats, I was pinned to the wall of nationhood – not only by outside pressure from Serbia and the Federal Army but by national homogenisation within Croatia itself. That is what the war is doing, reducing us to one dimension: the Nation. The trouble with this nationhood, however, is that whereas before, I was defined by my education, my job, my ideas, my character – and, yes, my nationality, too – now I feel stripped of all that. I am nobody, because I am not a person any more. I am one of the 4.5 million Croats.[15]

Thus, the threshold upon which we sit provides risk as well as opportunity. Globalisation is changing the rules of the game for all of us, and while it has great potential there is also danger. Globalisation is with us, and it is here to stay. The challenge for the 21st century is to harness the forces of globalisation for the good of Jewish-Christian relations. The growing interconnectedness and interdependence of Jewish–Christian relations, supported by the revolution in information technology is bringing all of us closer together. Globalisation affords an unparalleled opportunity to bring about further advances, building on the themes identified in my paper.

But there is no guarantee of progress. There are risks, for example, that instability in one part of the world will effect Jewish-Christian relations in another. Globalisation is not inherently good or bad - it is a reality, which we must shape. We must learn to think globally, and act internationally, nationally, and locally, to ensure that globalisation works for us and not against us.

We must draw inspiration from the pioneers of Jewish-Christian dialogue who fought so hard and achieved so much in the 20th century, and build on their work in the global society of today. This is not an optional extra, it simply represents the way in which history is developing. It is challenging all our structures, including the powers and structures of the institutional religions. It does not make them irrelevant but adjusts their role.

What does this mean in practice? It means that our initiatives should come together. Efforts to change theological education, congregational perceptions, interfaith understanding sometimes seem to be the concern of different groups – each of which sometimes hears only part of what was said. Educationalists hear one point; religious leaders another; congregants a third and so on. The lesson of the global society is that we each need to hear the same points and work together. For example, those who talk about education must also be willing to talk about institutional concerns.

Are these simply platitudes? Let me give one example taken from the Flexible Learning Network being established by the Cambridge Centre for Jewish-Christian Relations (CJCR).

The Establishment of a Flexible Learning Network

At present the CJCR offers an MA in Jewish-Christian Relations either on-site, in Cambridge or via Distance Learning through the internet. It is designed for people who have the time and ability to engage in this field of study but who are unable to travel to Cambridge. The Distance Learning Programme has become the flagship of the Centre since it is the channel for disseminating our ground breaking educational programmes.

There is one major limiting factor: since the courses are pitched at a post-graduate academic level they are not appropriate for all students. Some who apply to take the course do not seek an MA. Others do not have a first degree and are not sufficiently qualified to begin an MA degree.

Jewish-Christian relations now need a provider of broader based courses. This has been on CJCR's agenda since our inception, but we first need to establish a track record at a postgraduate level before addressing other options. Now our students our located throughout the world and with our experience of distance learning programmes it is possible to establish a Flexible Learning Network – one which can tailor courses for a variety of different audiences including clergy, teachers and those involved in pastoral work to name but a few. The potential is enormous.

I am sure you can think of other important and necessary projects. Together we can develop programmes which will affect a wide range of areas such social, political, civil, cultural, and educational as well as religious life. This will fulfil the challenge of Jewish-Christian relations today and will help maintain the momentum that has been built up in recent years.

Giant strides have been made but we are talking of a dynamic and relentless process. We will never be able to sit back and say, "The work is done. The agenda is completed." On many major issues, we find ourselves on the same side of the fence, faced with the same challenges. The agenda is changing and new agendas are no less vital and pressing.

So, despite great advances, Jewish-Christian relations still face major challenges as well as opportunities. Rising to meet these challenges requires a concerted effort, and today it requires a global effort.

Notes

1 F. Gavin 'The Christian approach to the Jews', *Christians and Jews* (New York: International Missionary Council, 1931), p 49.
2 *The Message and Reports of the First Assembly of the World Council of Churches* (London: SPCK 1948), p 77.
3 *Lambeth Conference 1948*. Vol 1 (London: Lambeth Palace, 1948), p 31.
4 E. Flannery, 'Seminaries, Classrooms, Pulpits, Streets: Where we have to go' *Unanswered Questions: Theological Views of Jewish-Catholic Relations*, ed., R. Brooks (Notre Dame: University of Notre Dame Press, 1988), pp. 128-9.
5 *Vatican Council II: the conciliar and post conciliar documents*, ed. A. Flannery (Dominican Publications: Dublin, 1981), p. 741.
6 idem.
7 *The Truth Shall Set You Free: The Lambeth Conference 1988* (London: Church House Publishing, 1988), p 303.
8 Matthew 28:19.
9 *The Message and Reports of the First Assembly of the World Council of Churches*, p. 78.
10 ibid., p 76-7.
11 T. F. Stransky, "Holy Diplomacy: Making the Impossible Possible" *Unanswered Questions: Theological Views of Jewish-Catholic Relations*, ed., R. Brooks (Notre Dame: University of Notre Dame Press , 1988), p. 66.
12 *Mission to London Papers* (Unpublished: Lambeth Palace, 1952), p 28-30.
13 *The Truth Shall Set You Free: The Lambeth Conference 1988* , p 305.
14 1975 Guidelines to *Nostra Aetate*.
15 Vladimir Tismaneanu, *Fantasies of Salvation: Democracy, Nationalism and Myths in Post-Communist Europe* (Princeton, NJ: Princeton University Press, 1998), pp. 89–90.

Maintaining Momentum in a Global Village

John T Pawlikowski

In the now more than half-century since the end of World War II we have seen an ever increasing number of documents issued by ecumenical groups, international church bodies and individual denominations at local and international levels. These have come largely from Catholic and Protestant church groups, though the Orthodox churches are related to documents released by the World Council of Churches and the National Council of Churches in the United States. In the past few years there have been some promising stirrings within the Orthodox churches regarding Christian-Jewish relations, including a potentially significant statement from Patriarch Alexii II, spiritual leader of the Russian Orthodox Church, during a conference organized in Moscow last October by the Russian affiliated organization of the International Council of Christians and Jews. All of these documents and statements, beginning with the historic Seelisburg document published in 1947 by the ICCJ through Vatican II's *Nostra Aetate*, through documents such as the groundbreaking statement of the Synod of the Protestant Church of the Rhineland, the now two volume of statements by Pope John Paul II, to very recent documents from the Evangelical Lutheran Church in America, the United Methodist Church and the United Church of Canada, have moved Christianity away from its traditional understanding of the Church as the replacement of Israel in the covenant with God to an affirmation of continued Jewish covenantal inclusion and an enhanced appreciation of the positive roots of Christianity in the Judaism of Jesus' day and beyond.[1] A new collection of documents is now being prepared by Eugene Fisher, Franklin Sherman and Alice Eckardt.

It is impossible in a brief presentation such as this to summarize the many documents now before us. So my goal will be to highlight some of the issues raised in them and to indicate where genuine progress has been made and where these documents remain incomplete. In so doing I aim to provide a basis of hope rooted in the profound changes that have occurred as well as provide a continuing challenge, in a special way for the younger scholars among us, to continue the momentum of the past half century so that this new millennium will truly find Jews and Christians becoming a blessing to each other as we journey together with our Muslim brothers and sisters and people of other faith traditions in the new world of the global village.

The first issue raised in the various documents is the basic affirmation of Jewish covenantal inclusion. After nearly two millennia of Christian popular and theological proclamation about Jewish displacement from the covenant for having rejected and murdered Jesus, about Jewish perpetual homelessness as a punishment for this rejection, the Christian churches have undertaken a radical about-face. Jews are now to be understood as integral members of the covenant. *Pace* most of the Church Fathers. Documents such as *Nostra Aetate* and the Rhineland Synod Document have taken us back to Romans 9-11 where Paul, though he recognizes a certain tension in his proclamation because of the parallel proclamation of newness in Christ, clearly affirms the need for Christians to regard Jews as covenantal brothers and sisters after the Christ Event. Dr. Eugene Fisher has rightly pointed to a distinctive feature of *Nostra Aetate*.[2] It is a feature common to many of the Protestant documents as well. Unlike other institutional church statements there is little reference to documents of the tradition (church synods, councils, popes, etc.). What church leaders appear to be saying in these documents through the absence of references to the tradition is that the tradition in fact went badly astray in presenting the theology of the Christian-Jewish relationship. The only option is to wipe the slate clean and begin anew, using Romans 9-11, despite its imperfections, as the basic foundation. Speaking of *Nostra Aetate*'s chapter on the Jews, Canadian theologian Gregory Baum argued at the 1986 meeting of the Catholic Theological Society in Chicago that it represents the most important and radical change in the church's ordinary magisterium at Vatican II.[3]

The leading German theologian Johann Baptist Metz has insisted over the years that the implications of the theological rethinking of Judaism begun in *Nostra Aetate*, the Rhineland Synod document and other recent statements, extends beyond the Christian-Jewish dialogue. After the

Holocaust, this rethinking involves a "revision of Christian theology itself."[4] As we look at the theological picture within the Christian churches today, I would say that Metz's argument has fallen on deaf ears thus far. One looks in vain for citations from these Christian-Jewish documents whether from the Vatican, the World Council of Churches or particular Protestant denominations in their other statements or publications focusing on Christian identity today. Since, in the past, this identity has been centrally shaped by a theology of the Church as fulfilment, and in some cases displacement, of the Jewish people in the covenant, it is vital that these documents which assert continued Jewish covenantal inclusion begin to impact Christian theological reflection as such. This lack of coherence in the Christian vision of Judaism and the Jewish people has been noted at times by Jewish participants in the dialogue. Do *Nostra Aetate*, the Rhineland synod document, the United Church of Canada's "Bearing Faithful Witness" and their sister statements have significance only when Christians are in conversation with Jews? Or are they brought into the picture when Christians are reflecting among themselves about the basic identity of the Church. Only if the latter becomes the norm can we say that these specific documents on Christian-Jewish relations have been truly received within the Christian community.

Let me cite two examples of this resistance which I have personally witnessed. In the preparatory drafts for the international ecumenical gathering held at Santiago de Compostela, Spain, several years ago, the vision of Christian self-understanding was dangerously close to displacement theology. Yet little or no objection was raised to this perspective by the Christian leaders involved in the process until some of us connected with the Christian-Jewish dialogue raised a fuss. In our intervention with Cardinal Edward Cassidy we argued that, as Catholics, we could not accept the preparatory text because it was contrary to *Nostra Aetate* and the subsequent 1974 and 1985 Vatican statements as well as to the many speeches of John Paul II on the subject. Eventually the final document was altered in a way that backed away from the displacement motif. However, in no way did it draw upon or reference the major Church documents on Christian-Jewish relations.

A second example occurred during the October 1997 meeting at the Vatican on the Church and anti-Judaism. This meeting was part of the Jubilee process within the Catholic Church. It was intended to prepare a dossier for the Pope in connection with his planned apology for Catholic interreligious failings (which in fact took place on the first Sunday of Lent last year). During this meeting I was struck again and again by how the bishops and Vatican leaders who formed fifty per cent of the participants in this meeting seemed unaware of the fundamental teachings of the Second Vatican Council and the present Pope regarding Christian-Jewish relations. One bishop argued that the purpose of the Jewish people was to teach Christians how to suffer! My only reaction was, thank God the sessions were closed to the press! Obviously many Catholic church leaders had not assimilated *Nostra Aetate* any more than had Catholic theologians.

Statements such as the United Methodist Church's "Building New Bridges in Hope" as well as *Nostra Aetate* carry implications that while controversial in some Christian circles, need to be confronted directly. As I have already asserted, the first of these assertions – that the Jewish covenant remains valid after the Christ Event – challenges many classical expressions of Christology. But if God remains faithful to the initial covenant with the Jewish people, if we are to assert (to quote the recent United Methodist document) that "God is steadfastly faithful to the biblical covenant with the Jewish people" and that "both Jews and Christians are bound to God in covenant, with no covenantal relationship invalidated by any other," then does this mean that Jews can attain salvation apart from the Christ Event? Put in other words, do Christians, as part of their fundamental commitment to the gospel, have an obligation to evangelise Jews? On the Catholic side, Cardinal Joseph Ratzinger recently affirmed the gospel obligation to evangelise Jews (and all other non-Christians) even though he would reject any heavy-handed approach. And documents coming out of the annual Lausanne Conference of Evangelical Christians as well as the special meeting of Evangelical Christians in Bermuda several years ago affirmed this Christian mandate even more strongly. And even the United Methodist document just quoted insists that "As Christians, we stand firm in our belief that Jesus was sent by God as the Christ to redeem all people, and that in Christ the biblical covenant has been made radically new... Essential to the Christian faith is the call to proclaim the good news of Jesus Christ to all people."

If we can credit the recent Vatican document *Dominus Iesus* for anything, it would be that it moved the question of evangelization in reference to Jews to the front burner. In this document the Vatican's doctrinal congregation headed by Cardinal Joseph Ratzinger makes two fundamental assertions that are critical to the evangelization question. The first is that we cannot speak of two or more parallel ways to salvation. There is only one road, in and through Jesus Christ. The flip side of this assertion is *Dominus Iesus'* insistence that on the objective level those who do not accept Jesus Christ are in a grave situation relative to their ultimate salvation. Despite the claims of some Catholic leaders that *Dominus Iesus* does not apply to Catholicism's relationship with the Jewish people, the doctrinal congregation's statements would seem to be universal. Surely if it had wished to formerly exclude the Jews, *Dominus Iesus* could have stated this explicitly. And the recent notification from this same Vatican doctrinal congregation regarding the teachings of Fr. Jacques Dupuis, S.J. about interreligious relations repeat these same two points. So, despite the efforts of Cardinal Cassidy and Kasper as well as a number of other cardinals and bishops around the world to defuse the negative impact of *Dominus Iesus* and argue that it is only a minor document in terms of interreligious dialogue, it appears that the Vatican doctrinal congregation is continuing to use it as a framework for the Catholic position towards all non-Christians.[5]

The second implication of *Dominus Iesus* is that when all is said and done, Catholic Christians have nothing really new to learn from the dialogue with Jews or any other non-Christian groups – whatever is positive in other religions is there because of Jesus Christ. Yet the 1985 Vatican *Notes* on catechesis and preaching relative to Jews and Judaism insists that Christians have something positive to gain from a study of Judaism and a dialogue with the Jewish People. This same assertion is made by Pope John Paul II in his weekly general audience on November 29th where he maintains that when Christians bring their faith to interreligious dialogue they need to recognize in humility the religious experiences of others and "to discover and appreciate every ray of truth, from wherever it comes," in the sacred texts of other religions. This seems to me to represent a deliberate effort to counter the harshness of the statement in *Dominus Iesus* regarding the grave salvific situation of non-Christians which has caused so much pain generally in the non-Catholic community, including among Jews. It may be significant that in Pope John Paul's statement convoking the May 2001 consistory of cardinals, which will include a discussion of ecumenism, there is no explicit reference to *Dominus Iesus*. The question remains, however, in light of *Dominus Iesus* and the notification regarding Fr. Dupuis, do Catholic Christians at least have anything positive to gain from the encounter with Jewish religious thought? Or do they know it all already?

Despite this noble effort to moderate the highly negative impact of *Dominus Iesus* the ambiguity remains. The highly acclaimed Rhineland Synod document of 1980 rejects bearing witness to Jews in the same manner as the Church bears witness to people of other faiths. But it continues to proclaim Jesus as the "Messiah of the Jews" and does not really tell us what the special nature of the Christian witness to the Jews is to be carried out in practice.

The closest the Catholic Church has come to an explicit rejection of Jewish evangelization occurred in 1978. Professor Tommaso Federici, a highly respected lay theologian in Vatican circles, was selected to prepare a paper on evangelization and the Jews for the international Vatican-Jewish dialogue held near Venice.[6] In the oral version of his presentation, Professor Federici called for a formal renunciation of evangelical outreach to Jews, since Vatican II had declared them to be within the framework of the covenant. Yet in the published version of his lecture, which appeared several years later, he had replaced his call for formal renunciation with an appeal to repudiate "undue" proselytising of the Jews. In subsequent Vatican statements on evangelization, the issue of missionary outreach to the Jews (which has never had the same priority for Catholics as it did generally for Protestants) has been passed over, leaving the impression that Catholicism's approach at present is deliberately ambiguous. According to my own interpretation of this policy of "studied ambiguity," the Vatican is well aware that formally to relinquish evangelical outreach to the Jews has profound Christological implications that it is unwilling to confront at this time. This is the case as well, I believe, in the vast majority of Protestant churches. The Vatican, unlike some of the Protestant denominations, does not encourage the proselytization of the Jews. Yet it does not wish to declare this effort theologically dead because of the far-reaching implications of such a declaration. The furore that has arisen in some quarters at evangelical Protestantism over the formal renunciation of missionary outreach to Jews illustrates how profound a challenge such a renunciation would represent for traditional Christian faith. As I have written elsewhere, the extent to which we create theological space for Jewish faith, against which Christianity has defined its identity, to that extent we moderate, albeit implicitly, the absolute claims of Christian faith.

So I believe the issue of evangelization is back with us in the dialogue.

This time I believe we need to consider it thoroughly rather than pushing it to the margins. Where that will lead us I am not at all certain. For Jews have regarded the commitment to proselytising a fundamental non-starter for authentic dialogue. It is my conviction that Christianity stands to lose its dialogical credibility if the issue of evangelization is not sorted out better that it has been thus far.

The second assertion that follows from the various Christian documents is that Christianity cannot be presented as the simple fulfilment of Judaism. In the history of Christianity, the churches have often denigrated Jews and Judaism in theology, preaching, liturgy and art. In better moments they have argued that the Jewish tradition contained inchoatively religious perceptions that became fully understood only in the New Testament. The Old Testament was presented as a foil, or a best, as a prelude to Christian belief. Post-biblical Jewish thought, including Jewish critical perspectives from the first century of the common era and beyond, played no role in Christian theology. The common line of argument has been that anything worthwhile in Judaism has been subsumed into Christianity through Christ. This would seem to be the approach advocated recently by the Vatican doctrinal congregation.

In recent years most of the new Christian documents on the Church's relationship with Judaism and the Jewish people have emphasized how positively Jesus and the early Christian community were rooted in the Judaism of its day. *Nostra Aetate* began this process, but it is advanced considerably, for example, in the Vatican *Notes* of 1985. Yet other church documents continue the superiority motif. In the new Catholic catechism, for example, there are passages that continue to reinforce the classical view that Christian "love" totally exceeds any notion of love found within Judaism despite the fact that the scholarship of the past several decades has rendered such a view utterly simplistic. Here again we must consider non-implementation of the Christian-Jewish documents within the broader framework of Christian theology. The one area where there has generally been a marked change is in denominational textbooks at the primary and secondary school levels. The recent examination of textbooks by researchers such as Philip Cunningham give encouraging evidence of a transfer of the dialogue documents' insistence on the rootedness of Jesus and the apostolic church in Judaism to basic Christian education.

Let me make just one observation here in connection with a point made by Edward Kessler regarding *Dabru Emet*. He points out quite correctly, and it is a point I have not heard before in connection with this groundbreaking document, that there is no mention of the Jewishness of Jesus. While I had not considered this before, I do think this is a genuine lack in the document. It omits an important point of connection between Jews and Christians. It also opens the door to a much wider discussion based on our fundamentally new understanding of the nature of the separation of the church and synagogue which has begun to emerge in the writings of such scholars as Daniel Boyarin, Anthony Saldarini, Robert Wilken, Alan Segal, Lois Feldman, Robin Scroggs and Marianne Dacy. I grew up, as did many other Christians in this assembly, with the notion that the church has been established pretty much as we know it within Jesus' lifetime. The Christian community, in other words, was a distinct entity by the time Jesus died. But we know this not to be the case. There is growing consensus that we cannot even begin to speak of a distinctive Christian identity until after the Jewish war with Rome which ended in 70 CE. And we now know that Christians continued to participate in synagogue worship (in what capacity we do not know) well beyond that, in some places even for several centuries. This continued participation certainly has implications for both Christians and Jews in terms of how we view ourselves. *Dabru Emet* is silent on this as are all the Christian documents. These new findings certainly will form part of our homework for the coming decades since they are beginning to generate a re-imaging of the basic relationship with such terms as "fraternal twins," "siblings," "partners in waiting" and "co-emergence" now being openly proposed.

The basic point that needs emphasizing, and which few of the existing documents make clear, is that the new understanding of the Christian-Jewish relationship touches the very heart of Christian self-identity. One of the best statements I have seen along these lines of late was composed by Stanislav Obirek. It is found in a letter to the General of the Society of Jesus from the Krakow Congress of "Jesuits and Jews" that met from December 27-31, 1998. The words of that document are a fitting conclusion to this section of my paper:

> How can we assimilate the impact of the Jewish-Christian dialogue into every aspect of our theology? In particular, how can we bring our appreciation of the Jewish identity of Jesus to bear upon our Christology, and our recognition of the permanent witness of Judaism as a living faith to bear upon our Ecclesiology and upon our understanding of what

inculteration means in the multiple cultures of our world today? How do we reflect upon the Jewish roots of Christianity, the presence of Jews in our societies, on their vocation and their understanding of covenant? What do our insights about Jews and their insights about Christians imply for a Christian understanding of religious pluralism?[7]

The next issue I would like to consider is how the documents deal with the painful history of antisemitism and its role during the Holocaust. Generally speaking the documents, both Catholic and Protestant, have acknowledged antisemitism as a widespread reality in the churches, which has scarred their very soul. Statements such as the Evangelical Lutheran Church in America's repudiation of the teachings of Martin Luther on the Jews, the Council of Churches' statement in the Netherlands, the French Catholic Bishops' Statement and the Vatican document *We Remember* certainly acknowledge the presence of antisemitism in Christian history. As a generalization, I would say that many of the Protestant documents do a better job connecting Christian antisemitism directly to regular church teaching and practices than do Catholic ones. *We Remember*, as I have written elsewhere[8], seems to identify the problem with wayward people who had gone astray by following strange teachers rather than admit that many of these wayward people honestly believed they were following popular church teaching as they heard it proclaimed in sermons and depicted in church art. I remember visiting Strasbourg Cathedral a couple of years ago while speaking at a conference at the European parliament. This cathedral is noteworthy for its depictions in stone on the side façade of the church as a vibrant young woman and the synagogue as a decrepit old woman, bent over and blindfolded, holding a broken Torah. Strasbourg is not the only such depiction but it is the most famous. And in the pre-literacy days it no doubt had a powerful impact on ordinary believers. I wondered what the cathedral guide would say about this depiction during the official tour. I thought he might pass over it. He did not. Rather he proclaimed that these images show the unity of church and synagogue. I wanted to shout out an expletive, but clerical propriety kept me restrained. But this illustrates our problem. Despite the statements about the history of Christian antisemitism in the various documents it remains profoundly difficult for Christians to integrate this reality into their ordinary understanding of the church. The late pioneer in Christian-Jewish relations Fr. Edward Flannery once remarked that Christians have torn out of their textbooks the chapters of history which Jews know the best. Another test of the success of the documents will be if and when these chapters on Christian antisemitism will be returned to the regular educational materials in Christian schools.

Regarding the related issue of the Holocaust the documentary picture is mixed. Some statements such as the Rhineland Synod statement and the French Catholic Bishops' document do link classical Christian antisemitism with the Holocaust. Others, such as *We Remember*, insist that Nazism was a phenomenon quite distinct from traditional Christian antisemitism. The truth is that on the ideological level it is quite correct to say that Nazism represents a new phase in group hatred that ultimately would have eliminated all religious groups. But if we stop there we will miss the connection, particularly at the grass roots level, where classical Christian antisemitism was decisive in leading Christians to become collaborators or bystanders as the Nazis launched their frontal attack on the Jews of Europe. I have argued that classical antisemitism provided an indispensable seedbed for the success of Nazism in countries that were overwhelmingly Christian. I might add that *Dabru Emet* is not particularly helpful in relation to this issue. In asserting in bold type in its first sentence on the Holocaust that Nazism was not a Christian phenomenon, it unintentionally can take Christians off the hook even though in the later part of this paragraph it qualifies this initial assertion to a degree.

Limited as some of the documents are, they have combined to engender a growing interest in Holocaust education within the churches. The recent publication from the US Catholic Bishops' Conference on the implement-ation of *We Remember* in American Catholic education is one welcome example of such a trend.[9] Another is the work of the National Catholic Center for Holocaust Education based at Seton Hill College near Pittsburgh, as well as the creative efforts of Beth Shalom here in Great Britain. So I am somewhat encouraged on this front.

What is almost totally absent in any of the institutional documents is the realization that the Holocaust poses a fundamental challenge for all religious thinking. Jewish scholars have generally taken a lead here, but some Christians such as Roy and Alice Eckardt, David Tracy, John Roth and Franklin Sherman have joined their Jewish colleagues. Let me be clear. In my judgment post-Holocaust theology involves something more than a rethinking of the covenantal relationship between Christians and Jews, though surely such rethinking remains a central part of post-Holocaust theological challenge. But beyond covenantal redefinition the Holocaust calls us to think anew about the basic meaning of God, Christ, the Church and ethics. Such reflection has begun to take place but it is not acknowledged in any of the documents of which I am aware.

My third major area of concern is worship. Some documents such as the 1985 Vatican *Notes*, the United Church of Canada document, and a more recent statement from the Catholic Bishops of England and Wales, do take up the issue. By far the most comprehensive attempt to integrate the new thinking about Jews into the liturgy is to be found in a document issued in September 1988 by the Catholic Bishops' Committee on the Liturgy in the United States.[10] This document, focused on preaching, goes through the entire liturgical year, suggesting how key readings of each season need to be presented in light of the new understanding of the Catholic-Jewish relationship. My regret is that this document, as good as it is, seems to have had minimal impact on courses in preaching and in preaching institutes that are held throughout the United States, especially during the summer. I have examined some course bibliographies, books on preaching and the program for the preaching institutes and have found scant, if any, mention of this document. Here is a document that calls out for further implementation.

But even this document, as good as it is, does not deal with the very structure of Catholic liturgy. So much of that liturgy, is geared to a "fulfilment Christology" that at best renders Jews and Judaism a prelude to Christianity. The fact that the Hebrew Scriptures are not read in the Easter season in many denominations when the church is retelling the story of its birth leaves the average worshipper thinking that these readings have no constructive place in Christian self-definition. And I have to wonder whether people leaving Christian houses of worship at the end of Holy Week believe what *Nostra Aetate* and the other major Christian documents have underlined, that Jews and Christians remain "intimately bonded," to paraphrase the words of John Paul II. Holy Week remains the real test in my judgment as to whether the many affirmations by the Christian churches regarding continued Jewish covenantal inclusion have indeed infiltrated the heart of Christian faith. My sense is, despite some progress, they have not.

The liturgy continues to use texts from the New Testament which easily generate continued stereotypes of Jews and Judaism in the many liturgical and preaching commentaries on the market today. Let me cite just three recent examples. The distributor of one of the most widely used parish bulletin sheets (J.S. Paluch) had in its introduction to the Scripture reading for the third Sunday of Lent 2000 the following statement: "Throughout John's Gospel, Jesus consistently transcends those things central to the Jewish tradition. Central to their tradition was the temple, so for Jesus to offer himself as a "new" temple at the beginning of the gospel leads very naturally into the rest of the gospel." An even worse example is the commentary on the very same texts found in the quarterly publication of another major American liturgical publisher GIA Publications of Chicago. It reads: "Jesus is determined to replace the tables of legalism tended by the merchants of hypocrisy. These tables, like the Temple, will be replaced by him, the new Temple of the New Covenant whereby he provides the passage to the Holy One. As assured as his replacing the wedding water at Cana with superlative wine, the replacement of the old temple with the new one would be just as earth shattering." A third example, which does show some sensitivity to the new developments in Christian-Jewish understanding, comes from the *Loose-Leaf Lectionary of the Mass* published by The Liturgical Press. The reading in question is Hebrews 8:6-13 which has Jesus declaring "the old covenant" obsolete. One wonders whether such a passage should in fact remain part of the lectionary given the fact that Vatican II clearly chose Romans 9-11 over this passage which is never cited in *Nostra Aetate*. The commentary attached to the reading says "The old Israel apparently observed the covenant simply as a set of laws, according to Hebrews, without any corresponding interior commitment." But the commentary does go on to say, "But we have enough evidence in the times before of Christ of the prophets insisting that the covenant should be interior to question whether it was over a poorly external matter."[11] So this commentary obviously is struggling to make sense of the passage in light of the spirit of *Nostra Aetate*. But how many congregants will hear only the initial part of the commentary and tune out the qualification. Again, I repeat, should such passages be retained in the lectionary? I would argue not in the light of *Nostra Aetate*.

Finally, in the liturgical area, we must begin to ask together as Christians and Jews what it means to worship in this post-modern age, in an era of Holocaust, genocides and mass starvation. These are the kinds of questions that Liam Tracey has tackled and that Arnold Eisen and David Power have brought to our attention. I might mention here that the Cardinal Bernardin Center will sponsor Jewish-Christian conversation on worship revolving around Arnold Eisen's book[12] in October this year in Chicago.

In closing, let me mention two more areas that have been mentioned in the institutional statements. The first is the importance of the land tradition in Judaism. A number of Protestant and Catholic documents have positively acknowledged this tradition, including the Jewish people's special link to Jerusalem. In an important statement several years ago Pope John Paul II clearly recognised how central Jerusalem remains to religious identity in Judaism. The preface to the Accord between the Holy See and Israel specifically alludes to the history of Catholic-Jewish encounter which includes the Christian theology of Jewish dispersion. So this essentially political document is at its root a theological document as well.[13] There are also numerous statements on concrete issues in the Middle East conflict. Generally speaking, the Protestant statements coming from the World Council of Churches and regional and denominational Protestant/ Orthodox entities have been quite critical of Israel. The Catholic statements, whether from the Vatican or from national Catholic bodies, have tended to be somewhat more favourable to Israel, although I detect a growing shift in Catholic circles to a more critical posture regarding Israeli policies.

As my colleague Edward Kessler has already indicated, we must place the Christian-Jewish dialogue in a global context. This means, first of all, an awareness of the major global challenges now facing humanity. I am encouraged to see the dialogue beginning to take up such issues as the death penalty (Jews and Catholics in the USA) and ecology (the Vatican and the International Jewish Committee for Interreligious Consultation). Issues such as these, including the international debt question and the ideology of the global market which John Paul II has recognized as the ideological challenge of our day, must be part of the Christian-Jewish dialogue as well. We cannot confine ourselves to theological and narrowly religious issues if we are to make our dialogue significant for the world at large. In this context we need to recall, for example, that the Christian-Jewish dialogue in the United States arose out of a joint Catholic-Jewish-Protestant struggle for justice for America's working class. That common commitment needs now to be renewed on a global level.

We must also make every effort to bring the issues of the Christian-Jewish dialogue to the world outside the North Atlantic region. Christian-Jewish understanding has central implications for religious understanding everywhere, not only in the North Atlantic region, as an article in *The Ecumenical Review* of the World Council of Churches once argued. In this vein I commend the efforts of Hans Ucko of the World Council of Churches who has been making efforts to bring the dialogue to Christians of Africa and Asia. His efforts will bear fruit this coming November when IJCIC and the World Council of Churches sponsor a Jewish-Christian dialogue in the Cameroon's.

The institutional statements have brought us a very long way in just a half century. This is indeed a remarkable achievement and we should truly rejoice in what has been accomplished in such a short time given nearly two thousand years of a tortured relationship. But many challenges continue to face us which shall need courage to confront. Indeed, as the American poet Robert Frost has said, "I have promises to keep and miles to go before I sleep."[14]

Notes

1   Cf. Helga Croner (ed.), *Stepping Stones to Further Jewish-Christian Relations: An Unabridged Collection of Christian Documents*. London/ New York: Stimulus Books, 1977; Helga Croner (ed.), *More Stepping Stones to Jewish-Christian Relations: An Unabridged Collection of Christian Documents 1975-1983*. New York/Mahwah: Paulist Press. A Stimulus Book, 1985. Eugene J. Fisher and Leon Klenicki (eds.), *In Our Time: The Flowering of Jewish-Catholic Dialogue*. New York/Mahwah: Paulist Press. A Stimulus Book, 1990. Allan Brockway, Paul van Buren, Rolf Rendtorff and Simon Schoon (eds.), *The Theology of the Churches and the Jewish People: Statements by the World Council of Churches and its Member Churches*. Geneva: WCC Publications, 1988. Eugene Fisher and Leon Klenicki (eds.), *John Paul II on Jews and Judaism*. Washington: USCC Publications, 1987. Eugene J. Fisher and Leon Klenicki (eds.), *Spiritual Pilgrimage: Texts on Jews and Judaism 1979-1995*. New York: Crossroad, 1995, United Methodist Church, *Building New Bridges in Hope: Statement of the United Methodist Church on Christian-Jewish Relations*. New York: General Commission on Christian Unity and Interreligious Concerns, 1996. Evangelical Lutheran Church in America, *Guidelines for Lutheran-Jewish Relations*. Chicago: Department for Ecumenical Affairs, Evangelical Lutheran Church in America, 1998. The United Church of Canada, *Bearing Faithful Witness: United Church-Jewish Relations Today (Study Document)*. Etobicoke, O, Canada: The Committee on Inter-Church and Inter-Faith Relations, 1997., Alice L. Eckardt, "How are the Protestant Churches Responding Fifty Years After?" in John K. Roth and Elisabeth Maxwell (eds.), *Remembering for the Future: The Holocaust in an Age of Genocide*, Vol 2: Ethics and Religion. Houndmills, Basingstoke, Hampshire, UK: Palgrave, 2001, 533-543.

2   Eugene J. Fisher, "The Evolution of a Tradition: From *Nostra Aetate* to the *Notes*," in International Catholic-Jewish Liaison Committee (eds.), *Fifteen Years of Catholic-Jewish Dialogue*. Rome: Libreria Editrice

Vaticana and Libreria Editrice Lateranense, 1988, 239.

3   Gregory Baum, "The Social Context of American Catholic
     Theology," in George Kilcourse (ed.), *Proceedings of the 41ˢᵗ Annual
     Meeting: Catholic Theological Society of America*, 1986, 87.

4   Johann-Baptist Metz, "Facing the Jews: Christian Theology after
     Auschwitz," in Elisabeth Schussler-Fiorenza and David Tracy (eds.),
     The Holocaust as Interruption. Concilium 175. Edinburgh: T & T Clark,
     1984, 27.

5   In recent addresses to the International Liaison Committee co-
     sponsored by the Vatican and International Jewish Committee for
     Interreligious Consultation (IJCIC) in May 2001 and to the annual
     meeting of the International Council of Christians & Jews in
     Montevideo, Uruguay, in July 2001 Cardinal Walter Kasper stated
     quite strongly that the Catholic Church has no mission to the Jews.
     He also began to develop theological argumentation to justify this
     position, arguing in part that Jews are in a totally special situation in
     terms of relations with the Church because they possess authentic
     revelation. It is hoped that Cardinal Kasper will further amplify his
     theological argumentation in future writings. Without such a
     theological basis the assertion that there is no mission to the Jews
     from the Catholic perspective rests on rather shaky ground. Philip
     Cunningham has developed a comprehensive analysis of *Dominus
     Iesus* and Catholic-Jewish relations in an essay *"Dominus Iesus* and
     Catholic Magisterial Teaching on Jews and Judaism" in a volume
     developed by the theology faculty at Boston College to be published
     by Orbis Books.

6   Tommaso Federici, "Mission and Witness of the Church," in
     International Catholic-Jewish Liaison Committee (eds.), *Fifteen Years
     of Catholic-Jewish Dialogue*, 46-62; For the implications of the
     Christian-Jewish Dialogue on the theology of religious pluralism,
     cf. John Pawlikowski, "Toward a Theology of Religious Diversity,"
     Journal of Ecumenical Studies, Winter 1989, 138-153.

7   Cf. B.W. Oppenheim (ed.), *Conference Proceedings: Examination of
     Conscience: Polish Church Confronts Antisemitism.* Los Angeles: Loyola
     Marymount University, 1999, 81.

8   John T. Pawlikowski, "The Vatican and the Holocaust: Putting *We
     Remember* in Context," *Dimensions*, 12:2, 11-16; and John T.
     Pawlikowski, "*We Remember:* Looking back, looking ahead," *The*

Month, January 2000, 3-8.

[9] Secretariat for Ecumenical and Interreligious Affairs, National Conference of Catholic Bishops, *Catholic Teaching on the Shoah: Implementing the Holy See's We Remember*. Washington: United States Catholic Conference, 2001.

[10] Bishops' Committee on the Liturgy, National Conference of Catholic Bishops, *God's Mercy Endures Forever: Guidelines on the Presentation of Jews and Judaism in Catholic Preaching*. Washington: United States Catholic Conference, 1988. Also cf. John T. Pawlikowski and James A. Wilde, *When Catholics Speak About Jews*. Chicago: Liturgy Training Publications, 1987 and Eugene J. Fisher (ed.), *The Jewish Roots of Christian Liturgy*. New York/Mahwah: Paulist Press, 1990.

[11] Cf. Bulletin for March 26, 2000. Shiller Park, IL: J.S. Paluch, 1; Commentary on Readings for Sunday, March 26, 2000 (Third Sunday of Lent) *GIA Quarterly*, 11:2 (Winter 2000), 2; and *Loose-Leaf Lectionary for Mass*, November 1, 2000-January 31, 2001. Collegeville, MN: The Liturgical Press, 274.

[12] Arnold Eisen, *Rethinking Modern Judaism: Ritual, Commandment, Community*. Chicago: University of Chicago Press, 1998.

[13] "The Vatican-Israel Accord: Their Implications for Catholic Faith and Teaching," in Eugene J. Fisher and Leon Klenicki (eds.), *A Challenge Long Delayed: The Diplomatic Exchange Between The Holy See And The State Of Israel*. New York: Anti-Defamation League, 10-19.

[14] Robert Frost, *Stopping by Woods on a Snowy Evening*. See www. robert frost.org.

Dabru Emet and the Future Direction of Jewish-Christian Relations

David Fox Sandmel

In the course of this book there are several brief references to "Dabru Emet: A Jewish Statement on Christians and Christianity," and in this chapter I intend to examine this seminal document. Dabru Emet ('Speak Truth') represents a promising direction for the future because it articulates a bold and innovative Jewish engagement with Christianity. In addition, I will comment on other concerns that I believe will effect Jewish-Christian relations in the 21st century.

In order to understand Dabru Emet, the most important thing to remember is that it was written by Jews for Jews. Like Vatican documents, whose meaning is only clear when read in the context of the Roman Catholics authorities speaking to a Roman Catholic audience in the language of the Roman Catholic tradition, Dabru Emet only makes sense when read with the premise that Jewish writers are speaking first and foremost to Jews. Christians may be listening in to the conversation, and should, since it is, to a great extent, about them. But the key question when reading Dabru Emet is, "Why would Jews say this to other Jews?"

Dabru Emet was written by a diverse group of Jewish scholars. David Novak received his rabbinic ordination at the Conservative movement's Jewish Theological Seminary and teaches at the University of Toronto. He is now identified with the Union for Traditional Judaism, a comparatively new Jewish movement that split from the Conservative movement over what it sees as the latter's abandonment of its commitment to halachic process. Tikva Frymer-Kensky is a professor at the University of Chicago Divinity School. Before that, she taught for many years at the Reconstructionist Rabbinical College. She also has close ties to the Jewish

Theological Seminary (JTS), where she studied. Michael Signer was ordained at the Reform movement's Hebrew Union College-Jewish Institute of Religion, and taught for many years at its Los Angeles campus. He currently teaches at the University of Notre Dame. Peter Ochs teaches at the University of Virginia. He is a little harder to locate on the Jewish spectrum. He too has ties to JTS, but has described himself to me as "funkadox". My background is Reform. I became involved in the project after the initial draft of the statement had been written and have managed the process that moved Dabru Emet from rough draft to finished product. I was intimately involved in crafting its final form – some of the wording is mine as is the title – and have served as the spokesperson for the project since its publication in September 2000. In addition to the four authors, Dabru Emet has been signed by over 200 rabbis and Jewish scholars from North America, Israel, and Great Britain, representing Reform, Reconstructionist, Conservative, and Orthodox Jews. The diversity among the authors and signers is one of the most remarkable aspects of Dabru Emet.

So, why did this group of scholars write Dabru Emet? Why would Jews want to say these things to other Jews? And why would they publish them as a full-page advertisement in the *New York Times* and *Baltimore Sun*? The answer to this last question is straightforward: we wanted to make a splash, to get the attention of the Jewish community. And to do that we had to break out of the confines of the rarified air of academia and interfaith gatherings and the normal modes of publication. For better or worse, it is to a major newspaper like the *New York Times* that the Jewish community pays attention, not to academic journals or even the Anglo-Jewish press.

The authors of Dabru Emet view it as a first step, not the final word. Indeed, Dabru Emet is, by definition, limited in what it can communicate. As a brief document of about 1,100 words (the maximum we could use and still have print large enough that people would want to read it), Dabru Emet makes broad assertions and speaks in generalities that can only point to some of the issues that demand further exploration. Dabru Emet is designed to provoke further study, to promote conversation, first and foremost, within the Jewish community, and, secondly, between Jews and Christians. And to support that conversation and flesh out what is contained in the brief statement, two additional resources have been produced. *Christianity in Jewish Terms* (Boulder, Colo: Westview Press, 2000), edited by myself and the authors of Dabru Emet, is a collection of scholarly essays that attempts to provide Jews with a Jewish point of reference and a Jewish language with which it can begin to grapple with Christianity. Another volume, *Irreconcilable Differences? A Learning Resource for Jews and Christians* (Boulder. Colo.: Westview Press, 2001), edited by myself, Rosann Catalano, and Christopher Leighton, contains essays co-written by Jewish and Christian educators and is designed for use by high-school, college, and adult learners. Dabru Emet and its supporting publications seek to challenge the Jewish community (academic, rabbinic, and lay) and to provide it with the tools to think about itself and about Christianity theologically, in ways that it has rarely, if ever, done before.

Why should Jews want – or need – to think about Christianity differently? First, Christianity has changed in the last fifty years. This is not news for those of us who are involved in Jewish-Christian relations; much of the Jewish world, however, is not aware of the theological transformation of Christianity since the Shoah. One of the purposes of Dabru Emet is to inform Jews of these changes. There are Christians who are similarly uninformed about post-Holocaust Christian theology; perhaps Dabru Emet will stimulate some of them to learn more about this phenomenon. Finally, in writing Dabru Emet, the authors wanted to affirm those scholars and theologians whose work is at the heart of this shift in Christian thinking, some of whom took great risks challenging fundamental aspects of church teaching and striving to change traditional thinking.

Second, if the Jewish community is not only to survive, but also to thrive – if there is to be Jewish continuity – then it must be able to respond to its environment. It is not an effective communal strategy to posit a Christian world that may have existed fifty or a hundred or five hundred years ago. Jews need to understand what their Christian neighbors are saying *today* about Jews, about what modern society should become, and about the place of Jews in that society. Jews need to be able to distinguish what forms of Christian belief are friendly to Judaism and which are not, and with whom we can form coalitions for social or religious agendas.

Historically, living as a minority among a Christian majority, Jews have learned about Christianity in non-Jewish terms. Behind Dabru Emet is the belief that it is now time for Jews to learn about Christianity in *our* terms, to hear how Christian belief sounds when it is taught in a Jewish language and vocabulary, and in categories that make sense form a Jewish perspective. This may enable Jews to understand Christianity, perhaps for the first time.

That Jews may now be able to think about Christianity differently than before signals that Judaism, as well as Christianity, has changed. Jews, like other people, are subject to the separation between science and reason on the one hand and faith and tradition on the other that causes a dissonance and a distancing between them and their tradition. As a community, however, Jews today are perhaps as powerful and as confident as they have been in over two millennia. The reestablishment of a Jewish national entity in the land of Israel and the emergence of strong and influential Jewish community in America are unprecedented in Jewish history. At the same time, the Jewish community is threatened by a collapse brought on by its own ignorance. This is compounded by its stubborn insistence on perceiving itself as a victim and on its use of that perception as a substitute for substantial understanding of itself based on a deep knowledge of its history and traditional resources for living in the world.

This brings us to the radical, counterintuitive aspect of Dabru Emet. Dabru Emet challenges Jews to reconsider attitudes toward Christianity in light of the changes in post-Holocaust Christianity. It also challenges Jews to learn about Christianity in Jewish terms. However, Jews cannot learn about Christianity unless they learn about the Jewish tradition as well. *At its core, Dabru Emet is also about Jews understanding themselves.* It is about reclaiming and recreating a vital, authentic, and self-confident Judaism that can enable Jews to thrive in a changing world and to contribute to it from the resources of the Jewish tradition.

The Jewish community of late has devoted a great deal of energy and effort to Jewish education. The rapid growth of day schools and adult education programs demonstrates that there is a craving within the Jewish community for a deeper anchor for identity than collective victimhood or a long-distance connection to the state of Israel. The return to Jewish learning is a positive trend – but it has been coupled, to some extent, with a turning inward and a turning away from involvement with other religious communities. Dabru Emet is based on the belief that there is a certain kind of religious learning that can only take place in the presence of the "other." When one studies in the presence of the other, one certainly learns *about* the other – about his tradition, about her reading of scripture, and the like. But there is also the potential to learn about one's self and about one's own tradition in a way that results in a deepened commitment to one's own particularity. When Jews and Christians study together, they certainly gain understanding that can replace old fears and stereotypes with respect and tolerance – a worthy goal in and of itself – but Jews and Christians can, in the process, become better Jews and Christians. This is counterintuitive, at least to Jews, who traditionally have been leery of encounters with Christians for fear of being proselytized. Dabru Emet challenges Jews to consider that there is something of value that they can learn *about their own Judaism* from Christians and Christianity.

Dabru Emet marks an important turning point in Jewish-Christian relations for other reasons as well. I know of no other statement from any Jewish group that addresses the question of Christianity from a Jewish theological standpoint. Jews have often reacted to statements from the Vatican and other Christian bodies, critiquing the content, and, as it were, giving them a "grade" on how well they measure up to Jewish expectations. Jewish scholars have certainly written about Christianity, often defensively, sometimes appreciatively. The fact remains, however, that no Jewish group has ever issued a theological statement similar to Dabru Emet.[1]

It is also significant that Dabru Emet did not come from any of the traditional sources in the Jewish community. It did not come from any of the seminaries, or from any rabbinic association, or from any of the denominational movements, or from the defense agencies that have previously taken the lead in Jewish-Christian relations. It should be noted that leaders of many of these organizations endorsed Dabru Emet. The initiative came from a group of academics, all of who are currently employed outside the Jewish community. While this may, in part, reflect the fact that academics are not subject to the same communal pressures and politics as those who work within the Jewish community, there is more to it than that. As Peter Ochs and I wrote:

> We were all educated, in part, in American universities, alongside Christian students and teachers of religion and theology, some of whom became friends and colleagues. And compatriots, too: fellow students of scripture and history and philosophy and ethics. Each of us had Christian colleagues whose concerns overlapped with aspects of our own Jewish pursuits: our concerns, for example, to nurture disciplines of reason as instruments of our religion and to revitalize the role of biblically based studies as sources of ethical thinking. We knew that Jews and Christians took different approaches to Bible studies: our approach was rabbinic, theirs was based on patristic and/or contemporary Catholic or Reformation models of

reading. But each of us found – to our initial surprise and against the expectations of other Jewish colleagues and kinfolk – that an expanding number of contemporary Jewish and Christian thinkers adopted analogous strategies for defending their biblical traditions against three common challenges. One common challenge was the emergence of radically secular, materialistic, and relativistic tendencies that diminish the influence of any biblical religion in the contemporary West... Another common challenge was the emergence of radical religious fundamentalisms as reactionary bulwarks against modern secularism...A third common challenge ... [was] the implosion of religious faith and confidence that has followed the Shoah. [2]

Thus Dabru Emet is unique in terms of its authors and as a document that presents a proactive and positive theological approach to Christianity. It represents what might be called a "second stage" of the dialogue, moving from the cautious first steps of overcoming past enmity and building trust to a deep exchange on essential theological issues.

I would like now to return to the point with which I started, that Dabru Emet is written by Jews for Jews and give one example of how that affects one's reading of the document. The first proposal states:

> **Jews and Christians worship the same God.** Before the rise of Christianity, Jews were the only worshippers of the God of Israel. But Christians also worship the God of Abraham, Isaac, and Jacob; creator of heaven and earth. While Christian worship is not a viable religious choice for Jews, as Jewish theologians we rejoice that, through Christianity, hundreds of millions of people have entered into relationship with the God of Israel.

Some Christians have been surprised that the statement that Jews and Christians worship the same God is by no means a given among Jews. After all, the Christian God-concept includes ideas like the triune nature of God and the incarnation – both of which are considered to be incompatible with the strict Jewish understanding of monotheism. The statement that Jews and Christians worship the same God is not a radical innovation on the part of the authors of Dabru Emet. Rather, they are continuing a line of argument that can be traced back almost 700 years in rabbinic thought.

But what does it mean to say to Jews that Christians worship the same

God as Jews? First, it counters the notion in the Jewish tradition that Christians are idolaters. At certain times and in certain Jewish communities, this had profound practical and legal ramifications. For most Jews today, it could have profound social and intercommunal ramifications, in terms of re-orienting our perception of Christian world. Second, if one is truly to understand this proposal, then one must learn about *both* Jewish and Christian ideas of God. Thus, to comprehend what lies behind the short paragraph in Dabru Emet, one must engage not only the Christian tradition but also the Jewish tradition and learn how each approaches God, what the commonalties and differences really are. This is an educational adventure from which one will emerge better informed not only about the other, but also about oneself.

Edward Kessler, earlier in this book, asked why the fact of Jesus' Jewishness is not mentioned in Dabru Emet. Dabru Emet is Jews talking to Jews. The Jewishness of Jesus is not new information for Jews; we have always known that. It is stated plainly in rabbinic literature and Jews have never denied it. In the Christian tradition, however, there is a history of denying the Jewishness of Jesus. The "rediscovery" of the Jewish Jesus has been a significant factor in the creation of a new Christian theology of Judaism and the building of a new Jewish-Christian relationship. Thus, while the Jewishness of Jesus has profound theological significance for Christians, it does not have similar significance for Jews.

A final question about Dabru Emet – can it be judged a success? In the short term, I think the answer is an unqualified "yes." The statement received a great deal of media attention when it was released. It has been translated into French, German, Spanish, Italian, Polish, Ukrainian, and Japanese (and other languages of which I am unaware). It is being discussed at conferences and in journals. And Jews and Christians are studying it separately and together in communities in America and Europe. The book *Christianity in Jewish Terms* is already being used in college courses,[3] and it is our hope that *Irreconcilable Differences? A Learning Resource for Jews and Christians* will be also be widely read and discussed. I think the best image for judging the ultimate success of Dabru Emet is that of a page of Talmud, in which the text occupies the center of the page and is surrounded by ever growing layers of commentary. Dabru Emet is a beginning, an important beginning; it is a call for an engagement through which Jews and Christians can approach not only each other, but their own traditions in such a way that each community is strengthened, and together they can work to repair the world.

While Dabru Emet represents a positive and challenging step forward for Jewish-Christian relations, there are other factors that concern me when I look to the future. One is my sense that for some in the Jewish community, Jewish-Christian dialogue has lost some of its appeal. On a superficial level, it is simply no longer perceived "new and exciting." A generation ago, engaging in dialogue was bold and courageous; that is no longer the case. There are other, more "sexy" issues and activities for rabbis and congregations to pursue.

Coupled with this is a general turning inward within the Jewish community. Some of this turning inward represents a sense that Jewish-Christian dialogue has been, if not a failure, then at best only a qualified success. The mainline Protestant churches, which were the first to become actively involved in dialogue, are seen by the Jewish community to have turned against Israel and to have taken up the cause of the Palestinians. This is viewed as a betrayal of the trust that was being built that reveals fundamental lack of understanding on the part of these Christians of the centrality of the state of Israel to Jews. Some might even suggest that this anti-Israel stance represents an essential anti-Semitism that is inseparable from Christianity. The Roman Catholic Church has, since the publication of Nostra Aetate, become the major Christian partner in the dialogue. The many positive steps and statements of the Vatican, including the visit of John Paul II to Israel are countered, at least in perception of many Jews, by crosses at Auschwitz, the canonization of Edith Stein, the beatification of Pius IX and Pius XII, and by some of the equivocal language in *We Remember: A Reflection on the Shoah*. The ongoing controversy over the role of the pope and the Vatican during the Shoah, and the seeming unwillingness to open the Vatican archives to historians make many Jews wary of the sincerity of Catholic efforts of reconciliation with Jews. For those who tend mistrust, it is as if for every step forward the Roman Catholic Church makes, its takes two backward. Even some of those who are not opposed to Jewish-Christian dialogue view it as a luxury that the community cannot afford at this moment. In the face of growing intermarriage rates, declining birthrates, and disaffection, all energy and resources should be put in strengthening the Jewish community by focusing on Judaism. While I am sympathetic to goal of preserving and invigorating the Jewish community, I think that engaging the Christian community is, at this stage of Jewish history and at this stage of the dialogue, essential to Jewish survival. The challenge then, is for the Jewish community to recognize that its vested interest in Jewish-Christian dialogue should not be limited to theologians, nor for purposes of "defense," but for its own health and future.

The other major challenge to Jewish-Christian relations is posed by the growing religious diversity within our communities. Will Herberg's famous book *Protestant, Catholic, Jew* (New York: 1960) was based on a perception of American society that no longer reflects reality. While the European situation is not the same as that in America, it too is experiencing a change is its religious composition. As other religious communities compete for our attention (and we for theirs), I believe that we will be challenged to defend the validity of continuing an exclusive Jewish-Christian dialogue. I do not have the space here to lay out the arguments to support this exclusivity. Suffice it to say that because of our entangled history, scriptures, and theology, Jews and Christians have things to say to and learn from each other that cannot be said or learned from any other dialogue partner. I am not suggesting that dialogue with other faith traditions is unimportant or without value. However, when a third party (or more) comes to the table, the nature of the discussion must change. As the new voices in our culture become more prominent, Jews and Christians will have to be able to articulate to ourselves and to others why this relationship is unique and why it must be preserved even as we develop relations with other communities.

In conclusion, as I look to future, I see both promise and challenge. The promise is represented by Dabru Emet and the potential for moving the dialogue to a new level of theological exchange. Such a move has been made possible by several decades of work by the pioneers of Jewish-Christian relations to whom we owe so much. The challenge is twofold. First, it requires convincing the Jewish community that it has a vital stake in the conversation with Christians. Second, it requires the development of a rationale for maintaining a separate Jewish-Christian dialogue even as Jews and Christians, separately and together pursue relations with other religions.

Notes

1   One notable predecessor of *Dabru Emet* can be found in Samuel Sandmel's "A Proposed Declaration: 'The Synagogue and the Jewish People.'" (*We Jews and You Christians* [Philadelphia and New York: J. B. Lippincott Company, 1967] 144-146). While it touches on many of the issues raised by *Dabru Emet*, it is the work of an individual, not a group. In another interesting development, it was announced earlier this year that in the late 1960's the French rabbinate had commissioned a small group of rabbis and scholars, including Emanuel Levinas, to write a document about how Jews might understand Christianity. The document was written, but never released, because the rabbinate could not reach consensus about it. Preliminary reports indicate that the French document bears much similarity to *Dabru Emet*. The document is to be published in the *Revue des Etudes Juives* in the near future, but as of the final editing of this article, it has yet to appear.

2   "Christianity in Jewish Terms: A Project to Redefine the Relationship." *Cross Currents*, Winder 2000-2002, 449.

3   I recently learned that it is being translated into Polish and Russian.

Conversation Three

Tradition's Role in Shaping Religion Today

Being Entangled in Stories: the 'logic' of Catholic tradition in a post-traditional society

Jürgen Manemann

Introduction

The purpose of this essay is to explore the 'logic' of Catholic tradition by examining the context of German society, especially since the reunification of Germany. I hope that some of the insights presented in this essay are applicable to other situations, too, so that this contextualization might serve as a way to shapen the significance of tradition in an era of globalization in general. The reason for this contextualization is deeply grounded in my understanding of theology or more precisely Christian theology.

From a Catholic point of view tradition and the question of God belong together. If we do not know anything of God, without facing our situation, we do not know anything of tradition without facing our situation. Kierkegaard said, "in order to experience and understand what it means to be a Christian, it is always necessary to recognize a definite historical situation."[1] Theology means speaking of God in our time, which necessitates a diagnosis of our time in order to discover what is going on in history and society.[2] In order to face the so-called 'signs of times', (Vat. II) theology must have the capacity to provide a broad and deep analytical grasp of the present in light of the past and vice-versa.

Christian theology is not a kind of metaphysics but is seriously challenged by history and society. In fact, for Christian theology there is no world history nor 'after it' or 'above it', salvation history. The history of salvation, we Christians are talking about, is the world history

(Weltgeschichte).[3] Every way of distancing ourselves from this history, from our society and from the suffering of others is in danger of creating idols instead of speaking of God.

Thus in the following reflections on tradition I am not going to provide the reader with different understandings of tradition in the history of Christianity, my task as a Catholic theologian examining foundational theology is to speak of tradition in the present context. I have largely built upon ideas of the so-called new political theology - and this theology is explicitly a theology after Auschwitz. The following is a tentative argument.

Toward the 'Second Modernity'

Considering the meaning of tradition in our context we first have to realise that this meaning has altered significantly.[4] We are told by some intellectuals that we are entering a new stage of modernity, called 'second modernity'. This is characterized through globalization, individualization, societies without employment and ecological crisis. Ulrich Beck, a sociologist from the University of Munich (who is also an adviser to leading German politicians) heads a group which works on the project of the so called 'second modernity'. Beck and his colleagues do not just diagnose the risks and crises of the 'second modernity' negatively, but their intention is also look for possibilities of new freedom. Thus, Beck argues that these crises are not necessarily negative because what will be lost may give rise to new freedom. Of course, this freedom is based upon risk but nevertheless represents freedom.[5]

According to Beck the 'second modernity' is illustrated by two events: Chernobyl and the removal of the Berlin Wall. Both call our rationality into question, but confuse our thinking process. Both confront us in a radical way introducing uncertainty and ambivalence at the heart of contemporary institutions, practices and discourses. Beck states that the centrality of incalculability, uncertainty and ambivalence heralds the emergence of a new stage of society, which he designates 'reflexive modernity'. Because of the radical uncertainty nothing goes unchallenged. In his analysis of the 'second modernity' Beck points to the end of tradition and proclaims his vision of an unencumbered self.[6]

New Productivity of Religion

For the subject of this essay I will examine how religion fits into the concept of 'second modernity', especially religions which are based upon traditions. A society in the era of the 'second modernity' is a society of uncertainty, which is defined intrinsically as a post-traditional society. A post-traditional society — as Beck points out — is a society which is no longer based on traditions but on the knowledge of the experts. The shift from a traditional to a so-called post-traditional society is celebrated by Beck as progress, because tradition is labeled with negative words like authority, obedience, circularity; whereas the liberation from tradition in general is described with words like freedom, emancipation, dialogue and so on. Finally the post-traditional stage seems to be the end of the bourgeois emancipation.

Of course, the theorists of this understanding of 'second modernity' are aware that our situation is double-edged. Due to the growth of uncertainty, fundamentalism, and racism, resentments may rise. Religion and tradition in general are regarded by the apologists of the 'second modernity' as part of a negative reaction. Instead of differentiating between religions and traditions, Beck and others celebrate an unencumbered self that should be able to act on its own. This self should become the foundation of our society and an end in itself. In this way religions based upon tradition, institution and community are regarded as something, which hopefully will have already been or will be overcome in order to build up a better democratic society.

But is this true? Is it really the case that a democratic society without tradition and religion is much more democratic and liberating? In my view, it is the other way around — in other words, a post-traditional society is much more in danger of being manipulated, as I will show in my following remarks.

Of course we recognize a vanishing interest in institutionalized forms of religion, but this does not necessarily mean — as Beck concludes — that there is a vanishing interest in religion in general in a so-called post-traditional society. Sociologists of religion point out that we have to take into consideration the opposite: an increasing interest in religion.[7] Religion does not vanish but its form is altering. Religion becomes more and more privatized and this privatization causes a patchwork-religion. Like a patchwork biography, religion is influenced more and more by personal choices, preferences. To formulate this in another way, religion becomes more and more heretical.[8]

The crisis of tradition in 'second modernity' is at the same time a 'God crisis' and vice versa. Johann Baptist Metz points out that our situation is characterized through a religious coloured atheism. This means that atheism is religious, but 'God-less' — it is grounded in religious phenomena, which are not tied up with the biblical God - the God of Abraham, Isaac, Jacob, the God of Jesus Christ. In this respect we can describe the present situation - according to Metz — a s follows: "Religion? Yes! God? No!"[9] Or to put it in other words, "we believe without God".

To summarize: we do not experience in our so-called post-traditional society a crisis of religion in general. We are not challenged by a secularized society: on the contrary, we are challenged by a post-traditional society with an increasing interest in religion: we are confronted with a new productivity of religion.

I would like now to express my doubts concerning the future of a post-traditional society as envisioned by Beck. Using the following quotation by Gilbert Keith Chesterton as a heuristical tool, we should be aware of the danger of an unquestioned theory of post-traditional society. Chesterton wrote: "When people cease to believe in something, they do not believe in nothing; they believe in anything."[10]

German Society after the Reunification

Since the Berlin Wall came down, followed quickly by the dissolution of the USSR, some intellectuals have spoken about the "end of history". For them the victory of liberalism and capitalism over communism, the victory of the West over the East, indicates the "endpoint of mankind's ideological evolution"[11]. But this triumphal proclamation did not last long.[12] Far from having now secured for itself a position as "the endpoint of mankind's ideological evolution", our liberal democracy in Germany has, by virtue of the victory it has won, actually entered a period in which it is likely tested as severely as it has ever been before. Why?

Until 1989 our democracy in Germany defined itself by its opposition to 'real existing socialism'. And now our democracy is troubled by the absence of this negative guarantor.[13]

To some extent living in crisis is at the heart of liberal democracy in general. A liberal democracy by definition is not allowed to guarantee its own foundations because the secular state should not give definitive justification to the freedom it guarantees. Thus, this justification is transferred to the responsibility of the individual.[14] Such freedom is based on the acknowledgement of otherness but also depends on resources to make interpersonal life possible. These resources are not provided automatically but need protection because they are in danger from modernization, with its tendency to destroy traditions and to accelerate individualization. To sum up: living in a liberal democracy requires us to live with uncertainty in the public.[15] But what happens if this uncertainty gets into our "habits of the heart" (R. Bellah)? Where can we find a source of meaning, of a new appropriate meaning? How can we resist building up idols in such uncertainty?

Today, after the reunification of Germany we are confronted with a "twilight of idols" (Nietzsche), especially with different types of neo-paganism focussed on the destruction of — what they call — the "Judeo-Christian tradition". One famous gnostic paganist in present Germany is the philosopher Peter Sloterdijk.[16] On the basis of a strong anti-monotheism Sloterdijk proclaims and celebrates the end of all forms of humanism, the end of any kind of anamnestic anthropology and the beginning of a new era: the era of post-humanism, an era of the superhuman.[17] Peter Sloterdijk welcomes "the upcoming production of man" and the search for "anthropotechniques", which we need for necessary prenatal selections (Listen to the German word 'Selektion'!).In his famous attack against humanism in 1999 Sloterdijk writes referring to Nietzsche:

> With this position that man is man´s breeder, Nietzsche breaks through the humanistic horizon since humanism is never allowed to go beyond the taming and educational perspective. The humanist accepts man as a given entity and then applies to him all his taming, training and educational tools. (...) Nietzsche´s suspicion against all humanist culture insists on lifting the secret of domesticity which surrounds mankind. He wants to identify the traditional owners of the breeding monopoly - the priests and teachers, who presented themselves as philanthropic - and their hidden function. Thus he wants to initiate a historically completely new battle (...). (...) the battle between humanists and superhumanists, philanthropic representatives of our species and those who favor breeding a completely

new human being (which Nietzsche calls the '*Übermensch*')."

Sloterdijk goes on to say that we have to start thinking about "the upcoming production of man and — generally speaking — anthropotechniques", which are, according to Sloterdijk, the topics from which modern thinking should not turn away. Sloterdijk takes these topics and starts to develop the metaphysical basis for a posthumanistic era - an era in which man, or more precisely, an elite builds man in its own image.[18]

Or let me call to your attention in this context a new aggressive paganism in the so-called 'New right'. This group is trying to develop a politics of exclusion and to initiate a new struggle of culture (Kulturkampf). It longs for cultural hegemony, which is regarded as the precondition for gaining political hegemony. The 'new right' is a complex of different movements and journals grounded on ideas of the Konservative Revolution, the intellectual right wing who fought the Weimar republic, with connections to neo-nazism.[19]

The apologists of the theoretical post-traditional society underestimate the drama of these processes, because they do not believe these reactions may be caused by what they envision as a post-traditional society. For them these reactions are relics of the first stage of modernization, but not of reflexive modernization. They are not aware that post-traditional society may be the reason for the 'twilight of idols'.

If the individual self in the post-traditional society must be its own source of guidance in several ways, then each individual must always know what he wants, desires and feels. He must act so as to produce the greatest satisfaction of his wants or to express the fullest range of his impulses. Moral guidance, for example, turns into the subjective goodness of getting what you want and enjoying it. Utility replaces duty; self-expression unseats authority, 'being good' becomes 'feeling good'. This kind of expressive individualism is very well described by Robert Bellah.[20] Such an individual is in danger of losing control because the possibilities of getting what you want increases dramatically, but he can not make use of all these possibilities. Thus, the individual falls behind pressure of time and becomes a *homo accelerandus* with hate against the future and the past which reminds him of lost opportunities. The solution seems to be a paganism aiming at the procreation of the superhuman which no longer depends on past, nor on the future.

Tradition and Self-Transcendence

The apologists of the post-traditional society have forgotten to remember two things: First, if new generations do not revolt against tradition we would still live in caves; but if revolt against tradition becomes universal, we will live in caves again.[21]

Resistance against traditions as well as a cult of traditions - both seem to be necessary. What would our society be without tradition? What would reason be without tradition?

Adorno writes, "today tradition confronts us with an irreconcilable contradiction; no (single) tradition can be invoked but if all of them are eradicated, inhumanity begins its forward march".[22] What does tradition mean in such a context?

It is not enough to characterize a human being through a permanent muddling through in a post-traditional society. Human beings are story dwellers. By living in stories and traditions we become human. Traditions provide us with an anamnestic ethic.[23] But we need criteria in order to distinguish between good and bad traditions. According to Stanley Hauerwas, the central criterion is that true tradition shapes actual lives and actual communities and results in truthful lives and lives open to the foreign - the strangers and their traditions, which we should make our own tradition.[24] Could this concept be of some help? I have some doubts.

I, for example, as a Catholic and a German should never make the memories of the victims my own story - instead of being allowed to make others' memories my own, I should make the true interests of others my own which are expressed in their stories. My story is first the story of the perpetrators and the bystanders but this does not mean not to remember the stories of the victims. Through the memory of the stories of the victims we can view our own story! And then we will see if our tradition with its stories is indeed able to face the stories of the others. Therefore, according to Darrell Fasching, we have to realize that the first test of each tradition remains its openness to questions and questioning. "The second requirement is that the (tradition) must permit one to follow the questions wherever they lead, even if that takes one beyond the (tradition) one is in; even if it entails the risk of damaging the faith one seeks to secure."[25] He also states that a "master story that does not permit itself to be called into question is ultimately demonic."[26]

The 'Logic' of Catholic Tradition

So what can we say about the Catholic understanding of tradition in the context of the aforementioned problems? First of all we have to be very self-critical in making tradition a basis for criticizing our society. If tradition means being entangled with history it is not and it should not be independent of historical and social influences. Regarding tradition as something beyond changes assumes an understanding of tradition as a container of instructions. Such a statical understanding of tradition has to assume that tradition is a complex of *caelestis doctrina* which was believed everywhere, everytime and by all. The criteria for such an understanding of tradition would be generality, originality and unanimity. This concept of tradition is guided by a longing for an eternal recurrence of the same. A faith based on such an understanding of tradition is in danger of becoming believed faith instead of lived faith.

Beck's criticism of tradition underestimates the complexity of tradition. Traditions are not fixed, immutable things. Beck claims that we can be free from tradition and that we should be free from tradition is incoherent:

> Even though some traditions are 'still of benightedness, chicanery, hostility, and oppression,' the Enlightenment project of attempting to think outside any and all traditions cannot be sustained. Wolterstorff claims that 'we shall have to acknowledge what the thinkers of the Enlightenment would have found appallingly unpalatable; namely, that examination of tradition can take place only in the context of unexamined tradition, and that in our examination, our convictions as to the facts are schooled by our traditions.' ... tradition is inescapable.[27]

From a Catholic perspective *traditio* has to be regarded as a communicative process and a communicative practice.[28] The Catholic way of transmitting tradition has happened often through ruptures and contradictions! In order to understand the energy of this tradition one has to regard that from a Catholic perspective tradition is deeply connected with the understanding of revelation.[29] As such, tradition is characterized through history, dialogue and eschatology. The eschatological dimension of tradition emphasizes very strongly that the church has to be seen as the pilgrimage church.[30] Tradition could be described as an ongoing process of God's self-communication in Jesus Christ through the Holy Spirit in the Church's annunciation.[31] The Church is defined as a listening Church as such it is not the subject of tradition but the subject of transmitting and testifying the tradition. Transmitting and testifying tradition happens through teaching, life and cult.[32] This is very important: Tradition is not restricted to the corpus of dogmas - it is tied up to the whole Christian life. It is obvious that this dynamical character of tradition is linked to the idea of *ecclesia semper reformanda*. Furthermore, there is a relationship between tradition and the so-called 'signs of the times'. Although the Church pronounces on the relationship between time and tradition, it does not ask whether this relationship can lead to mistakes. Here we have to start in order to gain a critical stance towards our tradition in the Catholic Church.[33]

Rupture is a necessary category of tradition. Through rupture a new paradigm with new perspectives may be possible, but not in Thomas Kuhn's sense, because this new paradigm does not necessarily replace the former tradition, on the contrary, it might include it as a rupture in itself. This could be defined as 'contradictory pluralism'[34] and it could be seen as a sign for tradition's critical noncontemporaneity. For me it is very important to recognize that tradition does not merely mean continuity but - and maybe this is much more important - discontinuity.

Subversive Memory

Tradition based upon discontinuity implies criticism and gives way to a challenging understanding of the center of our tradition: the *memoria passionis, mortis et resurrectionis* of Jesus Christ.[35] Thus we become aware that the remembrance of this past gives rise to dangerous insights into the established society but our Church seem to be apprehensive of the subversive contents of this memory. "Remembrance is a mode of dissociation from given facts, a mode of 'mediation', which breaks, for short moments the omnipresent power of the given facts."[36] It is interruption of one-dimensionality. This *memoria* interrupts our life and reveals our idols. Interruption seems to be the condition of facing idols. That's why Johann Baptist Metz could say that the shortest definition of Christian religion is interruption.[37] Both interpretations are inspired by Jewish philosophers. The first deals with dangerous memory and is based upon insights of Herbert Marcuse; the second, inspired by Walter Benjamin.[38] Tradition, as explained above is open to a so-called foreign prophecy: a *conditio sine qua non* for brushing traditions against the grain.

Hope for the Sake of the Hopeless

Such a tradition of a subversive memory is a counterpart to circularity and a longing for security and certainty. It makes us sensitive for risks and aware that the categories upon which our religions are founded, are not strong but weak: telling a story and remembrance. According to Johann Baptist Metz, Christianity is a community of memories.[39] This community also tells painful stories of shared suffering and of the suffering of others. And these memories require us to remember stories not only of suffering received but of suffering inflicted - these memories force our community to alter. In this respect our community binds us to the past and at the same time to the future. As such it could be characterized as a community of hope. A Christian perspective based upon the *memoria passionis, mortis et resurrectionis* of Jesus Christ would remind us, that first we should not remember a future for us and our children, but a future for those who were and who are undergoing misery. Remembering resurrection is at the same time remembering suffering because it means remembering a "hope for the sake of the hopeless" (W. Benjamin).

Thus the Christian *memoria resurrectionis* is to be understood not as a triumphal procession but as an expression of a solidarity with the dead. So we can say with Chesterton: "Tradition means giving votes to the most obscure of all classes, our ancestors. It is the democracy of the dead".[40] Theology has to keep the question open: What will happen to the dead? As the synod document "Our hope" (1975) states:

> To forget or suppress this question ... is to behave in a profoundly inhuman way. For it means forgetting and suppressing the sufferings of the past and accepting without protest the pointlessness of this suffering. In the last resort, no happiness enjoyed by the children can make up for the pain suffered by the fathers, and no social progress can atone for the injustice done to the departed. If we persist too long in accepting the meaninglessness of death and in being indifferent to death, all we shall have left to offer even to the living will be banal promises. It is not only the growth of our economic resources which is limited, as we are often reminded today, but also the resources of meaning, and it is as if our reserves here are melting away and we are faced with the real danger that impressive words we use to fuel our own history - words like freedom, liberation, justice, happiness - will in the end have all their meaning drained out of them.

This tradition leads to another uncertainty than the prophets of the post-traditional society are longing for. The movement of such an understanding of tradition is exodus. Thus uncertainty becomes its central moment and not certainty. Uncertainty is dangerous. Uncertainty could lead into despair. Nevertheless, tradition understood as dangerous memory is more afraid of indifference than of despair. But uncertainty does not only mean losing the orientation or despair, it is also an expression of freedom - of being independent of the powers which rule the world. Uncertainty could also be the reason for certainty, because this uncertainty requires me to be responsible for the other, which leads me into uncertainty but at the same time provides the foundation of a kind of certainty for the Other, which is totally different from the certainty we are speaking about and longing for. In this sense our tradition could liberate us from self-destructive powers and lead us to look for fragments of redemption. As I have already said, maybe that uncertainty leads us to despair, but profound thoughts could arise from despair. The alternative seems to me an optimism, the readiness to jump hastily from one conclusion to another, which may be regarded as an inevitable sign of narrow self sufficiency, which dreads doubt and is consequently always superficial. Tradition does not guarantee security — it is much more a kind of losing balance.

Tradition, understood as a dangerous memory of suffering, provides the knowledge that the need to lend a voice to suffering is the precondition to all truth, hope and justice. As long as there is misery we are required to hope. This tradition does not accept the declaration that our system is the 'end of history', to which, as modern cynicism has it, there is 'no alternative'; nor does it accept that our society is celebrated as post-traditional, because maybe the theory of the post-traditional society is more an expression of a repressed past than an analytical tool. Dangerous memory as the foundation of a Christian tradition is an expression of a conscience which consists in the ability to take into account the suffering of Others. This memory interrupts our "high-order-interest" in self-determination and self-preservation and our view of the world. Instead of being able to become an attorney for the dead, our so-called post-traditional society is linked together with future in a way in which future becomes the criterion of the present - through movement both, present and future, become more and more synonyms. As such the present must not justify itself because future does not need any justification – it is always right and stronger. Such a society must try to remove a memory of suffering which refuses making future the normative criterion.

Tradition as an anamnestic solidarity possesses an eschatological reservation with regard to all stages of progress and emancipation in history. This eschatological reservation could make us sensitive for different kinds of idolatry. Such a reservation does not accept unquestioned given facts. It raises questions. Questions which call into question man - and God. If the understanding of revelation and tradition are linked together, then a new perspective of revelation will influence the understanding of tradition and vice versa. Thus a tradition-based memory of suffering, which focuses on what is missed, would also have an impact on the concept of revelation in general. It would put this moment into the understanding of revelation. So speaking of God means speaking of God as a missed God. To me, this is very important for a theology after Auschwitz.

Memory and Institution[41]

If life, if the whole Christian life is defined as tradition than we have to acknowledge the importance of face-to-face encounter. Here we are challenged by the more concrete question: Who is the subject of tradition? Considering tradition as outlined above should make us hesitate before using abstract terms such as the 'Judeo-Christian tradition'. According to Gershom Scholem the identification of the German-Jewish relationship as a symbiosis is a counterfeited idealization.[42] If we speak about a symbiotical 'Judeo-Christian tradition' we also should take into consideration that this tradition was foremost a negative one. If we do not forget this negative connotation, then maybe we will have a chance to overcome this negative connotation. Nevertheless we should not stop using the term in order to fight the neo-pagan tendencies. But when we use the term we should be aware of its hyphen which emphasizes the differences.

For me, the time has come for the Catholic Church as a community of memory to face its tradition in terms of a contradictory pluralism. Taking into account the contradictory elements in our tradition we become aware that our community is not homogeneous but that it is able to face the non-homogenous, the other. Non-homogeneity is a result of the prohibition against representing God in pictures and images. Of course, communities use their traditions to make their identity distinct from others. Nevertheless, the community of such a tradition, of the '*ekklesia*' ('being called out') is at the same time a community created for the Other. For my Church the task would be to become a community of memory, of dangerous memory calling the Church into question because this memory demands a remembrance of the most radical protest against Christianity - Auschwitz. The danger is indicated by the following statement of Elie Wiesel, "the thoughtful Christian knows, that the Jewish People did not die in Auschwitz but Christianity".

That means that our Church should refrain from victimisation. Its identity should not rest primarily on the identification that the church belongs to the victim, but more on the identification that it belongs to the perpetrators and the bystanders. My Church is obligated to remember the God of Abraham, Isaac, Jacob, and Jesus for the sake of the hopeless because this God reminds us of that hope. He promises one for the others. So our tradition would remind us Catholics that we have to understand and interpret Jesus' message not just in an individual manner but also politically: "whoever gains his institution will lose it, and whoever loses his institution for the sake of the Kingdom of God will gain it in a new way."[43] Thus, the Church would not have its interest in its self-preservation but in the victims of the world. It would remember a messianic future, which does not extend our future but interrupts it.[44] It would not confirm our 'habits of the heart' as the apologists of a civil religion as well as the communitarians intend, it would demand a change of heart.

How to Come to Resistance by Remembrance

But will there be a chance of creating an anamnestic ethic in our accelerating and 'post-traditional' society? How could we create a culture of re-membrance and how could we come to resistance by remembrance?

According to Beck and others these traditions have come to an end. But do they know what they are talking about? "Traditions are not reified 'things' that can be known apart from practice, any more than languages are 'things' that can be known apart from linguistic performance and competence."[45] Have they really recognized what it means to speak of an end of these traditions? The end of these traditions leads to the end of the God of these traditions. If Beck would have read Nietzsche he might have hesitated to promote his understanding of a post-traditional society in that way. Or: didn't he understand the message of Nietzsche's madman?

Nietzsche does not only ask, "where has God gone?" The question, 'where is God?' has an echo. He thus raises the question, 'where has man gone?'[46] Especially today we hear this question in a very radical sense. But does man exist without God? Does man not need the question of God - even if he answers this question in a negative way? What would our society be without the word 'God'?[47] But without traditions the word 'God' is like a blinded face. It is interesting to recognize that the 'knowledge' of God provided by the biblical traditions is at the same time a non-knowledge. So what can we say? The word 'God' has a presence. But we do not know whether this word will have a future.

What can we do against the oncoming idols in the 'post-traditional' society? Unlike the holy God of the monotheists, the pagans and their gods affirm what they call life, nature and earth. Their gods are portrayed as instinctive and heroic and represent the will to power as something to affirm. In our poor time my religious traditions may force me to make untimely considerations: not to affirm power and security, not to have spiritual investments in the world as it is. They require changes because they make me aware of the fact that "anyone who wants the world to remain as it is does not want it to remain". (E.Fried).

Notes

1 See here: J.B. Metz, Im Angesicht der Juden. Christliche Theologie nach Auschwitz, in: *Concilium. Internationale Zeitschrift für Theologie 5* (1984): 76-92, 76.

2 See: J.B. Metz, Glaube in *Geschichte und Gesellschaft. Studien zu einer praktischen Fundamentaltheologie* (Mainz: Grünewald-Verlag, ⁵1992): 9-16.

3 See: J.B. Metz, Unterwegs zu einer nachidealistischen Theologie, in: J.B. Bauer (Ed.), *Entwürfe der Theologie* (Graz/ Wien/ Köln: Styria-Verlag, 1985): 209-235, 215.

4 See: J. Manemann (Ed.), *Jahrbuch Politische Theologie* Bd. 1: Demokratiefähigkeit (Münster/Hamburg: Lit-Verlag, ²2001).

5 See: U. Beck (Ed.), *Kinder der Freiheit*. Edition Zweite Moderne (Frankfurt a.M.: Suhrkamp-Verlag, ⁴1998).

6 See: U. Beck, *Die Erfindung des Politischen* (Frankfurt a.M.: Suhrkamp-Verlag, 1993).

7 See: K. Gabriel, *Christentum zwischen Tradition und Postmoderne* (Freiburg/Basel/Wien: Herder-Verlag, 1992); H.-J. Höhn, *GegenMythen. Religionsproduktive Tendenzen der Gegenwart* (Freiburg/ Basel/Wien: Herder-Verlag, 1994).

8 See: P. Berger, *Der Zwang zur Häresie. Religion in der pluralistischen Gesellschaft* (Frankfurt a.M.: S.Fischer-Verlag, 1980).

9 See: J.B. Metz, Gotteskrise. Versuch zur "geistigen Situation der Zeit", in: *Diagnosen zur Zeit*. Mit Beiträgen von Johann Baptist Metz, Günther Bernd Ginzel, Peter Glotz, Jürgen Habermas, Dorothee Sölle (Düsseldorf: Patmos-Verlag, 1994): 76-92, 77/78.

10 On a flyer from 1848 we find the following warning: "The Christians which do not believe in their Christian faith anymore, will be the furiest enemies of the Jews ... If the Christian people will not possess Christian faith ... then, Jews, make yourselves iron skulls because with bony skulls you will not survive history." (see: H. Steins, *Moses und die Offenbarung der Demokratie* (Berlin: Rowohlt-Verlag, 1998): 168.

11 F. Fukuyama, *The End of History and the Last Man* (New York: Free Press, 1992).

[12] See: R.B. Douglas, Liberalism After Good Times: The "End of History" in Historical Perspective, in: R. B. Douglas/ D. Hollenbach (Eds.), *Catholicism and Liberalism*. Contributions to American Public Philosophy (Cambridge: Cambridge University Press, 1994): 101.

[13] See: H. Dubiel, *Ungewißheit und Politik* (Frankfurt a.M.: Suhrkamp-Verlag, 1994): 93.

[14] See: E.-W. Böckenförde, Erfolge und Grenzen der Aufklärung, in: *Universitas. Zeitschrft für interdisziplinäre Wissenschaft 8* (1995), 720.

[15] H. Dubiel, *Ungewißheit und Politik*, op. cit.

[16] See: J. Manemann, Gnosis und Politik heute, in: *Kirche und Israel 1* (1997): 71-87.

[17] See: J. Manemann, Politischer Anti-Monotheismus. Zu Peter Sloterdijks Elmauer Vortrag, in: *Orientierung 19* (1999): 201-203.

[18] P. Sloterdijk, Regeln für den Menschenpark. Ein Antwortschreiben zum Brief über den Humanismus, in: *Die Zeit* 16.09.99.

[19] See: J. Manemann, An den Grenzen der Moderne. Zu Kulturkampf und Demokratiefeindlichkeit in der gegenwärtigen Gesellschaft, in: J. Manemann (Ed.), Jahrbuch *Politische Theologie* Bd.1, op.cit., 137-154.

[20] See: R. N. Bellah et al., *Habits of the Heart. Individualism and Commitment in American Life* (New York a.o.: Perenial Library, 1986): 77.

[21] See: L. Kolakowski, Der Anspruch auf die selbstverschuldete Unmüdigkeit, in: L. Reinisch (Ed.), *Vom Sinn der Tradition* (München: C.H. Beck-Verlag, 1970): 1-16, 1.

[22] Th. W. Adorno, Über Tradition, in: Th. W. Adorno, Ohne Leitbild. *Parva Aesthetica* (Frankfurt a.M.: Suhrkamp-Verlag, 1967): 29-41, 35.

[23] J. Manemann, Toward an Anamnestic Ethic After Auschwitz or How to Come to Resistance by Remembrance, in: M. Hayse/ D. Pollefeyt/ G.J. Colijn/ M.S. Littell (Eds.), *Hearing the Voices: Teaching the Holocaust to Future Generations. Proceedings of the 27ᵗʰ Annual Scholars' Conference on the Holocaust and the Churches, March 2-4, 1997* (Merion Station: Merion Westfield Press International, 1999): 55-63.

[24] See: D. J. Fasching, *Narrative Theology after Auschwitz. From Alienation to Ethics* (Minneapolis: Fortress Press, 1992): 96/97.

[25] D. J. Fasching, op.cit., 118,

[26] D. J. Fasching, op.cit., 120.

[27] T. W. Tilley, *Inventing Catholic Tradition* (New York: Orbis Books,

2000): 19.

28 See T. W. Tilley, op.cit.

29 See: "Dei Verbum". Die dogmatische Konstitution über die göttliche Offenbarung, in: K. Rahner/H. Vorgrimler, *Kleines Konzilskompendium. Sämtliche Texte des Zweiten Vatikanums mit Einführungen und ausführlichem Sachregister* (Freiburg: Herder-Verlag, 171984): 367-382.

30 Dei Verbum, op.cit., Art. 7.

31 Dei Verbum, op.cit., Art. 8.

32 Dei Verbum, op.cit., Art. 8.

33 Here it is important to recognize the use of the metaphor of the mirror: "All knowledge in the time of the Church remains knowledge seen in a mirror — and hence fragmentary. The direct relation to reality, to the face of God itself is kept for the eschaton. This is the only place in this chapter in which one can hear a gentle note of criticism of tradition, for when everything is seen and read only in a mirror, one must expect distortions and shifts in emphasis. In any case, this is theologia negative, which necessarily involves the setting of a certain limit to both kerygmatic and ecclesial positivity, without this line being further developed." (J. Ratzinger, Chapter II. in: Dogmatic Constitution on Devine Revelation, in: *Commentary on the Documents of Vatican II.* Volume III, ed. by H. Vorgrimler, New York/ London: Burns & Oates/ Herder and Herder: 1968): 183)

34 M. Seckler, Über den Kompromiß in den Sachen der Lehre, in: M. Seckler, *Im Spannungsfeld von Wissenschaft und Kirche. Theologie als schöpferische Auslegung der Wirklichkeit* (Freiburg: Herder-Verlag, 1980, 99-103, 100. A look into the decrees of the Second Vatican Council could make us aware that tradition implies also a contradictionary pluralism. Thus it is no accident that Vatican II provides us with a non-statical understanding of our tradition: Here tradition is worked out in the decree of revelation, this already indicates the interrelationship between the understanding of revelation and tradition. It is very interesting to recognize that not only the catholic tradition implies ruptures but also the understanding of tradition itself, because the description of tradition in *Dei Verbum* is a rupture in comparison with former ways to understand tradition.

35 See: J.B. Metz, Glaube in *Geschichte und Gesellschaft*, op.cit., 113.

[36] H. Marcuse, *Der eindimensionale Mensch. Studien zur Ideologie der fortgeschrittenen Gesellschaft* (Darmstadt: Luchterhand, ²²1988): 117.

[37] J. B. Metz, Der Kampf um die verlorene Zeit. Unzeitgemäße Thesen zur Apokalyptik, in: J. Manemann (Ed.), *Jahrbuch Politische Theologie* Bd. 3: Befristete Zeit (Münster: Lit-Verlag, 1999): 212-221, 214. Furthermore: J. M. Ashley, *Interruptions. Mysticism, Politics and Theology in the Work of Johann Baptist Metz* (Notre Dame: University of Notre Dame Press, 1998).

[38] See: J. Manemann, "Weil es nicht nur Geschichte ist". *Die Begründung der Notwendigkeit einer fragmentarischen Historiographie des Nationalsozialismus aus politisch-theologischer Sicht* (Münster: Lit-Verlag, 1995): 217-233.

[39] See: J. B. Metz, Glaube in *Geschichte und Gesellschaft*, op.cit.

[40] G.K. Chesterton, *Orthodoxy*, New York 1959, 48.

[41] See: J. Manemann, *Carl Schmitt und die politische Theologie. Politischer Anti-Monotheismus* (forthcoming October 2001 (Aschendorff-Verlag)

[42] See: D. Diner, Negative Symbiose. Deutsche und Juden nach Auschwitz, in: D. Diner (Ed.), *Ist der Nationalsozialismus Geschichte? Zu Historisierung und Historikerstreit* (Frankfurt a.M.: Fischer-Taschenbuch-Verlag, 1987):185-197, 185.

[43] O. Fuchs, Biblische Theologie und Öffentlichkeit, in: *Jahrbuch für Biblische Theologie.* Bd. 11 (1996): Glaube und Öffentlichkeit (Neukirchen-Vluyn: Neukirchener Verlag, 1996): 225-247, 237

[44] See: J.B. Metz, *Jenseits bürgerlicher Religion. Reden über die Zukunft des Christentums* (Mainz: Grünewald-Verlag, ⁴1984): 9/10.

[45] T. W. Tilley, op. cit., 45.

[46] See: J.B. Metz, in: F.-X. Kaufmann/J.B. Metz, *Zukunftsfähigkeit. Suchbewegungen im Christentum* (Freiburg/Basel/Wien: Herder-Verlag, 1987): 140.

[47] See K. Rahner, *Grundkurs des Glaubens. Einführung in den Begriff des Christentums* (Freiburg/Basel/Wien: 1984), 54-61.

Tradition in Transition: approaches to Jewish-Christian relations

Michael A. Signer

The Paradox of Tradition and Modernity: an illustration

Jurgen Manemann in his provocative essay urges us to consider the context of our situation as a significant horizon for analyzing our concept of tradition. Yet it seems to me that any discussion of tradition becomes complicated because the fluid nature of our contemporary civilization complicates any discussion of tradition in shaping the religious lives of Jews or Christians. Whether we call our own era "modern" or "post-modern" it seems to be defined by an ethos that places the autonomous self and rational inquiry unbounded at the center of an orientation toward secularity. Peter Berger, the American sociologist, claims that the sociological conditions of contemporary culture are best described by the term, *haeresis* , which means either "option" or "choice." The key difference between modernity and traditional societies arises in the multiplication of choices open to individuals. They come to think of their path of their lives less as "fate" and more as "choice."[1]

Since the eighteenth century the Jewish community has become an example of the perils of freedom that accompanies autonomous choice. For choosing is bought at the price of the stability offered by a tradition bound society. In this paper I would like to explore the paradox that modernity has presented to the Jewish people in Western Europe and North America. We shall first explore that paradox through an illustration of how technology and modernity frame the question of tradition. I will then describe the ways that the Shoah or destruction of European Jewry has become a point of significant re-orientation in Jewish attitudes towards modernity. In the concluding section of the paper I will propose that the tri-partite canon of the Hebrew Scriptures (TaNaKh) offers perspective for understanding the fragmented reality of the contemporary Jewish community.

The ability to retrieve and utilize knowledge is a point of meeting between the Jewish tradition and the technology of modern culture. As compatible as information retrieval and Jewish learning might be, the human encounter of the paradox of tradition in the modern context may be observed at the Institute for Microfilms of Hebrew Manuscripts in the National Library at the Hebrew University of Jerusalem. These rooms in the basement of the library provide access to microfilms and fiche of Hebrew manuscripts from every corner of the globe. This collection derives from the fear by Israeli scholars in the 1950's that the debacle of destruction of European Jewry and its institutions had endangered the patrimony of the Jewish heritage. Utilizing a form of technology developed during the interwar years—the microfilm—they sent out teams of scholars from Israel to photograph all manuscripts in European libraries. The collection process continues into the present——and has expanded the horizons for the retrieval of Jewish texts [and thereby tradition] in a geometric proportion. Even in the past decade the libraries from the former Soviet Union have made material available that will occupy scholars into the next century.

It is not simply the collection of materials in the manuscript room that peaks our interest into the paradox of tradition. The collection of material for scholars doing historical studies might not be perceived as anything out of the ordinary. *Ad fontes* was one of the mottos of historicist scholarship parallel with the rise of modern scholarships. There is no paradox in collecting ancient documents. What is unique about the Institute is that it enables a reader to sit in Jerusalem and peruse documents that are the only remains of Jewish communities that flourished only fifty years ago.

The paradox of tradition is indicated in the living experience that a modern scholar like myself has in the reading room. One morning I observed that the majority of readers were not wearing modern western European clothing, but the black clothing and yarmulkes of Haredi or ultra-orthodox Jews. Why would they engage in activities at the national library of a country whose government they regard as illegitimate? They sit at their microfilm readers just as I do. We share space and resources, but do we share any sense of time? Do we have any assumptions in common about the texts that we study? Does their approach to sacred texts share with those who are trained in modern European and American universities?

I asked one of the librarians about the Haredi presence in the room, and he responded that they now form a majority presence there on most days. He indicated that their interest was not in historical work. Many of them are members of Hassidic groups who want to publish texts by their religious leaders that have been previously unavailable. There are other Haredi Jews, he claimed, who were deeply engaged in the production of critical editions of Jewish legal texts. They had little interest in historical context but wanted to produce accurate editions so that religious life could be enriched by an exact transmission of the tradition.

I would aver that the presence of Haredim and the manuscript room at the national library illustrates the problematics of tradition. People who have profound suspicions about the modern world and reject its fluidity or pluralistic framework are ready to exploit its technology toward their own ends. Many of us also exploit that technology but we do not consider the modern world evil, but something that can be transformed by a more nuanced and complex model of its past.

Modernity and Tradition

My example of the Institute for Hebrew microfilms allows me now to provide some reflections on the nature of tradition within the Jewish context. The historian of philosophy Nathan Rotenstreich defines tradition as a "mode of generational relation, whose structure and meaning are inherently historical—with history understood as a succession of events that affect and relate people living at different times."[2] Within Judaism the primary "mode" of relationship has been through a combination of written texts and oral discussions that later become inscribed—and in turn then become the subject of more oral discussion. Even the Hebrew term for tradition, *masoret* refers initially to the attempt to fix the primary text of revelation—the Hebrew Bible.

Descriptions of post-biblical Judaism use the term "Torah" to mean divine revelation. However, the Rabbis who became the tradents of that revelation developed their hermeneutical framework based on both a written and oral form. Thus, we have "written Torah" referring to the text of Scripture and "oral torah" that denotes the rabbinic teaching.[3] The transmission of written and oral law as a unified body of traditions by reliable tradents has been a subject of discussion from the early rabbinic texts such as the first chapter of Mishnah Avot. [4] One of the central problems with these discussions of the transmission of tradition has been whether or not the social reality at any moment in time has affected the shaping of the tradition.[5] During the medieval period one can observe two complementary positions with respect to tradition in the writings of Maimonides. In the code of Jewish law, Mishneh Torah, he provides a full account of the laws of sacrifice that will be observed when the messiah restores. This presentation of the sacrificial laws indicates that their status as revealed law is not historically contingent. These laws are in suspension between the destruction of the Temple and the messianic era. His *Guide for the Perplexed* explained the traditions of sacrifice as pedagogic: the Israelites freed from Egyptian slavery could not comprehend abstract monotheism and were educated [in the literal sense] toward a pure monotheism. The purpose of the *Guide* was to offer a commentary on rationale for the origins of the sacrifice rather than to argue that the written and oral Torah was contingent upon historical circumstances.[6] The emphasis on a historical context as a criterion for the validity of rabbinic tradition would develop in Western Europe during the nineteenth century in the writings of scholars like Abraham Geiger and Zacharias Frankel.[7]

While the rabbinic tradition provided a dialectical relationship between the metaphysical notion of divine revelation and the realization of that revelation in the daily life, the written Torah shaped the over-arching narrative for the Jewish people. Jews lived in between: they could look back on their biblical ancestors as models of God's covenantal love as they separated themselves from the nations that surrounded them. From the end of the Biblical period and in the wake of the destruction of their sacred shrine in Jerusalem, their immediate situation was 'exile.'[8] In that exile they would remain faithful to God by observing the commandments with the hope God would restore them to their land and rebuild their ancient cities and shrine.[9]

The rabbinic tradition constructed an approach to the nature of continuity and change was irrevocably altered by the forces of modernity and secularization in Western Europe and the subsequent diffusion of those ideas into Jewish populations in Eastern Europe. Jacob Katz in his book, *Tradition and Crisis* has offered the most sophisticated analysis of the shifts within the Jewish community during the eighteenth and nineteenth centuries. The forces of Hassidism in the east emphasized an internal shift within the leadership of the Jewish community towards religious charisma. It was in Western Europe that a more fundamental shift came about with the emergence of the Maskil, the enlightened Jew. The Maskil is characterized by his emphasis on rationalism. The cultural models and modes of behavior of the non-Jewish culture became the hermeneutical lens for his interpretation of Judaism.[10] However, the rationalist affinity for western European culture did not bring about the dissolution of appropriating rabbinic texts that characterized pre-modern Jewry. It broke down what he calls a "homogeneous" nature of the pre-modern Jewish lens for applying these texts to the community. Historians of modern Jewry have traced the creative reformulation "the tradition" by every group within the Jewish community.[11] The group of Western European Jews who constituted themselves as "modern Orthodox" (they used the term *Gesetztreue*) developed a theology that denied historical contingency as an element for interpreting Torah, but the legal decisions written by Orthodox Rabbis incorporated elements of modernity that permitted Orthodox Jews to live within the community of German urban culture.[12]

The common element in the approach to the external or Christian society of Western European Jewry was a profound faith in the emergence of the modern state—a society organized by law rather than determined by caste or religion. Katz refers to this rationally oriented form of social organization as creating a "neutral basis above the religious difference...[creating] a third sphere—the neutral human one—to which members of both religions could belong."[13] The neutral sphere—rather than the 'naked public square' became a magna charta for Western European Jewry, a beacon of hope for Eastern European Jewry, and the growing reality of those Jews who came to America.

The Shadow of the Shoah: Tradition Broken or Mended?

We turn from this glowing and optimistic picture of creative approaches to the corpus of rabbinic texts protected by the modern state to focus on three themes that have changed Jewish perspectives toward the external society during the past half-century: 1] the betrayal of modernity as progress; 2] the reality of the state of Israel; 3] the addition of Jewish mystical texts as a 'normative' element in non-Orthodox Jewish thinking.

The Betrayal of Modernity

It was the nation state or group of nation states that participated in the destruction of European Jewry from 1939-1945. The Shoah demonstrated how clearly a nation of laws had no essential relationship to a democratic form of government. The devastation of European Jewry, gypsies and other vulnerable minorities revealed how a bulwark of civil legislation did not offer protection but provided a framework for their destruction. Elements that marginalized or demonized the Jewish population of Europe (those who practiced their religion or were affiliated only by birth) utilized the rational elements of scientific racism and the pre-modern elements of anti-Judaism. For the Jewish community that survived and their descendants a "historical" perspective has found it difficult to accept the distinction between the "secular" elements of scientific or racial Antisemitism and the "religious" elements of Christian anti-Judaism.[14]

A sense of betrayal of modernity has become common to all elements of post-World War II Jewry. For other groups of American Jewry, the shifting sentiment of Richard Rubenstein's biography has become exemplary even if they disagree with his theological approach.[15] His reflections begin with an encounter with Probst Heinrich Gruber. This meeting led him to reject the deuteronomist concept of Jewish history that became normative for the Rabbis: God exiles and punishes, but God will ultimately save. This rejection of the idea that God works within history moved him toward accepting an Eastern idea of God as the infinite nothing. Rubenstein indicates that this *theologia negativa* is quite compatible with ideas from the Kabbalistic tradition of Judaism. If the deuteronomistic God is no longer the potent force behind Judaism for Rubenstein, the Jewish tradition retains its power in its psychological or therapeutic power to provide protection against the anomie of modern society.

In the community of American Reform Jews the optimism of the universal messianic perfection of the social order expressed so eloquently by Hermann Cohen has been replaced by the post-modern theology of Eugene Borowitz.[16] Reform Jews have expanded their theological horizons from the "perfection of the world under divine sovereignty" [*tiqqun 'olam*] to the "perfection of internal characteristics" [*tiqqun midot*]. The recent document of Ten Principles passed by the Central Conference of American Rabbis and adopted by the Union of American Hebrew Congregations are grounded in a rejection of nearly one hundred years of identification with progress and modernity.[17] It is remarkable to observe how the American Jewish movement that was so powerfully embedded in optimism and progress could develop such profound suspicions of those values within less than fifty years.

The State of Israel and its reality

A modern Jewish state born three years after the Shoah presents its own "interruption" of the Jewish tradition. The term "interruption" does not imply that the birth of the state of Israel in 1948 is an aberration of the Jewish tradition. Within the context of interreligious relations discussions about the state of Israel produce a very contentious spirit. It is for that reason the recognition of the state of Israel by the Vatican has removed a serious roadblock to trust and dialogue for many Jews. Other Christian groups have perceived Israel as a nation among the nations as an entity apart from the Jewish religion. The common arguments about the role of the state of Israel in modern Jewish life are not germane to our analysis in this paper. I use "interruption" here in the same manner as suggested by Professor Manemann—an occasion to discern how varied the textual and oral transmission of Judaism might be, and how it might be possible to rethink the Jewish tradition in the situation of a modern state. Indeed, the birth of the state of Israel has provided an occasion for creative rethinking of rabbinic and medieval Jewish authorities about the nature of a Jewish society.[18] How could a modern state resonate to the rich realities of the tradition?

As a modern state Israel constitutes a major hermeneutical problem for the rabbinic tradition. Jews may have dreamed of a return to Zion for nearly 2000 years but it was the vote of the United Nations for the partition of British-mandate Palestine that transformed the Yishuv organization into the prototype of a modern Jewish state. The rabbinic tradition had envisioned a variety of eschatological scenarios that would bring about an end to the Diaspora. None of these had included a vote by the "nations of the world."

The state of Israel constitutes what Gershom Scholem and Emil Fackenheim have called the "Jewish return to history."[19] The word "return" refers to the notion that "history" constitutes the narrative of a national entity with a culture, forms of social organization, and laws. An important school of historians such as B.Z. Dinur, Yehezkiel Kaufman and Yitzhak Baer who arrived in Palestine before the birth of the state developed a dichotomous history of "Israel in its Land" and "Israel in the Exile."[20] The next generation of historians such as Samuel Ettinger and Hayyim-Hillel Ben-Sasson demonstrated how the years in exile had developed important institutions that developed out of the experiences in other cultures.[21] With the rebirth of their state these Diaspora institutions would be transformed into a unique Israeli experience. The arguments within modern Jewish historiography have divided colleagues who work in the field in Israel and the Diaspora. On one level, the state of Israel has provided for a rethinking of the narrative of rabbinic/biblical tradition from creation to the days of the messiah.

The state of Israel also has been an occasion for rethinking Jewish eschatology. In tractate Sanhedrin of the Talmud there are two possibilities presented for the end of the Jewish dispersion. One vision of the end requires divine intervention and demands no human effort. The second eschatology has a strong element of theurgy. It requires the initiative of human beings—the people of Israel— in order to stimulate God to provide for the "yoke of the nations" to be removed from Israel.[22] These discussions took place among rabbinic authorities during the Middle Ages and in the second half of the nineteenth century. They also provide the warrants for many arguments today about whether or not it is permissible to surrender "land for peace." The headlines of our newspapers do not reveal the deeply impassioned theological warrants from the Jewish tradition that provide a heated discussion among Jews in Israel and the Diaspora about these issues.[23]

One can also discern the tensions about the state of Israel in the language of the Jewish prayer book. The prayer for the state of Israel, read on Sabbath mornings after the lection for the Torah and Prophets, contains the phrase that Israel is "the beginning of the flowering of our redemption." A survey of the prayer books used throughout the Jewish community of the world will indicate the variety of creative resolutions to the link between a political state born in the full light of modernity and a biblical/rabbinic tradition that resists efforts to provide positive historical context.

Esoteric as Exoteric: Jewish mysticism as popular piety

One of the most surprising elements to emerge within the Jewish community over the last few decades has been the emergence of Jewish mystical literature or "Kabbalah" as part of popular piety. While many Jewish intellectuals (myself included) would like to dismiss this fascination with the esoteric as ephemeral, it appears that this phenomenon will pervade our communities for the near future. It captures the imagination of many Jews who have matured in the liberal Jewish communities with their emphasis on rationalism in theology and historicism as the criterion for religious practice.[24]

Gershom Scholem, the scholar who demonstrated that Kabbalah had been a significant part of the Jewish traditional literature would no doubt be bemused by the study of Hassidic literature and mystical explanations of the commandments. However, he also pointed toward those periods in the Jewish past when the esoteric became exoteric. His classic work on Shabbetai Zevi, with important modifications by Moshe Idel, foreshadows in many ways what occurs in the anomie of our own time. Interestingly, many who are turning to this literature within the Jewish community have been alienated from its life for many years. They sought their "spiritual enhancement" in the wisdom traditions of Buddhism and are now "returning" to their own Jewish communities for a more specific language and localized set of practices.

The reintroduction of Kabbalah is important for our analysis of the shaping of tradition in contemporary religious life of the Jewish community. It is part of the larger revival of charismatic or spiritual movements in North America, but it has also brought to the consciousness of many Jews an aspect of their tradition that they never knew was available to them. It is anti-historical and provides a mythic and narrative presentation of the immediacy of religious experience. Every religious act is linked to an external and partially knowable aspect of the Eternal. As Arthur Green has put it, in the era of the twenty-first century the movement of the Jewish community is no longer outward—but seeking the well-springs deep within.

A Heuristic Device: The Jewish Canon as Lenses for Interpreting the Tradition

We have now described how the Jewish tradition was construed prior to modernity. Then we have examined three trends that constitute an interruption to that tradition. Keeping in mind that our primary purpose is to examine the Jewish tradition within the larger context of Jewish-Christian relations, we can understand why both the pre-modern and post-Shoah worlds of Jewry might still be reluctant to engage in the process of Jewish-Christian reconciliation and dialogue. We all recognize that whether we began our work in interreligious dialogue prior to the Second Vatican Council or within the post-1960's era that our work has been—at best—on the margins of our community. In the Jewish community there are many people who understand what we do as a continuation of the tradition of *Shtadlanut*—making an effort to harmonize relationships between Jews and non-Jews to minimalize violence. In many ways the majority of Jews view us as the "Rabbi" who received Tevya's request for a prayer for the Czar—and the response, "May the Czar stay far away from us." Their concerns are focused within the boundaries of the Jewish community. Most Jews want to put their resources toward projects that strengthen educational institutions; fortify links between Israel and the Diaspora; and insure the continuity of the Jewish people.

In this concluding part of the paper, I will move toward a heuristic device that might help us in future discussions about the Jewish community and the lenses it uses to discern its tradition. Every group within the world wide Jewish community recognizes that there is an enormous task in the retrieval of tradition. Our analysis indicates that the interruptions we have described yield two broad lines of approach: post-modernity versus anti-modernity.

The anti-modern approach yields little promise for those of us who engage in Jewish-Christian dialogue. The "Fundamentalism Project" sponsored by Martin Marty and Scott Appleby has investigated the simultaneous appearance in late twentieth-century religious communities throughout the world of communities who understand themselves as the "perfecti" of their tradition.[25] It is interesting that aside from American Protestants who invented the term, most non-Christian groups resist the description. Surely the groups of Haredi Jews described in the manuscript room of the Hebrew University are not biblical literalists. They indeed are not. But they share with many other groups a common resistance to modernity and attempt to create an environment for their adherents that permit them as few transactions with the external world as possible. For these groups there is no dialogue with the outside world—there is only negotiation and transaction. In their instrumentalist view of the external world they are ready to use all technology possible, but not to engage the ideas or life-style of those who do not conform to their standards. Returning to the image of my Haredi companions at the Institute for Hebrew Manuscripts, then I would claim that they work in that room to add more material to a tradition that is immediately present to them. Were I to work on the very same manuscript, it would be to reshape the material into a contemporary appropriation.

Post-modernity is more complex phenomenon. I will use as my paradigm of post-modernity in Judaism, the group of philosophers who have gathered around Peter Ochs of the University of Virginia.[26] These Jewish scholars are eager to engage the classical texts of the Jewish tradition. They are profoundly suspicious of the enlightenment paradigm that sought universal laws and homogeneity attempting to reduce the difference between languages and traditions that diverged from Judaism. Indeed they seek an intellectual alternative to the western tradition of philosophy and are discovering that a broad definition of the canon of the Jewish textual tradition has supplied them with tools to retrieve Jewish ritual and thought. Using Talmudic argument and Kabbalistic exegesis of the Scripture they are discovering new possibilities for a Jewish approach to life within modernity. There are other scholars and Rabbis who might not identify with the approaches of the post-modern Jewish philosophers but whose work reflects a similar project of combining the rational and the mythic in order to renew Jewish life within its institutional contexts.

What the post-modern approach to tradition may illustrate is the move from a paradigm of hierarchy to one of dialectical tension. A post-modern approach does more than simply offer a positivist or historicist avenue of reading the Jewish tradition in which one phenomenon sublates or evacuates all other possibilities. It suggests that the theologian works through the texts of the Jewish tradition with a variety of polarities that are always in tension with one another. In their approach difference itself— the difference and distance between ancient and modern— is the point of departure. It is difference that suggests creative possibilities that grow from where the discussion began.

Let me map my idea of post-modern retrieval on to the three parts of the Hebrew canon. I have written elsewhere about my conviction that the most productive dialogue between Jews and Christians is grounded on face-to-face studies of texts in the Hebrew Bible through the lenses of pre-modern interpretations in both traditions. The disclosures that emerge from reading Augustine and the Rabbis or Rashi and Hugo of St. Victor allow for deep and nuanced discussions of the commonplaces and differences of Jews and Christians.[27]

The model of interreligious dialogue grounded on the three parts of the Hebrew canon that follows is not grounded in historical criticism of Scripture—but I do believe that a discerning reader of contemporary biblical scholarship and theology will find resonance in what I suggest. The tripartite division of the Hebrew canon does not imply that the characteristics ascribed to one section are absent from the others. The intertextual resonance between Torah, Neviim and Ketuvim is the stimulus to profound results of theological insight produced by its rabbinic exegetes for nearly two millennia. What I shall describe as a "central theme" in Torah will be found in Neviim or Ketuvim with equal weight and profundity. With that *"caveat lector,"* let me begin to describe my model.

Each part of the Hebrew canon raises some central themes. These themes, in turn, are the ground for questions that may be discovered in reading any part of the Hebrew canon. Finally, I believe that the central themes and questions raised by each part of the Hebrew canon find a unique resonance in eras of Jewish history.

The first part of the canon is Torah or Pentateuch. The Pentateuch's themes provide answers to two fundamental questions: What must I do? Why must I do it? Of course the Pentateuch provides the responses to far more elaborate and complex questions. But the narrative portions of the Pentateuch from the Creation story through the desert wanderings respond to the "why must I do these commandments?" It is to fulfill the human responsibility for its relationship to the covenant with the God of Israel. The "what must I do?" question has predominated Jewish focus of the Oral Torah. In moving from a paradigm of hierarchy that the "What" as necessary and the "Why" as marginal to dialectic where the "What" and "Why" remain in dialectical tension, we need no longer have one trump the other, but can hold them both before us.

The second part of the canon is Neviim, the prophetic books. In these texts the modern reader learns how must I live in the context of society? The Neviim indicate what are the consequence of a society ordered to the covenant. The hints at these consequences are outlined in the period of the desert wanderings. There are promises and punishments that are revealed in the book of Deuteronomy. However, the prophetic books provide a more nuanced understanding of the social consequences of covenant in a self-governing entity with international pressures. When the punishments and promises are read in dialectical tension with one another——they provide hope for a future beyond the consequences of exile. In the Neviim, history means not just holding power, or national destruction and disaster—but exile and that is followed by redemption.

In the third part of the canon, Ketuvim, the reader discovers a rich variety of genres from poetry to proverbs to lament. One finds literature that defies easy genre classification such as the book of Job. For my own heuristic purposes the Ketuvim presents a very complex form of question that was one of the central themes of the Pentateuch: "Who am I?" This question of identity is then asked within the greater context of the two previous parts of the canon: What must we do? Why must we do it? And "What are the consequences of our behavior?

Now for the historical perspective: Each of these parts of the canon can be correlated with a distinct aspect of previous generations of those who sought to constitute the Jewish tradition. Clearly the pre-modern period occupied itself predominantly with Torah-oriented questions. The vast literature of Talmud, Midrash, Piyyut, Responsa and codifications of Law are responses to those fundamental questions. Themes from Neviim and Ketuvim are also present in the magnificent liturgical poetry of the medieval synagogue or the literature of chronicles that give testimony to Jewish martyrdom during the medieval period. With the dawn of modernity, the questions of Neviim became the predominant themes: From Mendelssohn through Leo Baeck the question of how one lived within the context of society and the consequences of the covenant are present. The genre of historical writing becomes part of the mainstream of Jewish religious writing during this period. Finally, in the shadow of the Shoah, the birth of the state of Israel and the emerging communities of North America and Europe the Ketuvim present their questions as the most urgent of our era. The question, 'who are we?' constitutes the on-going quest for most of contemporary Jewry.

Natan Rotenstreich has suggested that the explanatory sources for the

Jewish tradition shifted between the pre-modern and modern period from metaphysics to history.[28] This image too supports our argument. I would add that the on-going development in post-modernity would add yet another link of explanation: Gnosticism.[29] I do not imply here the pejorative notion of 'gnosticism' as dualism. Instead I would hold that 'gnosticism' in the post-modern era indicates that many Jews are seeking a unifying principle to constitute their Jewish tradition. They find the "images" and variety suggested by the Ketuvim—that wisdom provides the apex of knowledge which is preserved by ritual practice and the turn toward community rather than the angst of the solitary or defiant promethean soul of modernity.

The description of the model is, I admit, quite inchoate, but I do hope that Christians and Jews can find in them some stimulus toward a discussion of Jewish tradition within the context of Jewish-Christian dialogue. My teacher Jakob Petuchowski wrote an article that argued when Jews and Christians come together the first question that must be asked is "What kind of Jew stands before what kind of Christian?" In providing this analysis of the complex perspectives for understanding the Jewish tradition in the contemporary world, I hope to have supplied our Christian interlocutors with the living reality of twenty-first century Judaism and why—at times—it is so difficult to get the Jewish community to engage in this process.

Notes

[1] Peter Berger, *The Heretical Imperative* (Garden City, N.Y.: Anchor Books, 1979).
[2] Nathan Rotenstreich, "Tradition" in *Contemporary Jewish Religious Thought*, edited by Arthur A. Cohen and Paul Mendes-Flour (New York: Charles Scribers Sons1987), 1007.
[3] Martin S. Jaffee, "A Rabbinic Ontology of the Written and Spoken Word: On Discipleship, Transformative Knowledge and the Living Texts of Oral Torah" *Journal of the American Academy of Religion* 65:3, pp. 525-549 and idem, "Halakhah as Primordial Tradition: A

Gadamerian Dialogue with Early Rabbinic Memory and Jurisprudence" in *Interpreting Judaism in a Postmodern Age*, edited by Steven Kepnes (New York and London: New York University Press, 1996), 85-117.

4   For a discussion of the problem of authority and authorization in rabbinic texts see the work of Hindy Najman , "Legal Innovation in Ezra-Nehemiah" *The Interpretation of Judaism in Early Judaism and Christianity* (Sheffield: Sheffield University Press, 2000), volume 7: pp. 202-216 and *Sacred Writing and Sacred Reading: Invoking Mosaic Authority in Second Temple Literature* (Leiden: Brill, forthcoming). A modern theological appropriation of this problem is described by Peter Ochs' analysis of the writings of David Weiss Halivni, "Wounded Word, Wounded Interpreter" in *Humanity at the Limit: The Impact of the Holocaust Experience on Jews and Christians*, edited by Michael A. Signer (Bloomington, IN: Indiana University Press, 2000), 148-160.

5   A summary of approaches to the problems of the historical background to classical rabbinic text is in Hermann Strack/Gunther Stemberger. *Introduction to Talmud and Midrash* (Minneapolis: Fortress Press, 1992), pp. 50-61. On the role of historical studies in the emergence of Western European Jews into the modern period, cfr. Jay M. Harris, *How Do We Know This? Midrash and the Fragmentation of Modern Judaism* (Albany: State University of New York Press, 1995) and David Ellenson, *Between Tradition and Culture: The Dialectics of Modern Jewish Religion and Identity* (Atlanta, GA: Scholars Press, 1994).

6   Isadore Twersky, *Introduction to the Code of Moses Maimonides: Mishneh Torah* (New Haven: Yale University Press, 1980).

7   Michael A. Meyer, *Response to Modernity* (New York: Oxford University Press, 1988).

8   Yitzhak Baer, *Galut* (New York: Schocken, 1947); Yosef Hayim Yerushalmi, *Zakhor: Jewish History and Jewish Memory* (Seattle: University of Washington Press, 1988).

9   On the development of this "master narrative" during the medieval period cfr. Michael A. Signer, "God's Love for Israel: Apologetic and Hermeneutical Strategies in Twelfth-Century Biblical Exegesis" in *Jews and Christians in the Twelfth Century*, edited by Michael A. Signer and John H. Van Engen (Notre Dame, IN: University of Notre

Dame Press, 2001), pp. 123-149.

[10] Jacob Katz, *Tradition and Crisis: Jewish Society at the End of the Middle Ages*, translated with an afterword by Bernard Dov Cooperman (New York: Schocken Books, 1993), 1-16. For an explication of Katz's contribution to the historiography of modern Jewry cfr. David H. Ellenson, "Jacob Katz on the Origins and Dimensions of Jewish Modernity: The Centrality of the German Experience" (forthcoming).

[11] See the writings of David Ellenson, particularly his biography of Esriel Hildesheimer, the founder of the Orthodox *Rabbinerseminar* in Berlin, *Rabbi Esriel Hildesheimer and the Creation of a Modern Jewish Orthodoxy* (Tuscaloosa: University of Alabama Press, 1990).

[12] David Ellenson, *Tradition in Transition* (Lanham, MD: University Press of America 1989)

[13] Katz, 255.

[14] This formulation of the Shoah as a betrayal of modernity has been explicated by Zygmunt Bauman, *Modernity and the Holocaust* (Ithaca NY: Cornell University Press, 1989) and in the theological formation of Irving Greenberg, "Cloud of Smoke, Pillar of Fire: Judaism, Christianity and Modernity After the Holocaust" in *Auschwitz: Beginning of a New Era?*, edited by Eva Fleischner (New York: Ktav, 1977), pp. 7-55.

[15] This account of Rubenstein's career and theology is based on the essays collected in *After Auschwitz: History, Theology and Contemporary Judaism* (Baltimore and London: Johns Hopkins University Press, 1962). In particular, I think that the essays "The Dean and the Chosen People" (3-13), and "Covenant and Divinity: The Holocaust and the Problematics of Religious Faith" (157-200) are must helpful.

[16] Eugene B. Borowitz, *Renewing the Covenant: A Theology for the Postmodern Jew* (Philadelphia: Jewish Publication Society, 1991).

[17] The declaration of principles may be read on the Internet at www.ccarnet.org or www.uahc.org.

[18] On this question cfr. *The Land of Israel: Jewish Perspectives*, edited by Lawrence A. Hoffman (Notre Dame, IN: University of Notre Dame Press, 1986).

[19] Gershom G. Scholem, *On the Possibility of Jewish Mysticism in Our Time* (Philadelphia: Jewish Publication Society, 1997); Emil L. Fackenheim, *The Jewish Return into History* (New York: Schocken

Books, 1978).

[20] David N. Myers and David B. Ruderman, *The Jewish Past Revisited: Reflections on Modern Jewish Historians* (New Haven, CT: Yale University Press, 1998).

[21] *A History of the Jewish People* (Cambridge: Harvard University Press, 1976) was edited by Ben-Sasson and Ettinger. It provides examples of the "Jerusalem School" of Jewish historians.

[22] See Babylonian Talmud, Tractate Sanhedrin, fol. 90 ff. Translations of these texts are provided in Raphael Patai's anthology of messianic and eschatological texts, *The Messiah Texts* (Detroit: Wayne State University Press, 1979).

[23] Aviezer Ravitzky, *Messianism, Zionism and Jewish Religious Radicalism* (Chicago, University of Chicago Press, 1996) and Alan K. Dowty, *The Jewish State: A Century Later* (Berkeley and Los Angeles: University of California Press, 1998).

[24] The observations in this section are based on my own musings and personal observations. However, I have profited from the writings of Martin Marty, Wade Clark Roof and Robert Wuthnow. Arthur Green's theological approach is to be found in two recent books, *See My Face, Seek My Name: A Contemporary Jewish Theology* (Northvale, NJ: Jason Aronson, 1992) and *These Are the Words: A Vocabulary of Spiritual Life* (Woodstock VT: Jewish Lights, 1999).

[25] Appleby and Marty produced four volumes of studies on fundamentalism between 1991-1997.

[26] *Interpreting Judaism in a Post-Modern Age*, edited by Steven Kepnes (New York: New York University Press, 1996) is a collection of work by post-modern Jewish philosophers. An example of Och's own hermeneutics of retrieval may be found in his own edited collection, *The Return to Scripture in Judaism and Christianity: Essays in Post-Critical Interpretation* (New York: Paulist Press, 1993).

[27] Michael A. Signer, "The Rift that Binds: Hermeneutical Approaches to the Jewish-Christian Relationship" in Lawrence Cunningham [ed.], *Ecumenism: Present Realities and Future Prospects*. Notre Dame, IN: University of Notre Dame Press, 1999), pp. 95-115; "One Covenant or Two: Can We Sing a New Song?" in *Reinterpreting Revelation and Tradition: Jews and Christians in Conversation*, edited by John T. Pawlikowski and Hayim Goren Perelmuter (Franklin WI: Sheed and Ward, 2000), pp. 3-25.

[28] See Rotentreich's essay in note 125.

[29] On the elements of Gnosticism in modern Judaism and Christianity see the illuminating and provocative study by Steven M. Wasserstrom, *Religion After Religion: Gershom Scholem, Henri Corbin and Mircea Eliade at Eranos* (Princeton NJ: Princeton University Press, 1999). The force of Gnosticism within the context of Jewish-Christian dialogue is described by Hanspeter Heinz, "The Celebration of the Sacraments and the Teaching of the Commandments in an Age of Religious Consumerism" in *Memory and History in Christianity and Judaism*, edited by Michael A. Signer (Notre Dame IN: University of Notre Dame Press, 2001), pp. 145-169.

Conversation Four

Presenting the Dialogue to the Public

Parallel Monologues: Catholics, Jews and Jedwabne

Konstanty Gebert

The last two decades have seen a slow and sporadic, but consistent increase in Catholic-Jewish religious contacts in Poland. Hitherto practically non-existent, the relationship between the two faiths has now a track record, at first glance consisting mainly of successive crises and attempts to overcome them. Conflicts over the existence of a Carmelite convent in Auschwitz, repeated anti-Semitic statements by Father Jankowski in Gdansk, or new crosses planted in Auschwitz and the seemingly impolite language used by Rabbi Joskowicz when discussing them with the Pope, have made international headlines. In the shadow of these conflicts, however, lies a history of more positive developments, from the activity of the Polish Council of Christians and Jews through a series of statements and initiatives by the Polish Episcopate, to inter-religious events in churches and seminaries. However, each time a new crisis develops, these achievements seem to count for very little. No functioning channels of communication between religious leadership on both sides exist, nor has the dialogue conducted over the last twenty years fundamentally altered mutual perceptions.

Most of these conflicts, including lesser ones which have not made it to the international media, are not primarily religious, but rather are derived from separate and irreconcilable visions of Polish-Jewish relations in the past, particularly during World War II. Typically, many Jews see Polish anti-Semitism as the main factor influencing these relations, culminating with the indifference of most Poles, and participation of many, in the persecution and genocide of the Jews committed by Germans in occupied Poland. They believe this anti-Semitism was primarily religious in its origins, and that therefore the Catholic Church, Poland's dominant Christian denomination, bears a heavy responsibility, at least for creating the moral climate in which a genocidal ideology could develop. In that perspective, the Church should acknowledge its sins of the past, express contrition, and remain ever vigilant in condemning and combating contemporary anti-Semitism, first of all in its own ranks.

Many —probably most— Polish Catholics do not think of it that way. They see traditional Polish tolerance as the main factor influencing Polish-Jewish relations. They believe this tolerance had created the basis for such relations: from the Middle Ages onwards Jews, persecuted elsewhere in Europe, found a safe haven in Poland. Those 'guests' then badly repaid the generosity of their 'hosts', by refusing to assimilate and by embracing 'anti-Polish' attitudes and ideologies, from capitalism to, especially, Communism. Polish hostility to Jews, if there is any, should be seen as an understandable, if possibly excessive, reaction of one unjustly wronged, with the Church trying to moderate things by teaching Christian love, even of one's enemies. In World War II Poles were outraged by alleged Jewish collaboration with the Soviet occupiers, and some might have acted out their revenge. Others might have harmed the Jews out of purely criminal motives, but the Polish nation as a whole tried to save Jews, not to harm them, and thousands died in the attempt. In that perspective, Jews should acknowledge their sins of the past, express contrition, and remain ever vigilant in condemning and combating contemporary 'anti-Polonism', first of all among themselves.

The fact that historical research essentially supports the 'Jewish' version of history, without neglecting the important issue of Jewish participation in, or cooperation with, the Communist movement, does not seem to have affected these general positions. Nor have successive Church documents (from the Pastoral Letter of 1991 to Primate Glemp's act of contrition of 2000) influenced the general position of the Church, or the Jewish perception of that position. The pioneering work of the Polish CCJ remains largely ignored on both sides, its Catholic members (the issue of other Christian denominations, also included in the Council, is not important for the purpose of this paper) representative of but a minority within their Church, its sole Jewish member considered something of an eccentric by most of his co-religionists. Given the fact that Catholic radio and print media routinely publish anti-Semitic content, that anti-Semitic publications are being sold on Church premises, and that anti-Semitic preachers may occasionally be admonished, but not removed, most Jews and Catholics in Poland would probably agree that negative attitudes toward the Jews are a legitimate Catholic position. The disagreement would then be solely over whether such attitudes express a historic wrong, or are in fact an attempt to correct one.

But such an opinion is in flagrant contradiction with the official declarations of the Catholic Church, both in Poland and abroad, as well as with what most authorities seem to agree is the Christian teaching. Interestingly enough, there does not seem to be such a contradiction with general Jewish declarations and teachings, although the Dabru Emet debate can be seen as a challenge to this mainstream position. Be it as it may, there is an obvious major discrepancy between how the Church in Poland is perceived on that issue, and how it wants to be perceived. Regardless of where the truth is in all that, it would seem that, at the very minimum, the Church should therefore maintain open channels of communication with the Jewish community, to avoid accidental misperception. This would not be dissimilar to the 'hot line' between Washington and Moscow during the Cold War and after, its existence supposed to be a safeguard against one side accidentally reaching the conclusion that the other is about to launch a nuclear onslaught, and reacting accordingly. And even if one is entitled to believe that inter-religious dialogue can progress beyond a Cold War model, it is not a bad starting point, given the circumstances.

In this context it seems useful to analyze the Christian and Jewish reactions in Poland to the discovery of the Jedwabne massacre and the public debate that followed. It can serve both as a litmus test of how representatives of both faiths perceive each other, and also as a case study of inter-religious communication. The author, a close observer and sometime participant in the unfolding events, can hardly claim to be a dispassionate analyst. As a Jewish journalist and once active in Christian-Jewish dialogue, he believes that the Church in Poland can overcome its anti-Semitic legacy and needs to do it, for its own sake and for that of setting the record straight. On a more immediate level, it needs to engage in damage control, in order to avoid creating a worse picture of itself than might be, in fact, the case. The Jewish religious community, whatever its own biases and shortcomings, does not seem to have a parallel problem, at least in this case — or, if it does, the author honestly is unable to see it. But then, given its size of less than 3500 members, it can hardly be an equal partner for the Church representing the at least 35 million Poles who are Catholics. It is the Church that sets both the religious and the inter-religious agenda. As such, it bears a special responsibility for it.

Jedwabne is a small town of some two thousand inhabitants in north-eastern Poland, in the Lomza region. Occupied by the Soviets in 1939, it was overrun by the Germans in the first days of their attack on the Soviet Union in 1941. The entire Jewish population of the town, constituting half of Jedwabne's inhabitants, was murdered on July 10 or soon after. Most were burned alive in a requisitioned barn, several hundred yards from the main square. In the Sixties a commemorative stone was placed at that site, with an inscription, which mentioned "1600 Jews burned alive by the Nazi gendarmerie and Gestapo." A more recent stone, erected after the fall of Communism in Poland, commemorates "180 people, including 2 priests, murdered on the territory of Jedwabne shire in 1939-56 by the [Soviet] NKVD, the Nazis and the [Polish Communist] UB". For almost ten years the two stones stood nearby each other, and apparently no-one noticed the contradiction, or bothered to comment on it. At the very minimum, the new stone excluded the Jews of Jedwabne from collective memory.

In April 2001 Jan Tomasz Gross, an émigré Polish-Jewish professor at New York University, published a slender volume of barely over one hundred pages, called 'Neighbors.' Basing himself on a Jedwabne *Yizkor buch* published in New York in 1980, on the proceedings of three trials which took place in Poland in the late Forties and early Fifties, on documentary footage of eyewitness accounts shot contemporaneously in Poland by director Agnieszka Arnold and on his own research, he proved that the Jedwabne massacre was in fact not committed by 'Nazis', but by the non-Jewish neighbors of the victims, Catholic Poles, acting under German instigation, but not compulsion. The book also indicated that similar mass murders were committed in other localities of the Lomza county at that time, following a similar modus operandi.

First reactions in Poland attempted to invalidate Gross's account. Adam Michnik, himself of Jewish origin, the editor in chief of the country's biggest and most influential daily, the liberal *Gazeta Wyborcza*, for several months forbade his journalists to cover the issue, persuaded that Gross must have been factually incorrect. At the other end of the political spectrum, the nationalist right-wing press, led by the Catholic daily *Nasz Dziennik* and the Catholic radio *Maryja*, insisted that this was yet another campaign of anti-Polish slander orchestrated by international Zionist and Masonic circles and their Polish stooges. For several weeks, only the conservative daily *Rzeczpospolita*, which was the first to cover the issue, would publish articles on the subject of the Jedwabne massacre.

The overall impact of the book, put out by a highly respected provincial publisher, was devastating. The mass public debate which followed, in the media and elsewhere, and is still continuing, is probably the most important debate of the post-Communist decade, with possibly only the controversy over abortion reaching similar levels of salience. In a May 2001 public opinion poll, a surprising 85% of those asked said they are aware of the debate. Although obviously centered on the historical facts revealed by Gross, and on Polish-Jewish issues in general, the debate turned to more general issues of Polish history and identity. As anthropologist Joanna Tokarska-Bakir put it, the discussion had put paid to 'Poland's myth of innocence.' The subject of this paper is not the debate itself, but the Church's reaction to it, and the degree, if any, to which it became an issue in Catholic-Jewish dialogue, or even communication. To appreciate that, however, the impact of the debate must be briefly addressed.

The debate on the Jedwabne massacre affected not only the Poles' vision of their history in World War II. It struck at the very heart of the fundamental Polish self-stereotype of the nation as innocent sufferer. According to this stereotype, Poles had always been victims of oppression, but never oppressed others. The great 19th century Romantic poet Adam Mickiewicz had put it succinctly: "Poland is the Christ of the nations." Poles, even if disagreeing on everything else, considered this formulation a simple statement of fact – and certainly the only too true history of their own sufferings, especially over the last two centuries, gave them no reason to doubt it.

Not only had Poles never hurt others, ran the accepted vision of Polish history; they had, to the contrary, altruistically fought in their defense. And again, the record confirms it: 19th century European history is punctuated by reports of Polish revolutionaries joining the struggles of the Italians and the French, the Hungarians and even the Russians against domestic and foreign oppression. And since Polish national ideology founded Poland's right to independence (of which it had been deprived over most of the last 200 years) on the righteousness of her cause, any critical vision of the country's attitude towards "others" was immediately seen as an attack on its very right to exist. This reflex reaction would return in the Jedwabne debate.

It should be noted, as an aside, that this reflex, though exacerbated in the Polish case, is hardly a Polish specificity. The Serbs routinely speak of themselves as "nebeski narod," the "heavenly people," whose innate goodness prevents them from doing harm to others. In both cases an attempted analogy with the Biblical status of the Jews is implicit, and at times explicit. Stanislaw Krajewski, co-founder and Jewish co-chairman of the Polish CCJ, once quipped that there is not enough room for two chosen peoples in one country. Both in the Polish and the Serbian case, it is assumed that these nations are almost by definition noble and thus incapable of hurting others because of the – only too real, let us stress this once again – suffering they have gone through; for suffering ennobles, and great suffering ennobles greatly.

But the view that suffering ennobles is in itself probably a noble fallacy. I have seen individuals go through suffering and emerge noble, but I suspect that many of them would have become noble anyway, suffering or no suffering. In group terms, however, suffering hardly ennobles; rather, it makes the group concentrate on its own pain, and become inured to and indifferent to the pain of others. This has happened both to the Poles and the Serbs, and in a way also to the Jews. Therefore I venture the thesis that suffering does not ennoble, but it makes one more prone to see one's own group as noble. Hence the self-perception trap the Poles fell into.

Furthermore, in Poland's case the period when, as a nation, it exerted an impact on other nations, ended in the late Forties, with the deportations of the Ukrainians. That period, therefore, slipped from the realm of memory, that is of subjective fact ('I remember...'), to that of history, that is reported conjecture ('I am told that...'). Finally, the years that followed were marked by the constant oppression, and occasional unbridled brutality of the Communist regime. In a nutshell: the Poles had every reason to feel victimized again, and felt no need to consider whether others could have been their victims.

But memory lingered on. In previous debates on Poles and Jews in World War II, which periodically erupted over the last fifteen years, the defensiveness of many Poles on issues such as the "szmalcownicy," i.e. individuals who blackmailed Jews in hiding and/or turned them over to the Gestapo, was clearly tinged with bad conscience. On the other hand the fact that sometimes sweeping and unfair accusations are made against Poles, portrayed as partners with the Germans in the Shoah, in flagrant disregard both of the country's resistance record, and of the thousands, as testified by Yad Vashem, who did save Jews, did not help a critical self-examination. The Jedwabne debate, however, was vastly different.

First, it was not concentrated around the issue of whether what the historical record says happened actually did happen. For the first time, revisionists and negationists were forced onto the margins, while the mainstream accepted the historical record as presented by Gross and grappled with it with impressive honesty and courage – at least to a point. Second, again in contradistinction to what obtained earlier, this was not a debate between Poles and Jews, but an internal Polish debate, rooted in the concrete case of the Jedwabne massacre, but ranging far beyond it. Both those remarkable characteristics were possible due to a new climate of self-assurance in Poland, itself a consequence of the country's successful negotiation of the post-Communist transition. The 'man the trenches!' reflex, so characteristic of previous debates in which Poland's history was critically examined, was to a large degree absent this time.

But most important, however, was the fact that Jedwabne was a genuine shock to all segments of Polish society. Regarding the individual cooperation of some Poles with the German genocide, many Poles suspected — and not a few knew — that it was much larger than they were willing to admit. There was, however, not even an intimation of the fact that a group of ordinary Poles might have, as soon as the Germans gave them a push and a nod, tortured, raped and murdered their Jewish neighbors: women, children, elderly, looted their houses, and then continued to live on, as if nothing had happened. This shock, incidentally, was what shocked some foreign observers, who have fallen prey to a reverse stereotype to that of Poland's innocence: they seemed to believe most Poles would routinely slaughter Jews given half a chance. Incidentally, while Poles expected extremely negative foreign reactions once the book was published abroad, what happened was somewhat the reverse: there were positive public reactions to the fact that Poland was capable of courageous and honest soul-searching. Polish Jews, on the third hand, as it were, both have kept a historical memory of the Jedwabne massacre, and also realized that, for historical reasons which need only briefly to be addressed here, the horrors of the Lomza region were much more the exception than the rule in wartime Poland.

Before the war, the Lomza region was one of the few rural strongholds of the ONR (Oboz Narodowo-Radykalny, the National-Radical Camp), an extreme-Right anti-Semitic movement. This created a climate of permanent tension in relations between Poles and Jews. Organized boycotts of Jewish businesses, and violent attacks on Jews, were more and more common. It needs to be stressed that the ONR was considered by the government as a subversive organization, and that the police usually endeavored to protect law and order. We also have testimony from rabbi Jacob Baker, who left Jedwabne as a young man three years before the war, about the generally good climate of interfaith relationships in town. This does not change much the overall picture of increasing violence. The ONR was supported by at least part of the Catholic church. During the almost two years of Soviet occupation which followed Poland's defeat in 1939, Polish nationalism and the Church itself suffered very heavily at the hands of the NKVD. A segment of Poland's Jewish population had elected to cooperate with Soviet authorities. And though other Jews constituted up to 30% of those deported, as politically unreliable, to Soviet Central Asia and Siberia, the very sight – unheard-of before the war — of some Jews in positions of power (as policemen, or representatives of local authorities) confirmed Polish perceptions of Soviet communism as a Jewish plot. Traditional religious and economic anti-Semitism in the region was thus given a new, more immediate rationale (though we know of very few cases of Jews from Jedwabne itself cooperating with the Soviets).

The role of the Church during the massacre itself seems to have been entirely passive. According to the *Yizkor buch* testimonies, a Jewish delegation had pleaded with the local priest on the eve of the massacre, begging him to protect the town's Jewish population, but to no avail. Massacres of Jews had over the previous few days occurred in nearby villages, and the Jews of Jedwabne had good reason to fear for their lives. According to the present parish priest Father Edward Orlowski, his then predecessor had, on the day of the massacre, asked a German officer to at least spare the women and children, and was told to mind his own business, which he then proceeded to do. It should be noted that, though the massacre occurred at German urging and with German support, it does not appear that Germans were actively involved in carrying it out.

Father Orlowski to this very day totally rejects the notion that the fathers and grandfathers of his parishioners were responsible for the murder. Speaking in May 2000 to a reporter from the Polish Jewish monthly *Midrasz*,[1] he stated that at most "they turned them [the Jews] in" and added: "It does not matter if one is a Jew or not. Had someone come to me and confessed, I could not have approved of him, even had he been a freedom fighter. Beat your breast and compensate for the wrongs if you may." In an interview with Polish TV Channel 1 in March 2001, he was even more explicit. Answering the question of whether anyone had ever confessed to him participation in the massacre, Father Orlowski first invoked the secrecy of confession, and then added: "I have been parish priest here for thirty years and let me tell you: not one conscience has been moved."[2] True to form, Father Orlowski boycotted the 60th anniversary ceremony on July 10, 2001. He did, however, receive on that day a surprise visit by Rabbi Jacob Baker. According to both clergymen, they reminiscenced about the good times before the war. Father Orlowski's position was endorsed by the more extreme Catholic and Right-wing media, as mentioned above, and by the local bishop Stanislaw Stefanek. To his credit, Bishop Stefanek celebrated Holy Mass in Jedwabne to commemorate the victims of the massacre in early fall of 2000, when the institutional Church was still silent on the event. Later, however, he took a different position, which will be described below.

In October 2000, after the debate had been raging for half a year, the Polish CCJ was the first institution to address the issue from a religious perspective. Jewish co-chairman Stanislaw Krajewski, speaking at a meeting in Warsaw,[3] called for "the official acknowledgement of the truth, and for paying homage to the victims." He added, "It should be made clear that the [future] ceremony is organized on behalf of all Poland, and it should be attended by the Polish leadership: the president, the Primate of the Roman Catholic Church in Poland, and the prime minister. A successful ceremony will be tantamount to success in the Christian-Jewish dialogue. The Church's *teshuva* will bear fruit."

Echoing his words, the Christian co-chairman father Michal Czajkowski said in a press interview:

> Doubtlessly some act of honest expiation in the spirit of the Pope's act of contrition of March 12 [2000] is necessary, for this was truly a horrible murder of Jews committed by their Polish Catholic neighbors… We are glad at the reaction of the Lomza bishop, who had performed holy mass on that spot, but this is not enough. What is needed is a more official and public act of expiation for this terrible crime.[4]

The CCJ continued to play a role in the Jedwabne debate, organizing an interfaith service to commemorate the victims in Warsaw's St. Martin's convent in March 2001 and a public discussion in Warsaw's Catholic

Intellectuals' Club the next month.

In the early stage of the debate the need for such a public act of *teshuvah*, with full Church participation, seemed obvious and unquestionable. By the same token, the role of the Church in the events leading to the massacre and in the massacre itself, as well as its position in the current debate, was usually not examined. In an otherwise profound article published in the Catholic monthly *Wiez* in March 2001,[5] and therefore written prior to that date, Archbishop Jozef Zycinski of Lublin, considered one of the leading liberals in the Episcopate, conducts an in-depth socio- and psychological analysis of the circumstances of the massacre. But in it he pays only fleeting attention to the fact that the murderers were Christian: "The society or local community of Jedwabne was no anonymous crowd... Its cultural environment should also have been inspired by Christian ethics." He then offers the Biblical story of David's sin of commissioning Uriah's death (2 Sam 11:15-17) as a way of reading the Jedwabne massacre: "How many Uriahs does David have to destroy", he asks, "before we view David's tragedy in the same way as we view the tragedy of Jedwabne?" The fate of the victims is obviously less important here than the fate of the murderers, whose Christianity seems to be incidental, but Archbishop Zycinski concludes on a warning note: "Let us not search for some imaginary documents that could turn the tragedy of Jedwabne into a commonplace event."

By March, when this article was published, a double consensus seemed to have emerged from the discussion. On the one hand, the overwhelming majority of the mainstream media, and a substantial minority of Polish public opinion,[6] had reached the conclusion that the Jedwabne massacre was committed by Poles, and that an act of contrition was called for. On the other hand, the Right-wing and most Catholic media (with the exception of *Wiez* and *Znak* monthlies and *Tygodnik Powszechny* weekly) continued to question the facts, to play up the possibility of the crime having been committed by Germans, of understandable revenge for Jewish-Soviet terror as possible Polish motive, and to deny the need of accepting responsibility for the crime. In this they were supported by a majority of Polish public opinion. The institutional Church, however, had yet to take position on the issue.

Addressing the issue for the first time in a statement late in February 2000, the Primate of Poland, Cardinal Josef Glemp, seemed to belittle the event. If Poles had indeed participated in the killing of Jews in

Jedwabne, he said, "it was a local tragedy." This statement elicited a response from the rabbi of Warsaw and Lodz Michael Schudrich. In a hitherto unpublished letter, the rabbi wrote on March 1:

> I was very saddened and hurt to read words attributed to you concerning the tragic massacre of 1941 in Jedwabne. The occasion of the 60th anniversary of the death of hundreds of Polish citizens of the Jewish faith is an opportunity for us together to mourn the tragic loss of human life. This is not an occasion for us to discuss historical truth or to attribute responsibility for this incident. It is the obligation of religious leadership never to let us forget the murder of innocent human beings. That is why your presence [in Jedwabne] is important on July 10th. This is not a local tragedy - it is a universal tragedy.

Rabbi Schudrich then brings the principle of the *Eglah Arufa* (Deuteronomy 21:1-9) as relevant to this case. It concerns the necessary expiatory ceremony to be held when a body killed by unknown perpetrators is found. "Too much innocent blood of too many different peoples has been spilt tragically in this land – Schudrich continues. – If we, the religious leadership of Poland, do not stand together to mourn and to cry out against such sinful acts, who then will be there to fulfil the moral imperative set before us by our Bible? The sin of murder is committed in a moment, but the sin of minimising or forgetting a murder is a sin which is repeated with every next moment of life. The Bible concludes the commandment of the *Eglah Arufa* with the following admonition: 'Still, you must eradicate the (liability for) innocent blood from within you, when you do what is upright in God's eyes' (Deut. 21:9). May God bless us with the wisdom and sensitivity to know what is upright in God's eyes."

The Primate never answered Schudrich's letter. But, in a pattern which would become routine, he referred to it in his next public statement, a speech given in the Catholic radio *Jozef* on March 4.[7] Stating he had rejected political pressure for Church participation in a commemorative ceremony in Jedwabne,[8] Primate Glemp said:

> This is why I had appreciated the letter or the Rabbi of Warsaw, who bases the need of such an act in Scriptural text… This is the appropriate spiritual plane for shrouding oneself in sorrow for the innocently murdered. We will be glad to do this in Warsaw in a conjoint prayer of Poles and Jews, either in front of the monument of the Heroes of the

> Ghetto, or in one of the temples, or in the Synagogue… It is highly desirable for us as a Church together with people of the Mosaic Faith to ask forgiveness of God for sins committed according to the truth revealed in the Bible.

It is interesting to note that the rabbi never said that the ceremony he suggests should take place in Warsaw, not in Jedwabne, nor did he suggest some kind of joint atonement. And certainly his words were twisted out of context when, replying to Schudrich's criticism of Glemp's formulation of Jedwabne as a "local tragedy" (which, after all, was the reason the letter had been written in the first place), the Primate said: "Yes, as humanity we deplore blood innocently shed in any nation. The murders of innocents in Jedwabne, Katyn, Dachau, Auschwitz, elicit our pain as members of the human race, just as the murders in Rwanda, the Balkans, or among neighbours in Palestine."

"There's no doubt one can feel offended by comparing Jedwabne to the terrorism going on today in Israel," the rabbi commented to Eric Greenberg of *The Jewish Week*.[9] This author was also shocked by the comparison made between Jedwabne on one hand, and Katyn, Dachau and Auschwitz on the other. The latter were state crimes committed, respectively, by Soviet Russia and Nazi Germany. The former – a crime committed by Poles, to be sure, but at a time when the Polish state was occupied and could not exert its authority. The comparison is unfair to Poland.[10]

The speech in general was extremely contradictory. On the one hand, for the first time the Primate stated unambiguously that:

> The murder by burning alive the Jewish population, herded by force by Poles to a barn, is undeniable.…This is connected with recognising a generational responsibility, which consists in asking forgiveness of God for the sins of the ancestors, and in asking forgiveness of the descendants of those wronged.… The reasons of the formation of such degenerate and hateful attitudes of Poles toward Jews, not seen in other parts of Poland, must be researched.

And yet the speech is permeated by a polemic tone, as when the Primate wonders why is it that all the "amplification" of the massacre occurs just now, or when he chides Archbishop Zycinski for the conclusion of his Wiez article: "Yes, do not let us look for imaginary documents, but do not let us ignore reliable research." It is as if the Primate was finally not sure if he himself was right in his unequivocal characterisation of the massacre.

What is most striking, however, is the total lack of reflection – which Primate Glemp seems to share with Archbishop Zycinski – on the specifically Christian dimension of the crime. The fact that the murderers were Christians, and presumably well steeped in the religious anti-Semitism which was then standard Church teaching does not seem to provoke these clergymen to deeper reflection. They are concerned about the murder as they are concerned about evil anywhere ("...Auschwitz, the Balkans, Palestine..." "...how many Uriahs?..."), more so because it occurred on Polish soil – but it does not seem to pose them a specific challenge.

Criticism of their attitude, however, must be placed in context. On March 11 the bishop of Lomza came to Jedwabne and delivered a sermon which laid forward the case against any soul-searching at all, be it even on a general plane. The bishop said:

> We are witnessing an unprecedented attack on Jedwabne. In fact it is an attack on the understanding of World War II, on the understanding of the history of Europe and the world. Jedwabne is a symbol, is a sign. This is why Your Bishop stands amongst You, to pray together, for we are in the center of an unleashed cyclone which, in the intent of the initiators, will set minds ablaze again in a spiral of allegations and hatred... Over a year ago my friends in Warsaw, in discreet conversation, with lowered voices, told me: there will be a great attack on Jedwabne, it is about money... And indeed, as my friends had announced, a campaign incredible in its methods has been unleashed against Jedwabne... Who profits from war? Who makes fortunes out of war? We have seen how mainly the producers of weapons, of technical equipment, producers of food and of clothing profit from war... But there is also a new way of profiting from war, from harm. There is an expression now in the United States: Shoah business. I tried to understand what it means. I must admit no one has explained it to me to the end. But they tell me succinctly: the best business is made now on the blood of the innocently murdered Jews and we need to know whom we risk to incite when we speak out loud about these things. This is why such powerful mechanisms were set in motion. Jedwabne is neither first nor last. This campaign, predatory, deceitful and very modern in its technique, reaches far and aims far.

And though Bishop Stefanek also included in his sermon reflections about the line between good and evil "which goes across every heart," and stated that a "Sanctuary of Innocent Blood" should be erected on the site of the massacre, his message was clear. The accusations are deceitful and extortionary. Not only the faithful of the Lomza region need not do any soul-searching, they need to stand firm in front of this campaign of hatred.

The bishop was never sanctioned by any of his peers. When asked about his sermon by *Tygodnik Powszechny* editor in chief, Father Adam Boniecki,[11] Archbishop Henryk Muszynski, former chairman of the episcopate's Commission on Dialogue with Judaism, answered curtly: "I do not know the full text." Only the Union of Jewish Religious Congregations and Rabbi Schudrich expressed their criticism. In a statement issued three days after the sermon, they stated: "We are surprised and saddened by the fact that in the sermon given last Sunday [in Jedwabne] by bishop Stefanek of Lomza, the understanding of the [moral] challenge [of Jedwabne] was lacking. We were particularly surprised by the fragments speaking of "attack on Jedwabne" or money allegedly involved. This is a denial of the real problem and, in final analysis, a justification of the murderers." Quoting World War II hero Jan Nowak-Jezioranski, the statement warns: "If we will justify the crime, reduce its importance, lay responsibility for it on the victims, look for attenuating circumstances, then the entire nation might, in the eyes of the world, become an accomplice to the crime."

Yet the fact that Rabbi Schudrich's letter did elicit a response, if distorted and indirect, from the Primate, seems to have raised hopes and expectations. A few days after Primate Glemp's speech the Catholic news agency KAI conducted, for the first time, an extensive interview with rabbi Schudrich. The interview was subsequently criticised by some members of the Jewish community as overly conciliatory, but in terms of Catholic-Jewish relations in Poland it was a ground-breaking event.

Rabbi Schudrich first lays to rest the notion that there is a Jewish request for apologies from the Poles, or the Catholics. "Everyone must consider in his conscience what would be the best form of asking forgiveness. I will not impose anything.... If I did something wrong, I have to ask forgiveness of the person I wronged. It is not enough to ask forgiveness of God" said Schudrich, in an oblique polemic with Primate Glemp's insistence that forgiveness should first be asked of God. He went on to say:

It is painful for me that the word Jedwabne elicits bad feeling. One thinks of conflict, murder, victims, the people are divided. It does not matter what version of events the parties of the conflict endorse, but they mainly think of violence and tragedy which took place here. But this is not right. Why do not these people mention the 500 years of common history?... The very question [of whether the Poles can be considered equal to the Nazis] makes me protest... It is incredible that such statements can be made! This is not only against Poland, but against truth and history... [But] for Poles it should be more important what they will say to God and what will be their own approach to Jedwabne, than what will be said in the USA.

And finally, asked the question of whether Jews should apologise to Poles for crimes committed by Communists – an issue that had become very salient in the national-Catholic counter-offensive against the Jedwabne accusations – Schudrich replied, "we Jews need to admit that there were Jews in the service of the Communists, or even of the Nazis, who had committed crimes against Poles, and also against other Jews. But they never maintained that they acted in the name of the Jewish people."

Rabbi Schudrich's interview elicited very positive reactions from the Catholic side. Archbishop Henryk Muszynski dedicated a substantial part of his already quoted *Tygodnik Powszechny* interview to comments on the rabbi's statements. Of particular importance, according to Muszynski, was the fact that Schudrich acknowledged that some Jews in Communist or Nazi service had caused harm to other people. "This is a great challenge for us – he commented – to be able to admit and say exactly the same thing about the co-responsibility or even co-guilt of those Poles who in fact did participate in crimes... Rabbi Schudrich had, in a way, met us half-way, stressing the absolute necessity of our asking for forgiveness."

In fact, Schudrich had not said that; nor had he amalgamated the guilt of Poles and that of Jews. Still, it seemed that a real rapprochement was in the offing: "I had often said", Muszynski continued, "that Polish-Jewish reconciliation had not yet happened, that we are still in the phase of mutual recrimination. After Rabbi Schudrich's words [about the unacceptability of blaming Poles for the Shoah] I am willing to change my mind." Schudrich's words may seem, and indeed are, self evident, but to a Polish audience, with its not unjustified feeling that Polish victimhood in World War II is being disproportionately overshadowed by instances of Polish collaboration with the Nazis, this was very welcome vindication. And

Archbishop Muszynski responded in kind, offering the statement, that while "both we and Jews were victims" this did not occur "in the same way and in the same degree." "The Jew was sentenced to death and had to die; the Pole could survive as Untermensch." Again, a self-evident statement, but important for a Jewish audience:

> Rabbi Schudrich's statement may be a breakthrough in reaching full moral, and even historical truth, and therefore in cleansing through truth... here I see a certain analogy with Polish-German reconciliation [initiated by the Polish Episcopate's "We forgive and ask for forgiveness" letter of 1965]: here and there the initiative came from the victims."

These were extremely brave words, for if Poles and Jews, respectively, are equated as victims, them Poles and Germans are also, respectively, equated as perpetrators. And though the archbishop obviously strongly endorsed the rabbi's completely justified condemnation of blaming the Shoah on the Poles, he could not fail to see that this does not close the debate; it only sets the frame of reference. The archbishop also praised the Primate's reaction to rabbi Schudrich's letter "which creates the proper spiritual plane for joining, through common prayer, with the victims in conjoint mourning for those innocently murdered."

What really gave weight to Archbishop Muszynski's words, however, was his frank recognition of the historical facts. "Regardless of whether it will turn out that 1600 Jews, or 160 have been burnt, the crime remains a crime... The responsibility for each crime falls on the immediate perpetrator, yet those who are connected to him by religious or national bonds, even though they bear no personal guilt, can not feel free of moral responsibility for the victims of that murder." And here, as Archbishop Zycinski had done before him (but, curiously, without quoting him), Archbishop Muszynski offers the example of David's sin as a way of understanding Jedwabne.

The Schudrich-Muszynski exchange through parallel interviews marked the high point of Catholic-Jewish relations in the Jedwabne debate. And yet, even the outspoken archbishop did not see fit to engage in an analysis of a specifically Christian responsibility, if any, for the massacre.

For a couple of weeks it seemed that the Jedwabne debate, indeed, as Archbishop Muszynski had said, would become a turning point in Catholic-Jewish relations, and the commemoration on the anniversary of the massacre would indeed be an opportunity for "conjoint mourning for those innocently murdered." Bishop Tadeusz Pieronek, president of the Papal Theological Academy in Krakow, said confidently that "the Church is not at all interested in obfuscating the truth about Jedwabne. The manner of commemorating the anniversary is in the hands of the local bishop [i.e. bishop Stanislaw Szczepanek of Lomza], who will take care of it, and nobody will create any obstacles." And Archbishop Jozef Zycinski stated:

> The task of the clergy is to draw lessons from that tragedy...For the clergy to be able to shape a new awareness of Polish-Jewish dialogue, we need an unequivocal assessment of the dramas of recent history. I have the impression that the overwhelming majority of the clergy adopts the Herbertean[12] vision of moral responsibility."[13] Both statements were soon to prove rather far-fetched.

A clear moral statement did come, as usual, from the CCJ. Its Christian members issued a statement saying:

> Facts [about Jedwabne], known to a few historians and witnesses, have not permanently entered our collective memory, and have not moved our conscience. Nor have the become a call to penance for other evil acts committed against Jews, which we had removed from our conscience... We bend our heads in sorrow in conjoint prayer and we ask the Lord for the grace of contrition, forgiveness and reconciliation.[14]

The counterattack was not long in coming. It was led by Father Waldemar Chrostowski who, after having spent many years in Christian-Jewish dialogue, published in 1998 a violent article accusing Jews of unwillingness to repent for their own crimes, and denying any special Christian responsibility for anti-Semitism. The outburst eventually cost him the position of Christian co-chairman of the CCJ, but not that of adviser to the Episcopate on Jewish affairs. In a press interview,[15] Chrostowski stated that:

> ... reconciliation presupposes mutuality. Not that the guilt of Poles and Jews was identical or comparable, but simply because it is there... There certainly are things for which we should ask forgiveness of different people with whom we share a common fate. But there are also issues on which we Poles should also hear words of apology. This pertains also to the Jewish side. If such a gesture of reconciliation would take place, then the

role of the memory of what had happened in Jedwabne would turn out to be salutary for both sides.

Father Chrostowski was obviously not asking for a simple statement of fact, that some Jews had in the past harmed some Poles; this had been already said in Rabbi Schudrich's interview. He was clearly hoping for more, whatever that would be. He also implied that contrition is a kind of *quid pro quo*, and that without a Jewish "gesture" the memory of Jedwabne would not be "salutary." Even some Catholics were puzzled about his meaning. In a radio interview[16] Archbishop Tadeusz Goclowski of Gdansk had the following reaction: "I don't know what Professor Chrostowski was thinking about.... We will probably never be able to weigh the proportions completely: what was the percentage of guilt, whether there was more of it on this, or on that side.... Each crime is simply a crime and one has to look at it in truth." Very soon, however, it turned out that Chrostowski is being very well understood in some quarters. In a TV interview, Primate Glemp also stressed that in "forgiveness, especially in relationship with this nation, there is an element of mutuality" and stated, definitively, that he would not go to Jedwabne for the anniversary.[17] The required "gesture" had apparently not been made.

The counter-offensive continued. Father Orlowski in Jedwabne started selling anti-Semitic pamphlets, purporting to be a rebuttal of Gross's research; he eventually joined Ryszard Gontarz, an ex-Communist ideologue of the 1968 anti-Semitic campaign, in a short-lived Committee to Protect the Good Name of Jedwabne. The notorious Father Henryk Jankowski in Gdansk decorated the Easter Sepulchre in his church of St. Brigit with the following quote from the Gospel: "The Jews killed Jesus and the prophets and persecuted us as well." An outraged Archbishop Goclowski ordered the offending elements removed; the ADL in a special statement praised the determined reaction to Jankowski's provocation. Much more important, and unfortunately much less publicised, was another Easter Sepulchre, set up by Father Wojciech Lemanski in his church in Otwock near Warsaw. It presented a burned barn with the inscription "Forgive us." Father Lemanski stated later in a press interview, that the reaction of his parishioners had been overwhelmingly positive.

Primate Glemp's decision not to go to Jedwabne for the anniversary effectively scotched any Church participation in the commemorative event. After a meeting of the Episcopate in early May, it was decided that the

Church should hold its own commemorative services on May 27 in Warsaw. The date has no special meaning, but the bishops would be in Warsaw on that day anyway, to commemorate Cardinal Stefan Wyszynski, Primate Glemp's great predecessor. "July is not the most convenient month for such a ceremony and many bishops would not be present" said Primate Glemp in a subsequent interview,[18] most probably referring to the vacation season. It was announced that the mass would be held in All Saints' Church in Warsaw's Grzybowski square. This was the parish of a notorious anti-Semitic priest in the 1930s, Father Maurycy Godlewski, who during the war underwent a change of heart and helped baptised Jews (and, according to some accounts, also other Jews) from the ghetto his church bordered on. Currently, this church has another distinctive feature: it houses a bookstore with a very large selection of anti-Semitic publications.

The bishops "want to apologise for all the evil that has been committed by Polish citizens on citizens of the Mosaic faith," explained Primate Glemp. "Poles also have been wronged, they were for instance killed by Nazis for saving Jews, or they suffered from evil committed by Jews, i.e. when Communism was being introduced in Poland. I expect the Jewish side will make a moral reckoning and will have the courage of asking forgiveness of Poles for these crimes." Rabbi Schudrich, who was to be invited to the ceremony "had himself said that very many Poles died at the hands of the Bolshevik formation, which was supported by people of the Mosaic faith" said the Primate.[19]

Never mind that Rabbi Schudrich had said no such thing. The *quid pro quo* was laid bare: we apologise for Jedwabne, so you apologise for Communism. Nor was it an expectation by Primate Glemp only: Bishop Bronislaw Dembowski, for instance, expressed it during mass in Wloclawek on Poland's Constitution Day, May 3.

Responding to the Primate's statement,[20] Rabbi Schudrich was very circumspect:

> I am deeply moved by this extremely important, from a moral and spiritual perspective, step taken by the Polish Catholic church… We Jews can learn from Poles how to look at our own acts… I had said earlier that I regret the acts committed against Poles by Communists of Jewish origin. But Poles need to understand that these Communists with Jewish roots were also traitors of their own nation and their own religion. There are no believing Communists, these could only be traitors of the religion and tradition in which they were brought up.

It seemed that the rabbi was not listening. The Polish church, by explicitly demanding a *quid pro quo*, had very seriously undercut the moral and spiritual dimension of its decision. Furthermore, the statement that Jewish Communists were in fact not Jews — different from the rabbi's statement in March, when he had said that they did not act in the name of the Jewish people — provoked the outrage of some on the Jewish left and made others squirm uncomfortably. Denying someone's Jewishness is a very powerful statement, and Rabbi Schudrich had clearly not substantiated it.

Primate Glemp in an interview[21] soon expounded on his earlier statements, with some of the contradictoriness earlier seen in his speech for radio Jozef. "Our prayer [on May 27] cannot be limited to Jedwabne only. We know we have to expand it, for Poles had contributed to the extermination of Jews also elsewhere, acting as a mob deprived of conscience....This was an act of savagery, an animal act." Such a powerful condemnation of the Jedwabne massacre and its perpetrators had not been heard from any church dignitary so far. The Primate seemed genuinely horrified by their deed. But — he hurried to add — "similarly the Jew-Bolsheviks who persecuted Poles after the war did not do it as faithful of the Mosaic religion.... Similarly the Jedwabne murder had no religious undertones." The analogy seems to be somewhat faulty, as Communists — Jewish or otherwise — never claimed to be religious, while the Christian religion did teach its faithful that Jews are accursed as God-killers, which might have played a role in determining their behaviour. But the Primate went on to deny any knowledge of Holy Week sermons in creating anti-Jewish feeling in pre-war Poland:

> Polish-Jewish antagonism did occur then, yes, but on an economic basis. Jews were smarter and knew how to exploit the Poles, or that was the way they were perceived. Another reason of ill feeling towards Jews was their sympathy to the Bolsheviks. This was one of the basic resentments, but it was not derived from a religious context. In what regards ill feeling toward Jews, confessional reasons did not, in pre-war Poland, play any particular role. Jews were disliked for their bizarre folklore.

It is therefore hardly surprising that the Primate says: "I am surprised that, apart from the Roman Catholic church, no other confessions are mentioned [in the context of Jedwabne]." And furthermore: "We wonder if Jews should not recognise that they are guilty toward the Poles, especially for the period of collaboration with the Bolsheviks, for co-operating in deportations to Siberia, for sending Poles to jail, for the degradation of many of their co-citizens etc." The interview concludes, quite fittingly, with an attack on Father Michal Czajkowski[22] "who endlessly imputes to the Church and the hierarchy an anti-Semitism supposedly consisting of ill feelings towards Jews, derived from the faith we confess. I see no ill feeling toward the Jewish faith, nor have I ever noticed such a phenomenon as anti-Judaism. That is the past. But it is worthwhile to mention anti-Polonism."

This interview, of course, closed the possibility for any meaningful dialogue. By pure chance, the break could take place on neutral ground, for a scheduling conflict occurred. On May 15, Rabbi Michael Schudrich sent the following letter to the Primate:

> Thank you so much for your invitation of May 14, 2001 to join together with you for the prayer to be held on May 27, 2001. I am very grateful for this prayer that will address the pain and suffering of the Jews of Jedwabne and surrounding area. However, our holiday of Shavuot, the holiday which celebrates the anniversary of the giving of the Torah on Mount Sinai, begins on the evening of May 27th and therefore I must be in the synagogue at that time.
>
> I hope that we will be able to meet at another time.
>
> Sincerely,
>
> Michael Schudrich
> Rabbi of Warsaw and Lodz
>
> NB I have read with great disappointment that in the basement of the All Saints' Church there is a bookstore selling anti-Semitic works. I am a defender of freedom of the press but it is inappropriate to have such books sold from the building of a House of God. I hope and pray that this information is inaccurate or soon will be inaccurate.

Asked by a journalist to comment on this letter, which had been made available to the press, and in particular on whether it had any connection with the Primate's interview, Rabbi Schudrich answered cryptically: "In every decision there are different factors, large and small." The letter, as it had by now become customary, received no response. In a comment for

Polish TV[23] Primate Glemp just said: "If he comes he'll be there, if he doesn't, the prayer will take place. This does not depend on his presence."

Another issue, however, raised in the Primate's interview, soon became a major controversy. The Polish Institute of National Remembrance, which conducted the investigation of the Jedwabne massacre, wanted to exhume the mass graves to ascertain the number of victims and the manner of their deaths. Rabbi Schudrich objected on halachic grounds. "We have the full right to do this [i.e. exhume]" said Primate Glemp, "on the basis of the Polish law on cemeteries... [But] this has been suspended at the demand of the Jewish side, though Jewish law is not binding in Poland." After a series of negotiations, Polish legal authorities agreed to conduct only a partial exhumation, i.e. without moving any remains found, in order to minimise halachic infringement. As a result, neither the number of the victims nor their manner of death could be precisely ascertained. Jan Tomasz Gross violently criticised this decision, finding himself in an unlikely alliance with Primate Glemp, while the religious Jewish community in Poland and abroad found itself in the no less unlikely situation of praising the halachic considerations of the Polish Ministry of Justice.

The goodwill momentum, driven both by the extremely encouraging tone of the general debate, and the promising developments of the Schudrich and Muszynski interviews, seemed to be lost, mainly due to Primate Glemp's ill-considered statements. This author repeatedly stated in interviews, on the issue of whether Jews should apologise to Poles for Communism, his willingness to ask Primate Glemp forgiveness for Jacob Berman, a Polish Jewish member of Stalinist Poland's Politburo, if Primate Glemp asks him forgiveness for Boleslaw Bierut, a non-Jewish Polish member of the same body, and then President. In an article in *Gazeta Wyborcza*,[24] I detailed the reasons why I would not be present at the church ceremony on May 27. Apart from the scheduling conflict, which would have been sufficient in itself, I pointed out that not only the date, but the program, had not been discussed with the Jewish community. Furthermore, the fact that anti-Semitic publications were being sold on the premises of the very same church invalidates the sense of the entire event, which risked becoming "a wasted opportunity."

I was not the only one to have such misgivings. Father Stanislaw Musial SJ, a former secretary of the Episcopate's Commission on Dialogue with Judaism and probably the most powerful voice within the Polish Catholic church demanding an honest accounting for its words and deeds in respect to Jews, expressed his concerns in a press article:[25]

> In connection with the tragedy of Jedwabne I have for months been hearing and reading protests, some by my Theologian Colleagues, against asking for forgiveness... Let us not forget, however, that the Jewish neighbours have been murdered not by Methodists or Mormons, but by Polish Catholics... These people probably went to mass on Sunday. It was celebrated by a priest who on [the previous] Thursday had not saved the Jews and their tormentors — his parishioners — from the crime.

Musial expressed his concern that if the mass did not occur in a spirit of pure contrition, without any afterthought, it would not serve the purpose of true reckoning.

As it turned out, however, the critics proved to be too pessimistic. Though the event took place in a half-empty church, with barely half of the bishops present (Bishop Stefanek of Lomza was one of those who did not make it) and a dozen or so demonstrators protesting in front of the church "the arrogance of the Jewish lobby," it was a powerful event. The image of the bishops, clad in black cassocks without insignia of rank, kneeling on the church floor to pray "for those murdered in Jedwabne and elsewhere," remains a powerful and authentic expression of contrition.

Bishop Stanislaw Gadecki, current chairman of the Episcopate's Commission for Dialogue with Judaism, who had been strangely absent from the year's debate, opened by stating:[26] "As shepherds of the Church in Poland, we want to stand in truth before God and men, especially before our Jewish brothers and sisters, turning with contrition and sorrow to the crime which in July 1941 occurred in Jedwabne and elsewhere. Jews became its victims, and its perpetrators included Poles and Catholics, persons who have been baptised." The prayer was continued by other bishops, praying "for the Jews, the people of the First Covenant: may they heed the commandment to love God and their neighbours and may they never experience violence..."; "for those who underestimate the contribution of Jews to world and to national culture, and especially all those who nourish ill feeling or ill will to the Jewish people: may they accept from God the grace of turning their hearts toward true and fruitful reconciliation"; "for the Jewish and Palestinian peoples, living in the Holy Land and the Middle East: may bloodshed, conflict and violence swiftly and durably cease there"; "for the victims of all hatred, especially directed against the Jewish people, for those murdered and deceased in pain and distress: may they achieve eternal peace and bliss with God"; "for criminals and murderers who wherever, but particularly in Jedwabne and on Polish lands, committed atrocities and evil: may God in his mercy grant them forgiveness." The prayer concluded with Primate Glemp repeating the papal prayers for the Jewish people.

It is legitimate to criticise the wording of some of the prayers, especially the unfortunate formulation: "perpetrators including Poles and Catholics," which seems to belittle the Polish perpetrators' responsibility. In a technical way, however, the formulation is correct: many of the murders in the Jedwabne area, before and after July 10, were committed directly by Germans. Within the group of all the perpetrators, Poles — and Catholics — certainly were only "included." Still, most of the wording was appropriate and frank. What is more troubling is what was not said — that the massacre would in all probability not have been possible if not for the Church teaching of contempt. Moreover, that no mention was made of the few Righteous Gentiles, such as Antonina Wyrzykowska and Stanislaw Ramotowski, who at the risk of their lives saved their Jewish neighbours from those who wanted to murder them. The fate especially of Mrs. Wyrzykowska is distressing: hounded out of the town after the war when her role in saving Jews was revealed, she eventually was forced to flee to the US. Her daughter, who still lives in Poland, fears to show her face to a TV camera. To the townspeople, saving Jews makes Wyrzykowska a traitor. A plaque to honour her, Jedwabne mayor Krzysztof Godlewski told me in sorrow "would not survive the night."

These and other Righteous Gentiles from the region were given recognition in an emotional ceremony in Warsaw's Nozyk synagogue on July 6, the Jewish anniversary of the massacre. Sadly, Catholic Church authorities did not see fit to participate in the event. Nor did they participate in the official 60th anniversary commemoration in the town itself. It seemed that, as far as the Church is concerned, the May 27 ceremony was the end of the road. In June Bishop Pieronek was asked during an internet chatline organised by *Gazeta Wyborcza*: "Are you not bored of the endless discussions of Jews and their problems in the media?" "I am" — he answered.

And yet this neither should, nor need be, the end of the road. If indeed the Catholic Church in Poland expected that the Jews will reciprocate for its contrition for Jedwabne by expressing contrition for Communism, it obviously should reread both history textbooks and its own theology. At the very minimum, it should reconsider the practice of not responding directly to concerns voiced by the Jewish community. A compromise date and agenda for the Church commemorative event could have probably been worked out, had the community and its rabbi been contacted beforehand. And if indeed the expectation of Jewish contrition was sincere, then contacts with the Jewish community would at least have made the Catholic side aware of just how inappropriate such a demand is.

On the Jewish side, the temptation might exist to decide that Primate Glemp's statements showed the true face of the Church, and that appropriate conclusions need therefore to be drawn. As a minimum, however, Jews should recognise that this is just "a" true face of the Church, not "the" true face. The face seen in the Muszynski interview, or in the Lemanski Easter Sepulchre, or in the Musial and Czajkowski comments, is certainly no less true. And which face will ultimately prevail will also to an extent depend on how we want to perceive our partner.

Notes

1   Jaroslaw Lipszyc: Sasiedzi i ich wnuki, *Midrasz*, July 2000.
2   Author's notes.
3   Stanislaw Krajewski: A Time of Penance, in: *Thou shalt not kill: Poles on Jedwabne, Wiez*, Warsaw 2001. The speech was published in the news-weekly *Wprost* on December 3, 2000.
4   *Gazeta Wyborcza*, October 18, 2000.
5   Jozef Zycinski: The Banalization of Barbarity, in: *Thou Shalt not Kill, op. cit.*
6   A public opinion poll conducted in early May on whether Poles should ask forgiveness for the massacre saw 32% saying yes and 48% saying no.
7   Full text in KAI, March 5, 2000.
8   "The Church should not participate in such plans because instead of introducing peace it would become an instrument of struggle" – he explained.
9   *The Jewish Week*, March 23, 2001.
10 I develop this point, and other criticism of Glemp's speech in an article in *Gazeta Wyborcza*, March 7, 2001.
11 *Tygodnik Powszechny*, March 25, 2001.
12 Reference to the poetry of Zbigniew Herbert, stressing the supreme value of moral responsibility.
13 Both quotes *Gazeta Wyborcza*, April 9, 2001.
14 *Gazeta Wyborcza*, April 11, 2001.
15 *Zycie*, April 9, 2001.
16 *Gosc Radia Zet*, April 12, 2001.
17 TVN, April 13, author's notes.
18 KAI May 14, 2001.
19 All quotes *Gazeta Wyborcza*, May 4, 2001.
20 *Idem.*
21 KAI, May 14, 2001.
22 The Christian co-chairman of the CCJ and a leading figure in

Christian-Jewish dialogue. It should be remembered that neither Fathers Orlowski and Jankowski, nor Bishop Stefanek, had incurred the Primate's criticism.

[23] TV Puls, Wydarzenia, May 19, 2001.

[24] *Gazeta Wyborcza*, May 22, 2001.

[25] *Tygodnik Powszechny*, May 27, 2001; the weekly appears 4 days before cover date.

[26] All quotes *Gazeta Wyborcza*, May 28, 2001.

A Case History – Jedwabne: a response

Clifford Longley

Konstanty Gebert has to be congratulated for bringing forward the story of the Jedwabne massacre and its aftermath so eloquently, and, it strikes me, so fairly. It would have been easy to make of it nothing but a denunciation; indeed that is what I began to want it to be. Why let the church off the moral hook on which it has impaled itself so eagerly? It struck me at first that there was only one honest Catholic response to what happened at Jedwabne, and that was profound shame. There is only one thing to say and that is to express that shame. Those who do so have to express it both as Catholics and as Poles. They should call upon Jews - and the whole world - to bear witness to that shame. Is there a need to complicate matters further than that? Might the outcome of this affair have been less tangled, less emotionally fraught and less morally ambiguous had the issue been brought down to this simple formula?

If only. The objection to this reduction is that it is a dangerous over-simplification. There is even a case for going to the opposite extreme, and complaining that what is wrong with the tortuous complexities that Konstanty describes so well is that they are not complex enough. They leave too much out of the picture. My simple formula then becomes in itself an attempt to cover up the truth, not face it. Shame is not enough. Or rather, shame only becomes appropriate once we have excavated the foundation of facts and ideas on which we are to build it, right down to the bedrock.

For instance, it at once struck me about his account that there are two parties to this conflict, both in 1941 and now, and we are giving them the same names then and now. We are calling them the Jews and the Catholics, and assuming both a continuity between Jews then and Jews now, and Catholics then and Catholics now; and at the same time a discontinuity between Jews and Catholics then and Jews and Catholics now. To put it another way: the assumption is made that there is a community of Catholics inhabited by the Catholics of 1941 and the Catholics of 2001, and a community of Jews inhabited by the Jews of 1941 and the Jews of 2001. These two communities had a relationship then, and they have a relationship now, and both relationships are ones of mutual exclusion; neither relationship is edifying. Except in the narrowest geographical sense, there does not seem to be any community of which both Jews and Catholics are members, neither in 1941 nor 2001.

The term "Pole" seems to be used almost as an everyday synonym for Catholic, in this context: it is not claimed by or applied to the Jews. Yet from the outside, until Konstanty's description pulled me up sharply, I would have thought it was a truism that the Polish national community both then and now consisted and consists of both Catholics and Jews. Are not Polish Jews Poles? Is there no real identification of the Jewish community as part of the Polish nation? I write as someone who regards himself as fully Catholic and fully English, who would not dream of suggesting, and would be deeply shocked to hear it suggested by others, that Jews cannot be just as English as I am. Indeed, I would regard someone who suggested such a thing as coming very close to committing the crime of incitement to racial hatred.

What happened in 1941 happened within the national community, and is a problem to be dealt with in that context. I wonder if I dare remark in passing at this point that if there had been this sense of one national community, holding Catholics and Jews together, might the Jedwabne events have been avoided altogether?

A geographical country is just an area on a map and the people in it. But a *nation* is an "imagined community," an idea existing in the minds of its members. They inhabit and experience their country, which fertilises their imagination with memories of sights, sounds and smells. They absorb their identity through their individual senses as well as through their collective memories. To be English or American, say, is to be a member of a particular society, a nation, a community of people with certain basic things in common (though what precisely those things are may be in dispute).

The concept of an "imagined community" is one we owe to the American sociologist of government, Benedict Anderson. In his book *Imagined Communities: Reflections on the Origin and Spread of Nationalism*,[1] he argues that a nation exists in the imagination of its members because even in the smallest nation, no citizen can know all the other members of that nation, but nevertheless feels in communion with them:

> It is imagined as a community, because, regardless of the actual inequality and exploitation that may prevail in each, the nation is always conceived as a deep, horizontal comradeship. Ultimately it is this fraternity that makes it possible, over the past two centuries, for so many millions of people, not so much to kill, as willingly to die for such limited imaginings.

Hence the citizen of such a nation shares an identity with other people he or she does not know but can imagine. He does not feel that communion with members of other nations who live beyond the finite boundaries of that nation (who are also not known but are also, to an extent, imaginable). In the Polish case, of course, these finite boundaries are imagined boundaries - they exist in the minds of those who behold them, but would be invisible to a visitor from Mars. But they stand between Jew and Catholic just as much as if they were real frontiers with barbed wire and watchtowers. What was particularly telling in Konstanty's text was his recalling, half jokingly, a remark about the difficulty of having two "chosen people" in one place.

I find all this talk of "Polish-Jewish relations" deeply disturbing. I cannot find any parallel in my own experience which I could call "English-Jewish relations." Relations between Catholics and Jews in England are conducted within a shared common national identity. (The question of what we feel about that residual aspect of English national identity which is Protestant is a matter for another day).

There is a parallel to pre-war Poland (and residually, to modern Poland) in the situation in Northern Ireland. In 1996 the Catholic bishops of England and Wales brought out a document called *The Common Good and the Catholic Church's Social Teaching,* which, I am proud to say, I had a hand in. It was a call to politicians and voters to recognise that there was an overriding common interest shared by the whole community, which transcended partisan interests and the need to make a profit. The English found this a useful concept — they already had the outline of the idea, but not such a neat name for it. So the Catholic bishops' statement was a great success. Some people even said it helped throw out a Tory Government which was overly fond of market forces, and that it offered the foundation for Blair's famous Third Way. Shortly after it appeared, I heard of a discussion among Northern Ireland church leaders who were impressed by this sudden English interest in the concept of the common good and wanted to know if there was anything they could take from it, for home consumption.

But their discussion took an interesting turn, on the question - was there one common good in Northern Ireland, or two? Was there a common good of the Protestant (i.e. Unionist, pro-British) community and a common good of the Catholic (pro-Nationalist, pro-Irish) community, alongside it? And of course they soon realised the deep contradiction in what they were talking about. There can be only one common good, otherwise it is not common. And they realised that the definition they had been brought up with of their own community, be it Catholic or Protestant, was defined not only by whom it included but, more significantly, by whom it excluded. Those who are excluded are not our neighbours (even if they live next door). They stand outside the reach of our solidarity. If they are in trouble, well, that's their problem, not ours. They don't regard our problems as their business either. Catholic and Protestant leaders in Northern Ireland have at last begun to realise how easy, indeed automatic, it is to think like that. And how dangerous and destructive. What I am describing is in fact the basis of an incipient civil war, in which conflicts of interest can reach boiling point and then seem resolvable only by bloodshed.

Does this illuminate the situation between Catholic and Jews in pre-war Poland? I believe so. It seems to me, with great respect, that the great difficulty modern Catholics and Jews in Poland have in talking about it is because they do not recognise it in these terms. They do not see what happened at Jedwabne as Pole against Pole (that is to say, Catholic Pole against Jewish Pole). As Benedict Anderson's theory makes clear, we have great difficulty seeing the common humanity of those who are excluded from our community, living beyond its boundaries. This lack of sympathy - for which, in many circumstances, read hatred - for those excluded from us can sometimes be masked by great displays of sincere charity and compassion towards those who are included within our community. Their humanity is immediately obvious to us, and we respond as you would expect and want. We are compassionate, therefore good people, so we cannot be racist, as good people are not racist.

I shall not preach the parable of the Good Samaritan at Jews. It has been done already, by one of their own. But the point is relevant. We may not limit the concept of neighbour to "people like us." The Samaritan didn't, and he is held up to us as our example. I don't believe Isaiah would have any quarrel with that, either.

A great deal of the tortuousness and awkwardness concerning the memory of Jedwabne in modern Poland might have been avoided had it been discussed in these sociological and anthropological terms, instead of putting the emphasis on such moral concepts as guilt, responsibility and repentance. To my English mind, the moral issue is an issue of justice and is a straightforward one. Were the perpetrators of the outrage caught and punished? Are any of those who were not punished, still alive? If so, let us bring them to justice now, in a proper war crimes trial. But let us also be clear that those who did not participate in the crime are not guilty of it, not then and not now. You should not be punished for, and you cannot repent of, a crime you did not commit. Let us have no truck with the concept of collective guilt, because that too is racist. If no collective guilt, then no collective repentance. I was surprised that this obvious point seemed to have escaped both sides of the argument. I cannot apologise for what I did not do. I can feel profoundly sorry it happened; I can feel dishonoured by it; I can feel obliged to do everything in my power to stop it happening again. Shame yes, guilt no. Was I wrong in thinking that some contemporary Jewish participants in the debate over Jedwabne, as related by Konstanty, wanted modern Polish Catholics to feel guilty and they didn't? That needs a bit of taking apart, may I suggest?

To my central thesis it may be objected that, at least in pre-war Poland, it was the clear wish of both sides to maintain two separate national communities, and neither of them saw anything wrong with it. Both the Catholic-Polish self-understanding and the Jewish-Polish self-understanding required communal identification to be defined in such terms. Their community leaders encouraged it. Anything else would have felt threatening. I suspect it is here that anti-Semitism made its influence felt. It was not primarily a matter of personal malice towards Jews, though that surely came into it. Anti-Semitism told the Jews that the treasures of their faith were not valued by the wider Polish community, and the less they had to do with the wider Polish community, therefore, the safer those treasures would be from dilution or contamination. Sadly, that kind of separation is exactly the sort of circumstance which breeds mutual suspicion, ignorance and fear.

Do not let us forget that Jews would have had in their minds just such a caricature of Christians as Christians unfortunately had of Jews. Those things from their daily experience which enforced the stereotype of

Christians would have been seized upon; those things which contradicted the stereotype would have been neglected. And so in reverse. And the less they knew of each other, the more their image of the other was shaped by prejudice and stereotyping, and the less it was capable of being contradicted by reality.

I am by no means suggesting there was something that could easily have been done to correct this. Nor, heaven forbid, that it was the Jews' fault. Jews had a right to protect themselves in a hostile environment, and centuries of habit are not cancelled out in a generation. Nor am I suggesting that anti-Semitism was not a root cause. But there are too many parallels with Northern Ireland for me to think we are dealing with some moral malaise unique to Poles or unique to Catholics. In the Northern Ireland parallel the Poles were the Protestants (the "civilised" majority), and the Jews were the Catholics (the looked-down-upon minority). And it came very very near to a holocaust, believe me. Left to their own devices, there could well have been another Jedwabne.

Note

[1]   Benedict Anderson *Imagined Communities: Reflections on the Origin and Spread of Nationalism* (Verso, 1991).

Conversation Five

Worshipping in a Post-Modern Age

Adequate Words to Praise You: the experience of Christian worship at the turn of the millennium

Liam Tracey

"Hereabouts, signs are obliterated,
but habit holds."

John Montague, *Border Sick Call*

Introduction

This paper was born of the request of the organisers of the conference to reflect on some of the challenges facing liturgy in our age, more specifically the so called postmodern challenge. In reflecting on this task, I quickly came to the conclusion that this request itself was born of a number of untested presuppositions. The presumption that we know what liturgy is and that as liturgical scholars we are competent in analysing how liturgy works or functions in communities of faith. This led me to examine some of the foundations of liturgical studies as we practice it in the academy. To pose some questions to practitioners of the academic study of liturgy and to conclude what we are indeed capable of saying about liturgy and the postmodern age. In reflecting on these questions one must face what I as a liturgist see myself as doing when I engage in liturgical study and the methods that I have been trained to use is the task of this reflection. This investigation become even more complex when we begin to explore not just Christian worship, but also other faith experiences of worship.

Common liturgy?

Liturgy as a word is a common one in Christian circles and one that is used often in academic circles. But what does the word mean for those taking part in worship and those examining their practices. For those Churches who describe themselves as liturgical communities, it means a very definite shape to their public prayer, a structured unfolding of the calendar which they call the Liturgical Year and a sacramental system, with varying number of sacraments depending on the Church tradition and even which era in history you happen to be looking at, but normally with particular emphasis given to the celebration of the Eucharist. But there are other Christian communities who prize the element of freedom and spontaneity in their public prayer, who would reject what liturgists might call the common shape of liturgy. These groups may not even accept the word liturgy or would be uncomfortable with what it might suggest, regarding their public prayer.

The problem is even greater when one asks what does liturgy express? If liturgy is an expression of faith, do Christians share a common faith? Is it already a conclusion to presume that Christians performing the same actions and gestures mean the same thing by these actions? The words that we use in describing the public prayer of faith communities need to be examined a little further in order to begin to answer these questions. Liturgy for some Christian communities has a strong connotation of tradition, which some welcome and others reject. Orthodox communities prize their liturgy because it is unchanging, it links them to the tradition of the Church, something given and passed on from generation to generation. Other Christian communities, especially those influenced by the Reformation, reject the word because of its suggestions of external worship, which seems to allow little space for the inner attitude of the believer, the one worshipping. For them what is important is the personal stance of the one who comes before God in this action. These Christian communities prefer the word worship, or coming for worship, which for them allows the personal dimension of worship to be emphasised, which they see lacking in the word liturgy. Allied to this understanding of the task of the liturgy is who is the subject of liturgy, the group gathered to pray or the individual members of the group?

In short, in speaking about liturgy, is it clear that the same action and the same word mean the same thing? What kind of common heritage or worldview or even belief is being subscribed to, and are those taking part aware of it. Is there something absolutely fundamental that those taking part must subscribe to and cannot be renounced, for the celebration to be Christian liturgy? There are immediate attendant issues to these questions: how is liturgical reflection formed and who articulates what liturgy means? These questions which some might see as unnecessary and others as unimportant, strike me as important if an honest response to the question of a common liturgical quest is to be found.

As already noted, the Catholic tradition and many other "higher" liturgical traditions along with it, prefers the word liturgy. The use of the definite article "the" is often very prominent in descriptions of what goes on in their liturgical celebrations. The task of the Church is to perform "the" liturgy which is seen as timeless and unchanging, the objective power of performing the rituals correctly and following the prescribed form is held in high regard. Almost ignored or at least not considered, in these traditions is what is going on in the inner world of the one who has come to celebrate the liturgy. Or, as has happened in the history of Roman Catholic liturgy, the very fact of people's participation was ignored or made little difference to the working of the liturgy.[1]

In this paper I will use the two words interchangeably, with the intention of expressing the external nature of public prayer and the inner life of the worshipper that is often attributed to its workings.

What Do Liturgists Do?

Is my task as a liturgist to observe liturgy, trace its history and development, report on how it has been understood in the past and how it is understood today, am I to critique current forms and propose new ones or retrieve long forgotten ones or is it as the title of the paper requested for this conference suggests an attempt to understand what people understand themselves to be doing when they gather for liturgy, or what liturgical experts and church leaders tell them they should be experiencing when they gather for liturgy and what happens when experts and leaders disagree about the meaning of liturgy, what should the people believe then?

The object of liturgical study would seem to be as the great liturgical classic calls it *"The Church at Prayer."* But here, again, a warning bell needs to be sounded, liturgists and others quickly begin to speak of the liturgy of the Church. As noted above, greater space needs to be given to the fact that there are liturgies and Churches, and they differ on what we do in the public prayer of a gathered community. There is already a presumption in the writings of many liturgists across the broad spread of Christian communities that there is a foundational liturgy that underlies all kinds of liturgical expression and our task as scholars or as pastoral agents is undercover this basic structure. This basic structure is seen to be found in the practices of the early Christian community and this practice is then seen as rooted in Judaism. This bias is common in many diverse liturgists whether they be practitioners of historical, theological or social science methodologies. It is a bias that I would suggest that needs conversation and one that I would go on to claim that is flawed or at best unuanced. If we accept much of the recent work in the studies of Second Temple Judaism and the origins of Christianity and their findings of the plurality of both practices and beliefs can we continue to blithely speak of the continuity of liturgy.[2] This notion of liturgy is one that has driven much of the liturgical reform that has taken place in our communities over the last years, reform is equated with a return to the pristine clarity of earlier ages, usually located in a mythical synthesis of the fourth century or a belief that this was the practice of the early Church. What we now need to ask ourselves is which early Church and what privileges the fourth century above the fifth. This is without even considering what happened to the liturgical life of Christian communities in the Middle Ages, a period usually frowned upon or totally dismissed by liturgists. What is striking is that the core of liturgical practices is presumed to be the same, even when radical changes happen to the outer form. Paul Bradshaw notes:

> Recent research has demonstrated that the first three centuries of Christian history do not reveal the existence of a common liturgical pattern shared by all parts of the Church and derived from the apostles, which only subsequently became more varied from place to place as additions and deviations crept in. On the contrary, the further back we go, the more diverse Christian worship practice appears to become, and the latter trend is towards uniformity rather than away from it.[3]

If we are genuinely interested in constructing a liturgical theology that is ecumenical based how do we as liturgists welcome or explain or integrate the liturgies that sprang from the Reformation.[4] Do we ignore these worship experiences, and construct theologies that sees all authentic liturgy based in the fourth century and anything that is different as fundamentally flawed and deserving of being discarded.[5] If we accept these forms of worship as part of the common Christian experience of liturgy, does it not minimise that common core which is seen as the ideal liturgy, and one that all Christian communities should strive to achieve. An example might clarify this question, is the Sunday celebration of the Eucharist a normative part of the experience of Christian liturgy? Many people, especially some liturgical scholars would answer yes, it is normative. Where does that then leave Christian communities who celebrate the Eucharist on a less frequent basis, because of their tradition or as is increasingly happening in the Catholic tradition because of the norms surrounding the ordination of the presbyters.[6]

How can the discipline of liturgical studies aid the better celebration of the liturgy? Has the liturgical reform that has taken place in so many Christian communities over the last fifty years ignored the culture of those who come to celebrate and the situation humanity finds itself in a world that is quickly moving from a modern to postmodern consciousness. In other words, is the question that liturgists struggle with "How can we celebrate in a more adequate or better way" now replaced with the question "Why do we celebrate at all?"

Is the model of a relationship between liturgy and culture a false one and a truer one to be found in seeing culture as the context for all theology and liturgy? Can the discipline of liturgical studies and liturgy itself take the world in which it lives seriously, how might the discipline of the human sciences be integrated in our methods of study and reflection?

How Have Christians Celebrated?

Liturgical reform based purely on historical research has tended to excessively emphasise one particular epoch of Christian tradition (fourth to the sixth centuries) and used some of the ritual models found there as the basis of reforming rites. What is often ignored in this approach is how ritual itself evolves over time. The reading of history operated by this approach can be questioned and it can end up as reducing liturgical studies as purely documentary and anthological, or proving already established theses.[7]

Historical methodologies and there are many operative in the field of liturgical studies, have had precedence until relatively recently. Spanning from concern with rubrics (the conduct or unfolding of the liturgy) to cultural history to exploring the mutual impact of doctrine on liturgy and vice versa, history has been seen as the field of entry and the way to engage in liturgical studies. While liturgists rightly reject a rubrical concern as the object of their field of inquiry, the passage beyond rubrical concerns has not always been easy. The founders of the modern liturgical movement saw rubrics (a concern with exterior manifestations of worship) as a part of liturgy and not necessarily the part that interested them most. They sought to move onto the meaning of this cult, what did the Church understand itself to be doing when it engaged in liturgy became their concern from a number of point of investigation. This impetus in liturgical studies has led to the preparation of fine critical editions of sources, particularly liturgical books, its limits as often noted is that it leads to the admiration of the past with little attention to the present, because it is rooted in the rules of philology. The relationship of what was liturgy in the past and how liturgy is today is often ignored in this approach. It can explain the past but how it is rooted in a context of the past is often ignored.[8] What questions, factors and circumstances gave rise to these answers and these particular ritual expressions is often ignored in studies of this type. As the discipline of history changed, so too did many fixed norms in this kind of approach to the study of the past, can a fixed text be established apart from a cultural context, what and how are variants readings to be integrated into our understanding. Or fundamentally, is the past a textual reality? Other liturgical historians have sought to expand their field of inquiry. As the broader Church community sought to reform the liturgy, they responded by paying attention to the historical circumstances in which worshippers lived, and sought models and examples for today. However, this was seen as an application of what had been learnt in historical research. Liturgy for the woman and man of today is found by modifying what existed in the past. Some other liturgical historians explored beyond liturgical texts of the past and turned their attention to the context of culture and how it influenced worship over the course of the centuries. How did culture, be it Jewish, Greek, Roman, Germanic influence the lives and the spirituality and the liturgy of those who have gone before us? This approach allowed liturgists to see liturgy as a cultural reality, which grows, changes, degenerates and reforms. What has been less explored is the other half of this relationship, how has liturgy influenced the cultures in which it has found itself. As it assumed and continues to assume cultural elements, the liturgy can change their meaning and purpose. Ultimately a set of question regarding the normativity of the past arise, can what has been passed down be changed in order to respond to the demands and needs of today, if it can who has that authority and how much change can be operated? Is the response of Christian communities of the past a guiding principle in this work for today? All these methods ultimately show the need for a further reflection on the development of liturgy. Many liturgists looked to the field of theology as an appropriate place for an answer(s) on the meaning of liturgy. Rather than just study the past and even how the Church has responded to events in the past, liturgical history shows that liturgy is historical, is dynamic. This consciousness of the historicity of liturgy is a challenge to worshipping communities today, to allow their liturgy to move, to change, to be historical. As this sense grew among liturgists, the turn to theology and the desire for a liturgical theology to underpin liturgical studies became greater. As liturgists responded to the question "How has the Christian community celebrated over the course of the centuries?" they founded themselves facing "What does it mean?"

What Does Liturgy Mean?

As some liturgists moved beyond the discipline(s) of history, as the proper nature of their studies, they became interested in the role of liturgy in the articulation of faith or how liturgical discourse is theological or foundational for theology. Some even felt that this was the proper object of the discipline.[9] In seeking to understand the theological significance of liturgy, many liturgists have engaged in what they call liturgical theology, others have sought to reform the liturgical rites themselves in line with theological developments or insights. Both approaches are problematic. Those who engage in liturgical theology as I have noted earlier in this paper often get caught into what liturgy should be and construct their liturgical theology on the basis of this ideal liturgy. In the latter case it can lead to a lack of theological harmony in the rites itself, as competing theologies struggle for ritual expression and present themselves as the theological explanation of what is happening in the liturgical action. How liturgical theology relates to the broader theological project is often for liturgists and other theologians a confusing question and one that is shied away from rather than grasped and reflected upon. To take liturgy seriously, would mean having to face one of the key theological questions in a new way, how is the experience of God communicated in liturgical celebration and what kind of knowledge is offered to those gathered to celebrate. In other words, how is liturgy a theological source? Or perhaps, even how is theology a liturgical source? Is liturgy an authentic source for theological reflection? Both approaches to liturgy that we have explored till now: the historical and the theological have contributed much to the study of liturgy, but both have not yet defined the specific nature of the liturgical activity of the Christian community. What is lacking in the study of liturgy is the epistemological status of the liturgy itself. In exploring the liturgical praxis of the Church, some liturgists have explored liturgy as an experience and an expression of faith. This experience of faith gives rise to the celebration of the Christian rite. This attention to the relationship between faith and rite leads to the consideration of the use of the human sciences in liturgical studies.

Why Celebrate Anyway?

If historical studies allowed liturgists to move beyond the concept of liturgy as rubrical, theological reflection on liturgy has placed the relationship between faith and celebration as a central concern. The consideration of the role of faith in the celebration of the liturgy and its central sacramental rituals has led liturgists to consider the sacramentality of the Christian faith itself and an ever greater attentiveness to the role of symbolic language in those rites.[10] These considerations led liturgists to explore what is the relationship between what we say about the celebrations and their effect on those who participate in the celebrations. This reflection opens up the central problem in liturgy: liturgy is action, yet theology is by its nature a speaking or thinking with God. How does this speaking match with action and what means can we use to overcome that distance? That which is believed and reflected upon in theological discourse is present in the liturgical celebrations, or as some other liturgists put it, that which is salvific (the basic Christian statement about the world and its relationship with God) is present. Communication theory of various kinds has offered to many liturgists the way forward in this dilemma. But is liturgy merely a communication game and do these theories offer anything more than the other methodologies that we have studied? The question then becomes "Why do people celebrate?" Christian faith, which is a statement about salvation, has need of expression in symbolic language and ritual gestures. What happens and how does this happen in the celebration of the liturgy and how might we access it has become for many liturgists the central question of their discipline. This has led to greater engagement with the human sciences, especially with anthropology and the emerging discipline of ritual studies. If human knowledge and existence is expressed in metaphor and language goes this argument, the field of symbol and ritual are natural areas for liturgical studies.[11] Or what are the anthropological foundations for what we celebrate? These studies make the claim that they have the capacity to reunify what has been split into many areas of study, rather than see liturgical studies as something that is derived from other disciplines, they propose liturgy as an original and autonomous field of study. The turn to ritual as a way of understanding liturgy has not been without criticism.[12] Many still see ritual as something that is boring and dull, filled with endless repetition with little meaning. It suggests to some formalism that distance those who take part from the action in which they are engaging. Accusations of being irrelevant are generally not far from those who would engage in ritual. It is seen as the enemy of free expression and limiting people's ability to respond. Liturgists would claim that this is a wrong notion of ritual, where ritualistic behaviour is being confused with ritual. Don Saliers articulates well the turn to ritual:

The central issue is not "what are the theological truths contained and stated in the texts?" but "what is being said and done in the liturgical action with the use of these words?" This latter question cannot be answered by recounting the earliest version of the liturgical texts under study, or by analyzing the language of the prayers as such. Rather, the actual performance of the language is done by a community. Thus the "hermeneutics" of the assembly's social, economic, and political/ethical energies and patterns are central.[13]

Ritual studies promise much, but it is far too early to see whether this promise will be kept. Nor should the turn to ritual lead us to abandon historical and theological endeavours in the search to understand what liturgy is and what does it do. Unanswered by liturgists who have turned to ritual studies is whether ritual is accessible to study and are they assuming that ritual is a way to approach the role of the symbolic in human life and that what they are studying is meaningful. Of course, a provisional conclusion leads us to see that we must be attentive to all three questions together, the historical, theological and cultural question cannot be neatly separated or answered simply or settled once and for all.[14] Ultimately these questions and their answers rest on the assumption that we can access the object of or study. This emerging issue has been tackled by a number of liturgists and it is to one of them that we now turn our attention.

Access to Liturgical Knowledge

A key issue in Ritual and Liturgical studies, is who decides what it all means, what authority have they to do that and how can we as students of ritual behaviour come to quantify or describe that meaning? The American Jewish liturgist, Lawrence Hoffman, notes that religious ritual cannot be reduced to one single meaning and that this meaning is not easily identifiable.[15] Hoffman points out that in any religious ritual there are several meanings present at the same time. These various meanings Hoffman named as *private, official,* and *public.* Private meaning is that meaning which an individual participant gives to the liturgical action in which they are taking part, that meaning may well be very close or identical to the meaning attributed by experts or authority to the ritual action or it might well be very different. This realm of private meaning has been neglected, ignored or condemned by ritual experts and authorities. An example from the Catholic tradition would be individuals coming to liturgy and saying their prayers. Liturgists often see this practice as anti-liturgical and something to be striven against for all the best motives. What they fail to note is that this is a private and individual act of taking part in the liturgical action by this person. Hoffman notes that official meanings of liturgical actions are those meaning ascribed to them by experts, liturgical experts who tell us what the rite means and the hierarchy of tradition and authority of a particular tradition. This meaning, which is often invested with authority, may be right or it may be wrong, but it is given considerable weight and becomes a focus of agreement, Hoffman would claim that it is often a safe interpretation. Public meaning is different from official meaning in that it is an agreed upon meaning by a number of those taking part, but it is not the meaning preached by the experts.

The interpreters of the official meaning of the liturgy would like to think that it is this official meaning, which informs the participants view of the world. Hoffman claims that this is false and that it if often the public or individual meaning ascribed to a liturgical action that is normative for the participant. Paul Bradshaw and others have further refined this scheme of Hoffman, Bradshaw notes:

> Hoffman's classification could be refined still further. His "official" meanings, for example, could be subdivided into (a) the intentions that the original compilers of a rite might have had, and (b) the meaning subsequently attached to the rite by later generations of ecclesiastical authorities.[16]

These warnings should caution us when we attempt any description of what we understand people in worship to be doing. As liturgists we also have to admit that we have not reflected on sufficiently what people actually experience Sunday after Sunday, the meaning(s) that they attribute to that practice, individually and collectively, many liturgists still tell worshipping communities what they should experience. I am not advocating a liturgical fatalism that accepts any kind of poorly performed, badly preached and poorly sung liturgy as acceptable but I am suggesting that it is time that we consider the status and place of such liturgies as we struggle to improve the quality of all liturgies. It is a plea that the experience of those who participate in liturgy is attended to and reflected upon as important data in our reflection upon liturgy. Allied to this reflection is the need for a method of reflection, to enable us to make sense of what we observe in the liturgy and organised what we gather into a useful whole. My suggestion is that we are still lacking that organising model. In a sense, I cannot answer the question set me by the organisers of this conference, "What is the experience of Christian worship in this new century and millennium?" There are many experiences, some vocalised and reflected upon, but many just engaged in week after week, whose meaning has never been gathered and whose experience has not informed what we engage in as liturgists.[17]

PART TWO

CHALLENGES

In this part of the paper, I would like to very briefly outline what I see as some of the challenges that face the Christian community and I would suspect other faith communities and as a result face the task of worship. Some of them are particular challenges in particular parts of the world, others are global, all of them have impacted upon the life of the Church and will continue to do so in the next years and some of them will become ever more critical.

The Challenge of Culture

The dominant worldview and the culture(s) dependent on it are not necessarily conducive to the task of public prayer. Ideas such as community, sacrifice, repetition, practice, habit, are no longer part of people's common vocabulary. They have been replaced with individualism or an emphasis on personal fulfilment, novelty and constant creativity are the order of the day. Participation in public prayer requires that the participants in this public action acknowledge that there are other claims on their lives than their own. The challenge that culture and our cultural context makes on the liturgy is well summarised by Michael Signer:

> Our cultural context creates barriers for those who come to worship. Contemporary culture emphasizes individual achievement and competence rather than interdependence and community, whereas worship at its best submerges the individual entrepreneur in the relative anonymity of his or her worshipping group. Moreover, for many Jews and Christians, the liturgical atmosphere of synagogue and church is the direct opposite of their work environment. At work they feel competent and in control, recognized and rewarded for their individual achievements. In church and synagogue, they feel infantilized by the texts of worship where both language and theology deprive them of their sense of control.[18]

How might the task of promoting liturgy in our communities come to terms with this challenge of culture(s), is an urgent question facing worshipping communities today. This reflection is not an easy one and one that many baulk at, but are cherished symbols and familiar ways of prayer to be abandoned in the struggle to be relevant is a constant question congregations face, yet how can the ever increasing chasm between what we do in our worship and what we live for the rest of the week be brought into conversation. One immediate response is to continue the task of exploring how cultural factors have influenced liturgy in the past and even till our own day. It requires that we take the findings of historical research seriously and acknowledge that much of our liturgy is already a product of culture. As we write our theologies of liturgy do we take this insight to heart, how have human persons in other times constructed liturgy, how have they responded to the demands of the cultures in which they have lived!

The Challenge of Feminism

No institution, inclusive of the Christian church, has remained untouched in the Western world by the challenge of feminist thought and the women's movement. Janet Walton has written that:

> The study of feminism from the perspective of many disciplines, especially feminist theology and feminist social theory, has provided systematic understandings of the androcentric and misogynist bias that plagues human history. It is no surprise that in societies in which "the male" has been considered the norm and the "female," a sub-species whose primary value is to serve the norm, appraisals of human worth have been seriously distorted. Both women and men are affected. Women are demeaned and rendered invisible. Men are inappropriately inflated with the result that men perceive power as their right and domain.[19]

Many women find that their experience of worship is one that is demeaning to their sense of self, that the liturgy does not include or acknowledge their experience of the world and how they experience their relationship with God. The God that is worshipped in public prayer is a masculine God, predominately described and conceived in masculine images and named with masculine pronouns. To constantly take part in this worship is for some to demean their sense of God and so they take their leave of the worshipping community, others remain but live a tension that is not always experienced as lifegiving or helpful to their spiritual lives.

Feminist thinkers have also explored how the organisation of Christian communities, especially in terms of leadership and power, has developed over the course of the centuries. The role of culture, gender and tradition in this organisation is explored to uncover the model of person that often is at the base of this organisation, feminists would hold that often the model of women uncovered in this analysis is one that places women in a subservient role and ignore their experience, building instead on a male view of the world and cherishing a masculine way of being in the world as normative. This analysis has led feminist thinkers to reflect on how these constructs have often profoundly influenced how we see the Divine in our lives and as already noted has worked its way into the actions and language of public prayer. Attempts to remedy this situation, has led to controversy in many communities. How feminist ritualisation and liturgy attempts to influence and change worshipping communities into the future is unclear, as is their location in the canon of the broader Christian canvas of liturgical worship.[20] Feminism once again questions Christians on what liturgy is about and how they go about organising a public life of prayer that is inclusive rather than divisive, that has the ability to embrace diverse experiences rather than proposing one model as the only possible one.

The Challenge of Inculturation

If the feminist critique of liturgy is often seen as a preoccupation of Western Christians, the challenge of inculturation is seen as one of the most crucial issues facing Christian communities in the developing world. Inculturation is understood as the relationship that occurs between the proclamation of the Christian message in a given culture or set of cultures. Both the Christian message and the culture is understood to be influenced through this experience. The liturgist, Anscar Chupungco see three distinctive movements in the process of inculturation: that of interaction, integration and transculturation.

The stage of interaction is where:

> [...] Christianity and culture enter into dialogue. Inculturation is not

onesided: both parties have something to offer and something to take. It is in the course of this dialogue that Christianity critiques cultural values, patterns, and institutions. It is the stage when, in the light of the gospel, the components of culture such as values, rites, and symbols are examined for their suitability and usefulness. Though mutual respect governs this dialogue, it is clear that not everything in the possession of a given culture is suitable or useful for Christian purposes. Some cultural components might even be incompatible with Christian tenets. Apropos it is important to note that inculturation does not eliminate the countercultural character of Christianity.[21]

Following this first moment of interaction, Chupungco sees a second movement taking place, that of integration:

The second element is integration of pertinent cultural elements. These are entered into the scheme of Christian values, practices, and institutions. Often the cultural elements will need to be adjusted or modified in order to be integrated. Sometimes integration into the corpus of Christian doctrine and practices may even involve a change in the meaning of them while keeping intact their external shape.[22]

The third element of inculturation is what Chupungco calls, transculturation:

[...] the dynamic of transculturation, whereby the parties involved retain their identity in the process of interaction and integration. Inculturation enriches Christianity without prejudice to its nature as a divine-human institution. In other words, an inculturated Christianity will not be reduced to a mere component of culture.[23]

Chupungco sees the process of liturgical inculturation as:

[...] the process whereby pertinent elements of a local culture are integrated into texts, rites, symbols, and institutions employed by a local church for its worship. Integration means that the cultural components influence the liturgical pattern of composing formularies, *proclaiming them, performing ritual actions and symbolizing the liturgical message in art forms.*[24]

Chupungco's analysis, which is perhaps one of the most detailed and evenly argued continues to treat the liturgy itself as an acultural creation. When the liturgy comes to a given culture, it already comes in a cultural guise. How does a local culture even begin to decipher what is intrinsic to the gospel message and what is a cultural pattern that can be changed or even discarded is unclear and often an occasion for controversy. Far from being a concern for emerging and young Churches, it is now clear that liturgical inculturation is incumbent on all Christian communities as the world of today seems evermore remote from the world that is contained in the liturgy.[25] When cultures become ever more pluralistic as is the case in the West today, the issue become even more difficult, how do we welcome various cultural expressions into the liturgical celebration of a given community. As people from different ethnic backgrounds join a particular community, how are the various cultural expressions and heritages included in the liturgy of that place? The crucial issue for Christians today, I will suggest in the conclusion of this paper, is the relationship Christian communities have with their cultural contexts: is it assimilation, rejection or some kind of integration.[26]

The Challenge of Rubricism

If the previous challenges to liturgy that we have discussed are to be believed, liturgy is failing because it has not engaged enough in reform, it has not engaged sufficiently with the world in which believers live, the challenge of rubricism as I have called it, argues in the other direction. Liturgy, claims a number of authors, is experiencing difficulty precisely because it has changed and allowed itself to be tainted with the movement of secularising the sacred.[27]

> Richard Gaillardetz has written that we are living in an era when people want either "community without transcendence" or "transcendence without community." Those who seek "community" seem to want liturgies that are warm, intimate, hospitable, laidback, user-friendly: in short, devoid of the ceremonialism that characterized Roman Catholic worship during the centuries that followed the appearance of the "Tridentine" Missal of Pius V (1570). Those who seek "transcendence" seem to want liturgies that display decorum, dignity, reverence, mystery, awe, otherness: in short, celebrations that challenge the comforting American culture of affluence, intimacy, individualism, and membership in approved groups. The

communitarians argue that liturgies must mirror the people that celebrate them. The transcendentalists seem more comfortable with the idea that culture should be adapted to liturgy— not liturgy to culture.[28]

Allied to this trend to rubricism, is the trend marked in my own tradition of emphasising secondary externals. We have the return of prescribing the colour of the cloth that is to cover the altar table, who can open and close the tabernacle door, who can exchange the sign of peace with who and where one should stand at any given point. This approach to liturgy justifies itself in terms of the sacred and right behaviour for approaching and living with the sacred. It ignores that an altarcloth is fundamentally a cloth or that a communion paten is firstly a plate. Denying history, theology is subordinated to an apologetic role and certain brand of ritual studies is pressed into service as supporting its viewpoint.

The Challenge of Language

An ever growing challenge to the Christian project and hence to its liturgy is what is often called post[-]modernism. Post[-]modernism challenges some of the very foundations of liturgy. It throws into doubt the universality of thought, the ability of language to communicate, that there is a "self" and an "other" to engage in a dialogue. What kind of language is best suited to speak of the divine and our relationship with holy things, how might words be used to gather us together in the task of the liturgy is becoming an ever pressing problem for many worshipping communities. As people become more visual and Internet based, with its possibilities of "being interactive", can we "hear" and "read." Many communities are in a weak position to respond to these challenges, as their traditions have paid more attention to the kernel of liturgy and little attention to how the liturgy unfolds in the event itself.[29]

The Challenge of the Mystery

As Christians come to terms with the challenges of culture, the means they use to express their understanding of the relationship between the Divine and humans will continue to change and to grow. For those interested in the relationships between Christians and Jews, a particular challenge is to understand in a better way the relationships between Jewish and Christian liturgies. This understanding has to be explored on the level of history, theology and ritual studies. As the history of the interactions between Judaism and Christianity continues to be studied, a greater complexity of interactions and influences emerges. Continuity, mutual exchange and novelty are the constants that emerge. On the level of a theological understanding of what happens in the liturgical event, recent authors have drawn attention to some of the presuppositions inherent in some Christian liturgical theologies and in the liturgical books themselves. This is particular evident in some liturgical readings of scripture, which adopt paradigms of supersessionism. Often salvation history is cast as a simple pattern of promise and fulfilment.[30]

Conclusion

All of these challenges, which I have briefly sketched, are ultimately questions about the relationship that exists or should exist between liturgy and culture. It is my contention that some of them are falsely conceived because of the understanding of liturgy implicit in them. Liturgy is conceived as a divine creation, as a given, whereas I would suggest that in order to respond to the challenges that liturgy faces today, we must acknowledge that it is as much a human creation deeply embedded in the culture(s) from which it emerged and lived. With the resources of history, theology and the human sciences, communities can then face these challenges and the questions they raise with greater clarity and freed from the fear of betraying a non-existent past.

Notes

1 Not all liturgists subscribe to this distinction, see H. Wegman, *Christian Worship in East and West. A Study Guide to Liturgical History* (New York: Pueblo Publishing Company 1985) xiii: "Worship and liturgy are sometimes described as the outward form of a religion, the 'expression' of inner religious feeling. This description is partly right: faith and the experience of faith call for expression, for visibility and audibility in words and signs".

2 See the groundbreaking study of P. Bradshaw, *The Search for the Origins of Christian Worship. Sources and Methods for the Study of Early Liturgy* (London 1992).

3 P. Bradshaw, "Difficulties in Liturgical Theology", in *Pacifica 11* (1998) 185.

4 James White standard study of Reformation worship is still very useful, see J.F. White, *Protestant Worship. Traditions in Transition* (Louisville: Westminster/John Knox Press, 1993)

5 A classical example of this approach is the book by Marcel Metzger on the history of the liturgy, of his 154 pages, 16 pages deal with the Carolingian era to Vatican II! The word Reformation is never mentioned. See M. Metzger, *History of the Liturgy. The Major Stages* (Collegeville: The Liturgical Press, 1997). A much more satisfying and detailed history is that of Frank C. Senn. See F.C. Senn, *Christian Liturgy: Catholic and Evangelical* (Minneapolis: Fortress Press 1997).

6 The warning made by James White is perhaps instructive here.See J.F. White, *Protestant Worship. Traditions in Transition* (Louisville: Westminster/John Knox Press, 1989) 15: "The role of the historian of worship is to record what practices actually persist and to be descriptive about them. Our function is not to make normative judgements. For example, whatever one believes about the significance of the sacraments in Christian worship is irrelevant to actual practice, which may show them to be of relatively minor importance [...] The historian, then, must be descriptive, not

normative. In that way, others are helped to function as liturgical theologians so they may elucidate what the Christian faith is on the basis of Christian do when they worship. But the diversity of what Christians do when they worship cannot be overlooked."

[7] Warning against this approach, Marcel Metzger notes how the past can be proof read to justify current practices. See M. Metzger, *History of the Liturgy. The Major Stages* (Collegeville: The Liturgical Press, 1997) 13: "We will be careful to shed all priorities and prejudices, distancing ourselves from certain methods which were all too common in the still recent past when the history of the liturgy was at the service of theses, and therefore, was utilized in a deductive way. Numerous examples of these deviations can be found in old treatises of sacramental theology. The writers of such books started from definitions worked out by medieval theology or the Council of Trent and applied these categories to liturgical institutions of previous periods."

[8] Not all liturgists subscribe to this approach, indeed for some, exploring the liturgical heritage of the past leads to insights that could serve us well today. See C. Vogel, *Medieval Liturgy: An Introduction to the Sources* (Washington: The Pastoral Press, 1986) 4: "Liturgical uniformity did not exist in the Middle Ages, not even within a single ecclesiastical province. Different worship habits-some of them quite remarkable-coexisted within the same family of liturgies and different liturgical families were often employed within the same country or region. As a result of such long periods of liturgical anarchy, we must make a real effort at imagining the kind of ritual chaos that existed in the Latin Church before the XIII century and even down to the intervention of the printing press in the XV. Until the end of the Middle Ages, no amount of liturgical legislation could curb the prevailing situation".

[9] See K.W. Irwin, *Liturgical Theology: A Primer* = American Essays in Liturgy (Collegeville: The Liturgical Press 1990).

[10] For an excellent consideration of this movement in theology see L.M. Chauvet, *Symbol and Sacrament. A Sacramental Reinterpretation of Christian Existence* = A Pueblo Book (Collegeville: The Liturgical Press 1995).

[11] See L.M. Chauvet, *Symbol and Sacrament. A Sacramental Reinterpretation of Christian Existence* = A Pueblo Book (Collegeville: The Liturgical

Press 1995) 84-109. Mary Boys in her recent study shows the influence of this kind of thinking. See M.C. Boys, *Has God Only One Blessing? Judaism as a Source of Christian Self-Understanding* = A Stimulus Book (New York: Paulist Press 2000) 199: "Liturgy serves as a primary source of the symbols and metaphors through which we Christians make sense of our world and envision a world ruled by God's peace and justice-God's reign for which we yearn, 'thy kingdom come.' Liturgy stimulates the imagination by providing language-verbal and embodied-to express deep emotions such as grief, joy, desire, and hope".

[12] A fine introduction to the whole debate is N.D. Mitchell, *Liturgy and the Social Sciences* = American Essays in Liturgy (Collegeville: The Liturgical Press 1999).

[13] D.E. Saliers, *Worship as Theology. Foretaste of Glory Divine* (Nashville: Abingdon 1994) 141. Saliers goes on to quote Lawrence Hoffman: "The holistic study of liturgy may begin with the text but must eventually go beyond it-to the people, to their meanings, to their assumed constructs, and to their ritualized patters that make their world uniquely their own".

[14] See F.C. Senn, *Christian Liturgy: Catholic and Evangelical* (Minneapolis: Fortress Press 1997) xiv: "The appeal to cultural studies has differentiated liturgical studies from more traditional ecclesiastical disciplines, although one observes a recent willingness among biblical exegetes and church historians also to derive insights from historical-cultural studies. The consequence of this is to demonstrate the human provenance of liturgical forms and content; these are seen to be culturally conditioned and historically contingent."

[15] A classic statement of his position can be found in L.A. Hoffman, *How Ritual Means: Ritual Circumcision in Rabbinic Culture and Today*, in *Studia Liturgica* 23 (1993) 78-97.

[16] P. Bradshaw, "Difficulties in Liturgical Theology", in *Pacifica 11* (1998) 189.

[17] Lawrence Hoffman clearly outlines the direction a broad based liturgical study might take into the future. See L.A. Hoffmann, 'Reconstructing Ritual as Identity and Culture,' in P.F. Bradshaw, L.A. Hoffman, eds. *The Making of Jewish and Christian Worship* (Notre Dame: University of Notre Dame Press, 1991) 37-38: "This new paradigm, no less than the others, thus demands that we carefully

sift through sources, sorting out the prayers and practices that were around at a given time from those that were not. The next step differs, however, for the authoritatively reconstituted textual history is only the beginning. We now read the text as if we were anthropologists personally observing the ritual's enactment. We take into consideration also non literary evidence: the class structure evident in the layout of ritual space, the ritual actions that people would have experienced (standing for emphasis, bowing in subservience, and the like); the hierarchical arrangement of leaders; the experience of music; and so on-some of which we deduce from the textual descriptions, and some of which we get from allied fields like archeology. We also test out theoretical observations against the actual witness of people who really live then and who wrote about what they thought the rite in question meant."

[18] M.A. Singer, *The Poetics of Liturgy*, in P.F. Bradshaw - L.A. Hoffman (eds.), *The Changing Faces of Jewish and Christian Worship in North America* = Two Liturgical Traditions 2 (Notre Dame and London: University of Notre Dame Press 1991) 186.

[19] J. Walton, "Feminism and the Liturgy," in P.E. Fink (ed.), *The New Dictionary of Sacramental Worship* (Dublin: Gill and MacMillan 1990) 469.

[20] For an introduction to feminist liturgy and its challenge to worshipping communities, see J.R. Walton, *Feminist Liturgy. A Matter of Justice* = American Essays in Liturgy (Collegeville: The Liturgical Press 2000). The earlier studies of Marjorie Procter-Smith have become classical introductions to this whole area of liturgical reflection, see M. Procter-Smith, *In Her Own Rite. Constructing Feminist Liturgical Tradition* (Nashville: Abingdon Press 1990) and M. Procter-Smith, *Praying with Our Eyes Open. Engendering Feminist Liturgical Prayer* (Nashville: Abingdon Press 1995).

[21] A.J. Chupungco, *Liturgy and Inculturation*, in A.J. Chupungco (ed.), *Fundamental Liturgy. Handbook for Liturgical Studies II* = A Pueblo Book (Collegeville: The Liturgical Press 1998) 339.

[22] A.J. Chupungco, *Liturgy and Inculturation*, in A.J. Chupungco (ed.), *Fundamental Liturgy. Handbook for Liturgical Studies II* = A Pueblo Book (Collegeville: The Liturgical Press 1998) 339.

[23] A.J. Chupungco, *Liturgy and Inculturation*, in A.J. Chupungco (ed.), *Fundamental Liturgy. Handbook for Liturgical Studies II* = A Pueblo

Book (Collegeville: The Liturgical Press 1998) 339.

[24] A.J. Chupungco, *Liturgy and Inculturation*, in A.J. Chupungco (ed.), *Fundamental Liturgy. Handbook for Liturgical Studies II* = A Pueblo Book (Collegeville: The Liturgical Press 1998) 339.

[25] This had been noted by Susan White in a recent study. See S. J. White, *Christian Worship and Technological Change* (Nashville: Abingdon Press 1994) 33: "The idea that traditional forms of Christian worship might actually need to be 'indigenized' to the specific and cultural and religious needs of late-twentieth-century Western industrialized people is only recently beginning to be discussed".

[26] See M. Collins, *Evangelization, Catechesis, and the Beginnings of Western Eucharistic Theology*, in *Louvain Studies* 23 (1998) 142: "Finding 'fits' between people's life worlds and the reign of God requires spiritual discernment grounded in prayerful attention to the voice of the Holy Spirit speaking to the churches. Making good connections and introducing necessary distinctions still remains the basic challenge for those called to evangelize and catechize and reflect theologically in a world church".

[27] A helpful and balanced introduction to some of these writers is K.W. Irwin, *Critiquing Recent Liturgical Critics*, in *Worship* 74 (2000) 2-19. Also see the collected essays in S. Caldecott, *Beyond the Prosaic. Renewing the Liturgical Movement* (Edinburgh: T&T Clark 1998).

[28] N.D. Mitchell, *Liturgy and the Social Sciences* = American Essays in Liturgy (Collegeville: The Liturgical Press 1999) 7. The article referred to is R. Gaillardetz, *North American Culture and the Liturgical Life of the Church: The Separation of the Quests for Transcendence and Community*, in *Worship* 68 (1994) 403-416.

[29] I deal with this challenge in a more detailed way in a forthcoming collection of papers from the Kimage Mission Institute. See L.M. Tracey, *The Failure of Founding Stories?* (Forthcoming).

[30] See the fine study of M.C. Boys, *Has God Only One Blessing? Judaism as a Source of Christian Self-Understanding* = A Stimulus Book (New York: Paulist Press 2000) especially Chapter 12. Also J.Y. Crainshaw, *Wise and Discerning Hearts. An Introduction to Wisdom Liturgical Theology* = A Pueblo Book (Collegeville: The Liturgical Press 2000).

Issues in Jewish Liturgy

Marc Saperstein

Most of what I write will pertain to the non-Orthodox branches of Judaism; it is in these branches where liturgical change is possible. There are, to be sure, issues within modern Orthodoxy (as contrasted with ultra-Orthodoxy), especially focusing on women's issues such as the right of women to lead their own worship service, and thereby fulfill the obligation of public prayer, in an otherwise fully traditional mode.[1] But for the most part, the dynamism in this area is to be found outside the Orthodox communities.

Some of the battles were fought out more than a century ago. The new Reform movement in Germany turned to a vernacular liturgy, insisting—and they were on solid ground in Jewish law—that (with the exception of a very few passages) language was less important than the ability of the people to understand what they were praying. Hence the profusion of prayer books with both Hebrew and the vernacular (German, English, French, Dutch, and so forth), leaving to the individual congregation which prayers would be read in which language.[2] Once the words were translated, however, a new problem arose: people discovered that they did not believe in much of what they were praying. The prayers for the ingathering of the exiles in the land of Israel and the restoration of the line of King David (an integral part of the traditional daily liturgy) created significant problems for Jewish communities pushing for Emancipation in the countries where they lived.[3] Today a more straightforward example might be the prayers for the rebuilding of the Temple and the restoration of the sacrificial cult (integral to traditional daily, Sabbath and holiday services). Most Jews would say they have no interest in returning to the sacrifice of animals as the paradigm of Jewish worship (though some are presently preparing for this possibility in

Jerusalem). The Reform movement jettisoned the petitions for a rebuilt Temple; the Conservative movement is still somewhat ambivalent on this issue.[4]

Trends that seemed clear on the liberal side of the spectrum just a generation or two ago—minimizing Hebrew in favor of intelligibility, de-emphasizing the standardized liturgy in favor of "creative" services—seem to have spent their momentum; the tendency even in the Reform movement today is toward greater use of Hebrew and recovery of traditional liturgy. What then are the significant issues today?[5]

One set of issues pertains to the liturgical discourse. Most important is the question of gender-specific language. The Reform movement removed all male-oriented language pertaining to human beings in its new prayer book, *Gates of Prayer*, published in 1974, but retained masculine language for God. Its newest liturgical publications (from the 1990s) have dropped this as well. This includes avoiding the third-person pronouns he and his (sometimes producing some linguistic tangles and sacrifice of aesthetic quality) and of masculine metaphors such as king (including God's "kingdom"), father, lord. Here our Christian neighbors have it more difficult in one sense, for the price of gender neutrality seems far greater in a belief system where the Son is not just a metaphor but a male human being.[6] In another sense, Jewish liturgy is more impervious to this kind of change, for while it is possible in English to be gender neutral (e.g. by shifting from "king" to "sovereign" and recasting the prayers from third person to second person), it is impossible in the Hebrew language, where both pronouns and verb forms in the second and third person—as well as every noun and adjective—are gendered.[7]

A central prayer of the High Holy Day liturgy is a litany of petitions addressed to *Avinu malkenu*, "Our father, our king." In Reform congregations, the tendency today is not to substitute the gender-neutral "Our parent, our sovereign," but rather to use the Hebrew phrase even when reading the English translation: "Avinu malkenu, inscribe us for blessing in the book of life." But that does not solve the problem of gender language for God —it just shifts it into Hebrew, where it cannot be solved (except by substituting the feminine gender)—as if hoping that people will not understand or notice this, at the very time when the Reform movement is trying to commit greater resources to Hebrew study.[8]

Some of the prayers have been modified to undo the exclusion of women. The central prayer of Jewish liturgy begins by invoking "our God and God of our fathers, God of Abraham, Isaac, and Jacob." "Fathers" can easily be replaced by "ancestors." But should we go a step further and add, "God of Sarah, Rebekah, Rachel and Leah"? Most Reform and many Conservative congregations do this.[9] But the liturgical phrase is taken from the Bible (Exod. 3:6); should the changes be made in the Bible as well? Should gender-neutral language be incorporated into Biblical translations? Should explicitly female language be used in relation to God in addition to the male language? We are by no means free from this thicket of problems.[10]

Beyond the gender language, there is a broader issue of language pertaining to God: whether the traditional metaphors, most of them deriving from the Bible, are appropriate today. Contemporary associations with "king" are generally either "figurehead," or "dictator," and associations with "shepherd" are undoubtedly very different from those of Biblical times.[11] Should we abandon this language and search for new, contemporary metaphors—God as not the sovereign but the Central Processing Unit of the universe? Not our father or parent but our most "Significant Other"?

A second set of issues pertains to liturgical accommodations to new historical events. It has frequently been asserted that the Holocaust and the establishment of the State of Israel during the 1940s were among the most profound experiences for Jews since the destruction of the Temple, an event that had a major impact on Jewish liturgy. Can Jewish liturgy fail to respond to these events? Even in the Orthodox community, there is some uneasiness in reading the Book of Lamentations and reciting the traditional liturgy for the Ninth Day of Av—Jerusalem is in ruins, not one stone stands upon another, foxes and jackals roam through its streets—when the reality is so different today, yet there is deep ambivalence about changing the liturgy.[12] Should Israel Independence Day—a national holiday in Israel like July 4th in the United States— be observed also as a holiday in the religious calendar of Jews, and if so, what should its special liturgy be?[13]

What about Holocaust Memorial Day, Yom Ha-Shoah? Should a special day be devoted to it at all, or should it be assimilated into the traditional day of Jewish mourning on the Ninth of Av? Should it be commemorated through religious ritual and liturgy, primarily in the context of the synagogue, or in a more religiously neutral setting such as a community center or school auditorium, where secular Jews might feel more comfortable? Should it be observed as a Jewish event, geared exclusively to Jewish participants, or as a community-wide event, in which Jews join with Christian neighbors in fellowship and worship. What should it emphasize— the suffering and murder of Jews? The heroism of Jewish resistance and of Gentile protectors? Other instances of genocide as well? Should a standardized liturgy be developed—of traditional texts and/or modern, contemporary texts?[14] Are new ritual acts appropriate? Here we see the dynamism of liturgical creativity developing before our eyes. The problem is how to foster consensus and cohesion.[15]

This question of a primarily Jewish or a primarily inter-religious observance of Yom Ha-Shoah leads me to the last point: those areas in which liturgical issues impinge on inter-group relations. From the Christian side, one may think of the rather unfortunate publicity attending the statement made a decade or so by the Rev. Bailey Smith of the Southern Baptist Convention that "God Almighty does not hear the prayer of a Jew."[16] A little calm thought placed this in a respectable theological tradition; the syllogism is, after all, quite simple: "God responds to prayers only if they are offered in the name of Jesus (cf. John 16: 23–24 and 14:6); Jews do not pray in the name of Jesus; ergo…."[17] The original context of the statement is generally forgotten: a protest against a rabbi offering a prayer (without invoking Jesus' name) at a public event.[18] And the reverse of this situation can also be a cause for tension. Many American Jews felt offended at hearing the invocation and benediction at the January 2001 presidential inauguration conclude with Christological language.[19] The claim was that this excluded them. But is the attempt to prevent Christian clergy from praying in public as they see fit not an infringement on their religious rights? Perhaps this is a peculiarly American conundrum.

What about Jewish prayer and the non-Jew? Is there anything analogous to the "perfidious Jew" passage eliminated from the Catholic liturgy by Pope John XXIII? For many centuries Christians accused Jews of cursing them and blasphemously insulting Jesus in their daily prayers. The text of the "Birkat ha-Minim" has long since been modified to make it clear that Christians (except perhaps apostates) are not intended in that imprecation.[20] But Orthodox Sephardi Jews still pray the traditional language of the magnificent *Aleynu le-shabe'ah* prayer, praising God for not having made us like the nations of the world or given us a destiny like theirs, "For they worship vanity and emptiness, and prostrate themselves before a god who cannot save, while we worship the King of kings of kings, the Holy One, blessed be He." The offending phrases are biblical, and originally referred to idolatry, but some medieval genius figured out that the word "va-rek" (and emptiness) was numerically equivalent to the name "Yeshu," and I imagine that not a few Jews had this in mind when they said the words. As a result of Christian indignation (fostered by Martin Luther and others), the phrase was dropped from the Ashkenazic liturgy.[21]

Yet there are still passages that seem to emphasize the distance between Jews and the rest of the world. First there are the references to chosenness—*asher bahar banu mi-kol ha-amim*) ("who has chosen us from among all peoples")—that is omnipresent in the traditional liturgy.[22] After a period of ambivalence, the Reform movement has made peace with this phrase, leaving only the small Reconstructionist stream to banish it from its liturgy.[23]

On occasion there are moments in the traditional Jewish liturgy when this sense of a special relationship does threaten to become a self-congratulatory put-down of the Other. Thus a passage from the traditional liturgy for the Sabbath begins with Exodus 31:16–17, "The children of Israel shall keep the Sabbath . . . it is a sign forever between Me and the children of Israel. . . ." But then it continues beyond the Biblical language: "You did not give it to the nations of other lands, nor did you make it the heritage of the idol worshippers, nor do the uncircumcised dwell in its restfulness, but to Israel your people you have given it in love" —phrases omitted from the Reform and Reconstructionist liturgies. Are such formulations offensive anachronisms?

Do Jews have the obligation to include the larger, Gentile world within our prayers? Jewish prayer tends to be formulated within the context of a specific people, *am Yisrael*, not within the context of humanity as a whole. God may be the King, or the Sovereign, or the Ruling Spirit or CEO of the universe (depending on one's politics), but many prayers of praise and petition do not extend beyond the parameters of the Jewish people: "Blessed are You . . . who spreads the tabernacle of peace over us, over all His people Israel, and over Jerusalem;" "Grant abundant peace unto Israel, your people forever . . . and may it be good in your sight to bless your people Israel at all times and at every hour with your peace;" "May God grant strength to His people; may God bless His people with peace;" "May the one who makes peace on high make peace for us and for all Israel, and let us say, Amen."

In Reconstructionist and Reform liturgy, these phrases have been expanded to add, "and for all who fear your name," or even more universalistically, "and for all human beings." But does this really recognize the existence, let alone the authenticity, of other faith communities? And can expansive inclusiveness dilute meaning? I remember hearing Rabbi Chaim Stern, chair of the editorial committee that produced the Reform Movement's *Gates of Prayer* in 1974, describe a letter of congratulations he received from Professor Jakob Petuchowski of the Hebrew Union College–Jewish Institute of Religion which concluded, "With warmest regards and deep affection to you, Susan, and all human beings." Stern reported having "got the message": there are some times when including just the family is not inappropriate.

I have already mentioned the *Aleynu le-shabe'ah*, which comes at a climactic point near the end of the daily services. It begins with a strong emphasis on the distinctiveness of the Jewish people, which alone worships the true God. It then rounds a corner and turns into the most universalistic prayer in the Jewish liturgy, by expressing the hope that *all* the inhabitants of the world will know and acknowledge that "unto You every knee should bend and every tongue swear allegiance." But how is this different from the Christian universalism that Jews often find offensive? How does it sound to Hindus, or to Buddhists?

The same prayer also expresses longing for the day when "You will remove the abominations from the earth, and the idols will be totally cut down." Reading this a few weeks before the Cambridge conference, I thought, "Does this mean that the Taliban are bringing us nearer to the messianic age by destroying those ancient statues of the Buddha in Afghanistan?" My point is that, with all the advances and the remaining issues in Jewish-Christian dialogue, we have hardly even begun to think through the religious meaning of, let us say, Hinduism and Buddhism. And this is hardly on the radar screen of issues even for most of those who take Jewish liturgy seriously, not to speak of the broader Jewish agenda. In many ways, our liturgy still reflects the insularity of the ghetto, and it is not clear that there is any pressure— even in those movements open to liturgical change—to address this quality, or to recognize it as a problem.

Notes

1   For an overview, see Blu Greenberg, *On Women and Judaism: A View from Tradition* (Philadelphia: Jewish Publication Society, 1981), pp. 75–104 ("Women and Liturgy"); Rachel Biale, *Women and Jewish Law* (New York: Schocken Books, 1984), pp. 17–24 ("Prayer").

2   On prayer in the vernacular and the translation of prayer books, see Alexander Guttman, *The Struggle over Reform in Rabbinic Literature* (New York: World Union for Progressive Judaism, 1977), pp. 5–18; Michael A. Meyer, *Response to Modernity: A History of the Reform Movement in Judaism* (New York: Oxford University Press, 1988), pp. 24–25, 51; Stefan Reif, *Judaism and Hebrew Prayer* (Cambridge: Cambridge University Press, 1993), pp. 279–81.

3   See, for example the response by the German Biblical scholar Johann David Michaelis to the argument for the improvement of the civil status of the Jews by Christian Wilhelm von Dohm, in Paul Mendes-Flohr and Jehuda Reinharz, *The Jew in the Modern World* (New York: Oxford University Press, 1980) p. 37.

4   For an overview of liturgical changes in the nineteenth century, see Jakob J. Petuchowski, *Prayerbook Reform in Europe: The Liturgy of European Liberal and Reform Judaism* (New York: World Union for Progressive Judaism, 1968), pp. 216–20 (ingathering of the exiles), 228–30 (restoration of Davidic line of kings), 231–35 (sacrifices); Ismar Elbogen, *Jewish Liturgy: A Comprehensive History* (Philadelphia: Jewish Publication Society, 1993), pp. 297–32.

5   See the overview by Reif, *Judaism and Hebrew Prayer*, pp. 294–331.

6   Cf. Rosemary Ruether, *Sexism and God-Talk: Toward a Feminist Theology* (Boston: Beacon Press, 1983), esp. pp. 134–38.

7   Thus the formula beginning most Hebrew prayers is *Barukh atah*, "Blessed are You"—non-gender specific in English, but masculine in Hebrew. Similarly the verbs attributed to God: "who brings on the evening," "who has given us the Torah," "Grant us peace"—are all masculine gender in Hebrew. An alternative is to substitute

feminine gender adjectives, pronouns, and verbs, or to alternate, but not to recast the traditional liturgy in a manner that avoids gender language completely.

8 An "alternate" version of *Avinu Malkenu*, addressing the petitions to the feminine *Shekhinah, Mekor hayyenu* ("Divine Presence, Source of our life") and using the feminine form of the imperative verbs, was apparently first introduced in a High Holy Day Prayer Book of the Israeli Reform Movement (*Kavvanah ha-Lev*, Jerusalem, 1989), and appended to the 1996 revision of the American Reform Movement's "Gates of Repentance." See Eric Friedland, *"Were Our Mouths Filled With Song"* (Cincinnati: Hebrew Union College Press, 1997), pp, 212–13 ("an unusual and unexplained litany"). For an effort to avoid male-oriented language in a new liturgy even in Hebrew, see Marcia Falk, *The Book of Blessings: New Jewish Prayers for Daily Life, the Sabbath, and the New Moon Festival* (San Francisco: HarperSanFrancisco, 1996).

9 The new (1998) American Conservative Prayer Book *Sim Shalom* provides an option for the inclusion of the Matriarchs.

10 See the illuminating discussion of Jewish feminist God-language by Judith Plaskow, *Standing Again at Sinai: Judaism from a Feminine Perspective* (New York: HarperCollins, 1991), pp. 134–46, including the argument made by some in defense of female liturgical language in reference to God.

11 On the contemporary problems with the metaphor "king," see Gabriel H. Cohn and Harold Fisch, eds. *Prayer in Judaism: Continuity and Change* (Northvale, N.J.: Jascon Aronson, 1996), p. 211.

12 On Tishba b'Av in American non-orthodox liturgies, see Friedland, *"Were Our Mouths Filled With Song,"* pp. 326–32.

13 Note the rather incidental reference to this in Reuven Hammer, *Entering Jewish Prayer* (New York: Schocken, 1994), pp. 196–97, 241.

14 See Marcia Sachs Littell and Sharon Weissman Gutman, eds., *Liturgies on the Holocaust: An Interfaith Education Anthology*, revised edition (Valley Forge: Trinity Press International, 1996).

15 Many Ultra-orthodox Jews in Israel refuse to observe the Yom Ha-Sho'ah practice of stopping whatever one is doing and standing in silence for two minutes as sirens sound throughout the country; they consider it an "imitation of the Gentiles" (and indeed it was apparently modeled after British memorialization practice following

World War One during the British Mandate).

16   Rev. Bailey Smith, 1980 Religious Roundtable national affairs briefing in Dallas, Texas. This provoked strong reactions and condemnation by liberal Christians at the time; I found the above reference at http://www.religioustolerance.org/jud_chrr.htm.

17   Martin Luther used a different kind of syllogism regarding Jewish prayer: "God cannot let his saints pray in vain", the Jews have "prayed, cried, and suffered almost fifteen hundred years already, and yet God refuses to listen to them", ergo, there are not pious Jews, but only a "whoring and murderous people." "On the Jews and Their Lies," in *Luther's Works* 55 vols. (St. Louis, 1958– Philadelphia, 1967), 47: 167, and cf. p. 291.

18   "It is interesting at great political rallies how you have a Protestant to pray and a Catholic to pray, and then you have a Jew to pray. With all due respect to these dear people, my friends, God Almighty does not hear the prayer of a Jew." http://www.mindspring.com/ ~dennisw/articles/nations/7.htm, citing a *Newsweek* article by Kenneth Woodward. Cf. New York Times, Oct. 11, 1980; Tom F. Driver, "Hating Jews for Jesus' Sake," *Christianity and Crisis*, Nov. 24, 1980, pp. 325 ff.

19   The invocation, by the Rev. Franklin Graham (son of the Rev. Billy Graham), ended, "May this be the beginning of a new dawn for America as we humble ourselves before you and acknowledge you alone as our Lord, our Savior and our Redeemer. We pray this in the name of the Father, and of the Son, the Lord Jesus Christ, and of the Holy Spirit" (http://www.loper.org/~george/archives/ 2001/Jan/14.html). The benediction, by the Rev. Kirbyjon Caldwell, concluded, "We respectfully submit this humble prayer in the name that's above all other names, Jesus, the Christ. Let all who agree say, Amen" (http://www.loper.org/~george/archives/2001/Jan/ 13.html).

20   For a review of the literature on this malediction and its various textual versions, see Reuven Kimelman, "*Birkat ha-Minim* and the Lack of Evidence for an Anti-Christian Jewish Prayer in Later Antiquity," in E. P. Sanders, ed., *Jewish and Christian Self-Definition* (Philadelphia: Fortress Press, 1981), 2: 224–44; Stephen G. Wilson, *Related Strangers: Jews and Christians 70–170 C.E.* (Minneapolis: Fortress Press, 1995), pp. 179–83; Elbogen, *Jewish Liturgy*, pp. 45–

46. This component of the liturgy undoubtedly is what provoked the frequent Christian complaints that Jews curse Christians every day in their worship.

[21] See Abraham Millgram, *Jewish* Worship (Philadelphia: Jewish Publication Society, 1971), pp. 454–56; Elbogen, *Jewish Liturgy*, pp. 71–72. Compare Luther's discussion of this, taken from the apostate Anthony Margaritha, in "On the Jews and Their Lies," p. 257.

[22] E.g., in the blessing over the reading of Torah, the *Kiddush* (sanctification of Sabbath or festival over wine), *Amidah* for the festivals, and elsewhere.

[23] On the Reconstructionist rejection of chosenness, both theologically and liturgically, see Jeffrey S. Gurcok and Jacob H. Schacter, *A Modern Heretic and a Traditional Community: Mordecai M. Kaplan, Orthoxy, and American Judaism* (New York: Columbia University Press, 1997), pp. 137–38, 141–42.

Conversation Six

Christian-Jewish Relations in the Context of the Wider Interreligious Dialogue

Culture, Identity and Faith: Jewish-Christian relations in a multicultural context

James K. Aitken

My title may seem to some to be something of an anomaly. Why give priority to culture over religion, and why speak of multicultural rather than multifaith? Is it to imply that religions are little more than cultures, or that culture is now the driving force of modern society rather than religion and faith? Some would say that this is the case, and with the increasing secularisation of the nineteenth century, they would not be far from the truth.[1] In many societies today faith is no longer the prime or sole formative element; various other facets of society are formative too. The hold of the Church on politics and as a moral force has been lessened. An individual's method of adjudication, of rationalisation, or of explaining events and making moral decisions have departed from the teachings of the Church. There are of course exceptions in the issues involved (e.g. the role of the Church in the pro-Life campaign in the US) and the extent differs from country to country, but many would probably say that this is true of large parts of western Europe. Nevertheless, my title might rather be seen as a broadening of the topic: faith might well form or contribute to society and is at the same time formed by it. Religion remains a powerful force, and it is not possible to separate it entirely from other cultural forces around us. In view of the multiple nature of the communities that shape any modern society religion plays a part in shaping that society and serves as a tool for communities to express their identity. The question has, therefore, been justifiably asked, 'Religion: Baggage or Sextant?'[2]

A further anomaly is that there has been a growing unease with such terms as 'multiculturalism', particularly of how it has been applied in educational circles. Its critics are to be found on both the right and the left of the political spectrum. In considering Jewish-Christian relations in a multicultural context, however, the intention is to open up the dialogue and the educational aspects of the relations to wider questions that affect our understanding and our relations. At the same time this will lead to a consideration of the implications Jewish-Christian relations has for wider issues within society. These are questions that take us beyond the interreligious sphere, but they will also introduce topics that can help to explain the connection of Jewish-Christian relations to dialogue with those of other faiths. It raises issues of identity, education and civil responsibility that should be tackled in order to understand better our relations with each other (Jews and Christians), as well as to determine the bases on which we should consider our co-operation with or contribution towards wider interreligious affairs. Such wider issues, I shall suggest, have been important unstated influences in Jewish-Christian relations, but if we can begin to clarify the ways in which they operate within Jewish-Christian relations we might be able to appreciate better what our wider responsibility should be.

Multiculturalism, from which derives the 'multicultural' of my title, is a general term that covers many different reform movements that have responded to different histories and ethnic groups in western countries. Different nations have applied their own political methods to tackle the issues, but they share the same characteristics of responding to the problems of a multi-ethnic nation in which some cultures and groups are under-represented or misrepresented by a dominant group or groups. Accordingly it shall be used here as a foil for understanding the changing positions of different groups in Jewish-Christian relations, and then for seeing the role of Jews and Christians within wider society. The principles first of multicultural education shall be considered, and they shall be compared to the educational intentions of Jewish-Christian relations. The need of both schools of thought is to encourage confidence and self-esteem amongst those that feel excluded and to educate the majority to respect the other. Methods of achieving this in Jewish-Christian relations are then suggested by drawing upon the experiences of other cultures. Thus the multicultural context is employed both for the diagnosis of the problem and for finding some solutions. For the diagnosis of the problem, however, specific multicultural theories shall be applied, but for finding the solutions, given the broad criticism of multicultural methods, no particular theory shall be applied – instead the affects of wider society on

Jewish-Christian relations and their necessary response in the contemporary period will be examined.

Plurality of methods

The consideration of multicultural issues is an acknowledgement that forces influencing our involvement in Jewish-Christian relations are more than merely religious. There are a series of intellectual traditions from which we draw, and from which we continue to learn. Likewise the contemporary academic discourse in which we frame our discussion of Jewish-Christian relations is built upon many foundations. Modes of reading, of hermeneutics, affect most disciplines, but an awareness of the limitations of our knowledge, of even our ability to know anything beyond our own time-bound reading, has challenged traditional interpretations of texts and of history. The perspective, therefore, from which we speak has become much more important a question than in the past. It has fortunately not reduced scholarship to nihilism or to a championing of the self over some sort of objective truth. Rather, it has allowed the flourishing of new perspectives on history, such as social and cultural history, and allowed for different levels of appreciation, such as reception-history. At the same time disciplines continue to draw upon each other, perhaps to a greater extent than ever. When describing what we mean by any piece of literature, any thought, or any cultural influence, we are instructed by fields such as philosophy, theology, anthropology, sociology, linguistics, history (in its many forms), politics, and literary criticism. To describe therefore an inter-disciplinary field such as Jewish-Christian relations is a complex task, and one that cannot be reduced to simple truisms or monolateral explanations. M. Signer has expressed this well when he notes the diversity of traditions from which theological reflection now draws. It might bring into question the proud position of theology as the *regina artium*, but the very juxtaposition of traditions, the encounter between Jewish and Christian traditions in the dialogue, brings new theological insights.[3] Therefore, theological issues should not be the only or even prime topics under discussion, but the wider cultural and intellectual influences on our traditions.

The latest report (published in 2000) commissioned by the Runnymede Trust in Britain, 'The Parekh Report,' considers *The Future of Multi-Ethnic*

Britain.[4] It recognises the important role that religion plays in civil society, and the importance of religious identity for many people. According to the 'Report', this is enshrined in Article 13 of the Treaty of Amsterdam, which provides a legal basis for the European Union to combat discrimination on grounds not only of 'racial or ethnic origin' but also of 'religion and belief.' Religion, nevertheless, can itself foster prejudicial or racist beliefs, even though nowadays this may often appear from our perspective to be less explicit, and religious claims or propaganda can be used to bolster racist views, even if the religion itself does not espouse them. 'The Parekh Report,' therefore, is critical on two fronts. First, race equality organisations are generally secular in constitution, often viewed by religious groups as insensitive to forms of prejudice that attack religious identity. They often can fail, too, to understand the force of religion in discrimination. Second, whilst the Churches do participate in anti-racist programmes (seen, for example, in the annual Racial Justice Sunday in the UK), such activities are often separate, both intellectually and structurally, from those concerned with inter-faith issues. The Report strongly recommends that 'in all faith communities there be closer connections between anti-racism and work to improve inter-faith relations' (§ 17.4).

This is an important critique of our work, and indicates the need for consideration of social and political issues within Jewish-Christian relations. Sometimes one feels that Jewish organisations are much more ready to tackle both racial and interreligious issues than Christian. Furthermore, we might apply this critique to many structures within the Churches and other religious bodies: commissions of interfaith will usually be separate from those on liturgy, Scripture, pastoral care and so on. And yet these are the areas in which interreligious concerns have often been most vocal, criticising the lack of awareness by preachers, liturgists or biblical translators.[5] Leaving aside the problem of where to find the time and resources for such co-operative programmes, the question, nevertheless, to be raised from such a position is, What are the intellectual foundations upon which we build such work? On what basis do we aim to integrate the various approaches to a subject and how do we bridge the agendas of different commissions? If theology is truly no longer the *regina artium* and if Jewish-Christian relations is an inter-disciplinary enterprise, then it should be automatic that inter-faith issues participate in wider civil, social or ethnic questions. We need to find principles on which to organise that work so that it does not become unmanageable within our limited resources and time. We need also to develop a *modus vivendi* that draws on the particularity of Jewish-Christian relations and at the same time reflects the universality of a multicultural society. Given the centrality of education to Jewish-Christian relations, and work of such institutions as the Cambridge Centre for Jewish-Christian Relations and the Chicago Catholic Theological Union, we will begin with education.

Education

Multicultural education aims to assist ethnic minority students to achieve their best, affirming their culture, identity and worth within the school. It may, in its American form at least, involve the imparting of democratic ideals, educating students to participate fully in a pluralistic society, whether they are part of a minority group that has to learn the confidence for such participation, or part of a majority group that should learn the correct attitudes and behaviours towards those of other groups in order to achieve this pluralistic ideal.[6] As an educational movement it is no different from many others that have arisen in various countries to attain equality for excluded groups. Jewish-Christian relations can be seen as one such movement in its drive for better education about the particular faith groups and about the causes of religious prejudice. In that sense it performs the twin functions of multicultural education — it both affirms the identity of each group (especially Judaism in the eyes of Christians) and it tackles the prejudice of each group towards the other to allow room for an open society. It thereby has the potentiality, but perhaps so far only the potentiality, for achieving the recommendation of 'The Parekh Report.' But as an innovative reform movement it is open to criticism. Banks's words on multicultural education might ring true for many in Jewish-Christian Relations:

> A reform movement ..., which deals with highly controversial and politicized issues such as racism and inequality, is especially likely to be harshly criticized during its formative stages because it deals with serious problems in society, and appears to many individuals and groups to challenge established institutions, norms and values. It is also likely to evoke strong emotions, feelings and highly polarized opinions.[7]

The opposition within some religious circles, Jewish and Christian, to Jewish-Christian dialogue, and to the attempts to interpret tradition in the light of the relations, has indeed been apparent, and even if some of those criticisms should be taken into account, they do not deny the essential understanding initiated by the relations. As already intimated, critics of multiculturalism come from both ends of the political spectrum. The radical left critique is that multicultural education fails to reform the social system, that it promotes the various differences as if they are equal, and that it avoids the real reasons for oppression and victimisation. Instead of education, the critic would say, we need analyses of the institutionalised systems of racism, often blamed on the capitalist system. Usually such left critics are unable to provide alternative educational systems, since they see the school as merely a reflection of society, and argue instead for a revolution in society. On the right, the critics tend to emphasise a back-to-basics approach to teaching basic skills, and suggest that a multicultural educational system that raises self-awareness amongst pupils neglects those skills. As one proponent has put it, teachers can act more like counsellors than teachers.[8] Instead, the school should concentrate on helping pupils to develop the necessary skills for participation in a shared national culture, often distinguishing between schools as national institutions, and private sectors (e.g. religious colleges) that are responsible for cultural training.

Critics such as these tend to focus on the worst examples or the poorly implemented practices. Activities involving shared religious holidays, the making of multifaith calendars, and other demonstrations of practice are often paraded as poor examples of the system. The critics fail, however, to consider the theoretical considerations and the goals of a multicultural education. In Jewish-Christian relations superficial activities, including the making of multifaith calendars, are part of the process of understanding, and do have value (we all have probably learnt from such encounters in our time), but they do nonetheless remain superficial. It is correct to criticise an education that does not reach down to the heart of the problem. Leaving aside some of the obvious political influences on the critics of multicultural education, can we learn anything from their strong critiques and anything from the responses to those critiques for Jewish-Christian relations?

As in multicultural education, the two prime forms of education in Jewish-Christian relations, if it can be simplified, are the promoting of a positive image of the other (traditionally of Judaism) and the combating of negative attitudes and prejudices. Each of these should be considered in turn.

Affirming positive identity

This aspect in Jewish-Christian relations differs to some extent from that of multicultural education in that here the intention has normally been to affirm the identity of Jews in the eyes of Christians, rather than the norm in multicultural education when it has been for the minority culture to affirm their identity in their own eyes. Nevertheless, even in multicultural education, part of the intention is for the other to be raised in esteem in the eyes of the majority. Furthermore, in Jewish-Christian relations there still remains a task to educate both sides to be confident as partners in the dialogue, and to be comfortable in their own tradition in order to participate. *Dabru Emet* demonstrates too that it is no longer merely an attempt to affirm Jews in Christian eyes, but there is also a need for Christians to be affirmed in Jewish eyes. On a controversial note, one wonders whether many Jews or Christians are that confident or comfortable to engage in dialogue, despite the broad participation from many people. On the Jewish side the fear of assimilation and intermarriage is perhaps an understandable indicator of lack of security in dialogue.[9] Also the unwillingness of some Jewish activists (sometimes motivated by wider political interests) to acknowledge the steps made by many Christians and Churches, or to take a more informed understanding of Jewish history that recognises times of harmony or shared learning, is symptomatic. One might add too the popular belief that the Christians are the ones who must do the learning. There are obvious reasons for this insecurity, especially given the unprecedented horrors of the past century and the resultant decline of communities in many parts of the world, but although the reasons may explain the insecurity they do not excuse it. On the Christian side, there is discomfort first because of the part the Churches and individuals have played in the history of persecution, rendering many Christians struck by the pain of their own tradition, almost unwilling to be an equal to the Jew in dialogue. Some appear uncomfortable even to state with ease their Christian confession. Second, and arising from such pain in the history, many Christians are uncomfortable with their religious inheritance. How can we continue to express creedal formulations that have been the seed of anti-Jewish preaching? How can we continue to read religious texts that have been used as evidence for the superiority of Christianity over Judaism? Such are the questions often raised, but the answers, sometimes involving dispensing with much of the inheritance, seem to reflect more a lack of security rather than a confident grappling with it.[10] Hence, affirmation of the identities of both the Jew and the Christian still needs to practised, and some of these issues we will return to under the theme of identity. But will such affirmation, as the critics of multicultural education argue, render the person less well equipped for participation rather than better?

It is clear that the building of confidence is a necessary aim to this day. Those involved regularly in the dialogue do indeed seem to be comfortable in their positions (perhaps sometimes too comfortable), but they are few and they need to find ways of incorporating others. The critique that such affirming will result in exclusion and making people less prepared or able to step outside their tradition in order to engage with another is only partially true. It depends on how the process is undertaken. It is possible to set up, as the multicultural critics do, aunt sallies, choosing the easiest targets for criticism. Instead, a better form of building confidence within one's tradition can be suggested. The recognition that we are part of a wider multicultural society is an important beginning, as it allows Jews and Christians to recognise their great similarities in contrast to other groups within society. It can, however, also potentially be harmful when it encourages a disparaging of other religions, as might sometimes be heard in the debate on the inclusion of Muslims in Jewish-Christian dialogue. Proponents of multicultural education suggest that the goals should be the removing of prejudice and the provision of skills for participating in a democratic society. In returning to the methods by which in Jewish-Christian relations some of the inherent prejudices within the religions and their traditions have been tackled, we might begin to re-assess how we should teach our traditions, and thereby discover ways of building confidence in the dialogue. It will also indicate how it can enable participation in wider civic concerns and co-operation with other faiths and cultures.

Combating of negative attitudes - pragmatic readings

A suitable place to begin is with an understanding of communication and the language of that communication. Modern linguistics has increasingly turned its attention to the whole communicative process, noting the complexity of that process in each situation. Furthermore, attention has been devoted to the part the hearer or receiver plays in communication, to his/her presuppositions and to the extent of his/her knowledge for determining meaning. The part that pragmalinguistics (pragmatics) has played in forming our understanding of communication is important, and in societal pragmatics it is particularly relevant. Pragmatics 'as the study of human language use in a societal context'[11] is disposed towards social problems and in particular to finding ways of remedying socially-caused linguistic problems, a concern for our linguistic environment, or as one scholar has coined it 'linguistic ecology.'[12] It can help the language user be aware of the force of his/her language, and also allow an oppressed minority to transcend the conscience of their oppression through language. In a simple way its application can be seen in non-gender specific language and politically-correct speech. Whilst one can justifiably claim that 'he' in many circumstances is generic and not gender-specific, this would be a limited semantic description, which ignores the pragmatic force of how it can be understood by some of its users. The recognition (on which, see below) of the female element in speech can help to rehabilitate the personal identity of women.

Such simple 'linguistic ecology' has been practised in the field of Jewish-Christian relations, most notably in the careful use of the term Pharisee or the removal of the designation 'the Jews' in John's Gospel by some modern translations (e.g. REB). However, to concentrate on single words is but one element of pragmatics, since it is the force of a phrase, sentence, paragraph and discourse that is important, and how they are interpreted within society. To return to the biblical text and discuss or explain words or phrases is not enough, but the force of their reading has to be considered. This is in fact enshrined in our religions, since it is tradition that warns us of the dangers of misreading texts, and not the stark words of the text itself. The attempts to explain the social context of early Judaism, to explain what Jesus would have meant in the first-century, or to account for the polemics with which early Christian writers composed, are all futile in the face of an individual's capacity to read a text anew in their twenty-first century context. Historical explanation is superficial, if helpful for some, when we take into account the world-wide reading community in diverse circumstances. We perhaps need to tackle the wider communicative function of our religious traditions within modern society.

The message, then, that we wish to communicate is, on a universalistic level, civil harmony and social cohesion, and, on a particularistic level, the combating of antisemitism and other forms of religious prejudice. This communication is, therefore, between two circles or sets of people, between Jews and Christians, and between two levels, between the two faiths and wider society. There are two circles and two levels, but the particularistic level and circle is a focus of the concerns of the wider level and circle. The particularistic level of communication between Jews and Christians should reflect the same principles as the universalistic level, and can serve as a model for that universalistic level. In practical terms, Jewish-Christian relations should be able from its experience to inform wider society and other cultures how to co-operate and to settle differences by rational negotiation. And using the same principles Jews and Christians should be able to work with other religions. But what is the communicative force of Jewish-Christian relations today for those other groups?

There are a number of positive elements that have been achieved in the dialogue, and the message that this can potentially convey is important. The message of repentance, expressed most fully in Christian churches repenting of their history, even if for some there is much more still to be achieved on this front, and the ability to re-read one's tradition and to purge it of its latent anti-Judaism, are notable examples. The ability within Judaism to face and overcome its history of being persecuted, and to be open and participatory in modern society, is another factor. There is also the message of reconciliation, expressed in the meeting of two religions that have had a joint history of conflict and hostility. However, there are some negative aspects too in our contemporary relations, which do form part of the message being conveyed. The insistence on the same historical issues, a failure to note changes in attitude within the communities, and a continuing failure to reach out to wider segments of our communities do not convey hopeful messages for other religious communities. We need to promote a language of societal living, to offer a message that transcends mere obsession with texts and historical events, and engages with wider issues of inter-communal activity.

Combating of negative attitudes - multicultural readings

The influence of cultural pluralism, of the reception of a text both linguistically and culturally, and the development of modern hermeneutics has opened up many new paths into our traditions. One example is post-colonial theory, which is manifest in the reading of history and in the reading of texts. Postcolonialism rehabilitates the position of those oppressed under colonial rule, restoring to them their culture as an object of worth. It furthermore counters the colonial mentality of portraying minorities in a negative fashion, whether or not they were actually under colonial rule. It thereby serves as a model for the rehabilitation of minorities in society irrespective of the past history of that society, whether or not it has experienced colonialism, or whether it believes it has transcended colonial history.

What is striking about the recent application of postcolonialism to biblical studies is how much it mirrors biblical issues in Jewish-Christian relations. The misrepresentation of groups such as Arabs in New Testament commentaries (admittedly written by scholars of an older generation) is comparable to the portrayal of Jews through the writers on the New Testament. And the (ab)use of the Bible by colonialists has been highlighted by postcolonialist theorists,[13] just as the application of the Bible in the past to demonize Jews has been noted by Jewish and Christian scholars. As postcolonial theorists are engaged in a similar reassessment of the text as those in Jewish-Christian relations, perhaps there should be greater co-operation between our enterprises, and our longer experience of such analysis may be of service. We can at least acknowledge that some of our concerns are not unique to the relationship between Jews and Christians, even if their consequences have probably been most dire for Jews.

The result of this lack of uniqueness is that the focus of dialogue might moderately change. Rather than tackling the specific question of why Christians have persecuted Jews, we should once more move away from specifics and consider principles. Postcolonialism, as Jewish-Christian relations, has indicated the need for understanding the force of our readings, and how they have shaped mentalities. Perhaps rather than tackling individual questions such as the portrayal of Jews, or Arabs, or whatever, we should aim for a hermeneutic that has as its goal the restitution of the oppressed, the explication of the dangers of religious tradition, and the problems of a text, and its reading tradition. It is not the text or the words within it that are the source of the problem. It is the reception within communities, joined with a religious mentality and social conditions, that have incited trouble. Some texts do of course have a greater propensity for being misused, but how far have we tackled the question of why Christianity has been the oppressor? Is it merely what is in the texts? Perhaps by trying to rewrite the texts or by dispensing as some have with traditional Christology, we have not solved the problem but merely circumvented it. These are further examples of what I have called 'superficial' remedies. If Jewish-Christian relations were to consider from its own experience the potential harm in any religion, it may provide a model for other religious groups and communities. The appreciation of the problems of reading texts can be applied beyond the confines of Jewish-Christian interests to the texts of other religious communities.

But what of positive uses of the text? We came to this topic in relation to ways of building confidence and identity within each religious group. It is therefore appropriate not only to consider how to find remedies, but to put into practice some positive steps, particularly with the aim of considering the wider reading community. Related to postcolonialism is a tradition of Asian biblical hermeneutics that aims to transmit the message of the Bible into a culture that has quite different traditions. Two brief examples will suffice. One is an example of applying the Bible to the particular social context; in this case the biblical pattern of exile and return as a way of conveying some of the issues and emotions in Hong Kong when looking towards 1997,[14] when its status as a British dependency was to be transferred to the Chinese government. The second is a comparison between biblical psalms and Chinese poetry, showing how each performs similar functions.[15] Both of these examples show the transmitting of cultural models from one society to another, but more importantly show how one cultural tradition can be transmitted without losing all of its positive elements. The rehabilitation of the Bible in post-holocaust readings has also been an important example of how a text often considered problematic can be used for the good.[16] Admittedly most of these readings are of the Hebrew Bible rather than the New Testament, but it indicates how a reading tradition can be developed and how the texts can be incorporated within our tradition once more, without the unease that is sometimes felt. Such rehabilitation of our tradition helps to build the confidence of members of the communities and to affirm a strong identity. And it is identity that is perhaps most important in the shaping of our goals.

Identity - the politics of recognition

In multiculturalism and in other forms of 'minority politics', such as feminism, there is a demand for recognition, arising from the conviction that one's identity is defined by the recognition or misrecognition of others. A society that promotes a demeaning image of a minority (be it women, ethnic groups etc.) can force that minority to accept that picture of themselves, and therefore proper recognition can be a part of the process of rehabilitation for the minority concerned. That process is seen in the modern belief in an egalitarian society in which equal dignity for all is the foundation of living. At the same time a belief in the individual's personal identity, their authenticity, has arisen. One proponent of this, J.G. Herder, has extended this notion of individualised identity to the *Volk*, to cultural groups, each of which should be allowed to express and maintain their own identity (cf. post-colonial theory). In the debate on multiculturalism already referred to, it is a dispute between these two apparently contradictory positions: the universalistic equal dignity for all, and the personalized identity in which difference between identities are sustained. The universalistic ideal is opposed to the personalized identity because the latter violates the principle of non-discrimination, encouraging differences and sometimes granting special privileges to one cultural group. The principle of the personalized identity, on the other hand, can lay a charge against that of equal dignity since such a concept of a homogeneous group does not give credit to the differences, and usually involves the minority succumbing to the standards of the majority.

The resolution between this paradox is instructive for Jewish-Christian relations. It is perhaps less of a resolution than a solution. The universalistic ideal of equal dignity for all should prevail, but should not take upon itself *a priori* that there is an equality of cultures, a complete neutrality. Some traditions are in contradiction to others, such as that seen in the Salman Rushdie affair, when the religious ideals of a religious group was in opposition to the principles of another society and its beliefs. Therefore, we need somehow to preference some over others, and not assert that all are merely equal or equivalent. It is also very hard to accept a culture that is so different from our own if it is accepted *a priori*. It may be philosophically possible, but emotionally, even intellectually, we cannot without trying to judge and evaluate it. The necessary process is what

Gadamer has called a 'fusion of horizons,'[17] where we learn to have a broader horizon, to change our basis of judgement and bring in a background of another culture. This is inevitably happening with changing social conditions, as we will argue below, but it should at all times be the aim of dialogue and understanding. We change our horizons in order to understand from a different perspective the worth of another. This takes us beyond the question of Jewish-Christian relations, by asking us to change our horizons for every encounter, and it is reflected in Asian biblical hermeneutics. However, within Jewish-Christian relations historical questions such as those of our shared origins (Jesus the Jew; the same God) remain historical since they do not attempt to appreciate the contemporary religious experience, they do not fuse the horizons.

Identity - Changing identity

'The Parekh Report' charts the changing ethnic constituencies of Britain, and the increase in ethnic groups in higher education. This helps to demonstrate the continually changing nature and the complexity of every community, affected by difference in gender, generation, religion and language. In Britain the change is very clear with immigration, especially from the former colonies, and the changing social and economic conditions of ethnic groups. At the same time there is exchange between different communities within society, and an individual's identity might partake of more than one culture, a process of adoption that is accelerated by globalisation and improved communication, both in transport and in information-exchange (e.g. the internet). Devolution has also affected identity, even if it is perhaps by opposite means to that of globalisation. Societies are built on historical collective memory, which is not to exclude a group with a different memory, but to note that new additions to society affect that collective memory. The collective memory, therefore, is changed from generation to generation and with each new wave of immigration.

Part of this change in identity can also be accounted for by increasing secularisation, but the effect of sizeable proportions of members of religious groups other than the traditional state religion (in Britain, Anglican Christianity) could have a similar consequence to secularisation in moving the focal point of decision making away from the Church. The previously stable situation, in which the Church hierarchy (as well as social hierarchy) and the legitimisation of faith defined the role and boundaries of people's activities, has passed. In the context of Jewish-Christian relations the issues concerning the two religions must seem meagre when faith plays such a little part in many people's lives in the West, and when there are so many other religions to contend with. The identity of the two communities will inevitably, if slowly, change too. Christianity being no longer the dominant discourse has perhaps contributed to the change in Christian attitude to other religions and to its own history. And Jews in many countries now cannot be said to be living under a dominant Christian environment, although the historical Christian traditions might still prevail in various forms (not least antisemitism). Both communities are shaped by an awareness of other religious traditions, and at the moment in Europe the existence of Islam is perhaps the one most in mind. The shared memory of Jews and Christians in their historical co-existence for centuries is being challenged by the new situation.

In the absence of a consensus for social principles can there emerge from the many identities an agreed method of co-operation or respect? Undoubtedly religion can be a dividing force, and, as the relative position of each religion within society changes, it can have a destabilizing effect when a religious community feels under threat. The situation of the Balkans is a demonstration of the hazardous dividing-function of religion, given the correct social circumstances. The issues that have been promoted in Jewish-Christian relations have been respect for individuals and other religious traditions, recognition of the value in other traditions, and negotiation and healing on issues of disagreement. These are values that can be found in most religions, and should be the starting point for social cohesion in multi-ethnic society. In the first place, they are values that both Jews and Christians should bear in mind themselves. There are inevitably to be changes in the relations as new specific topics come to the fore with each generation, and as the identity of each community changes. To keep these values in mind may ease the pain that some may feel if cherished opinions are questioned. Second, the values promoted in Jewish-Christian relations are examples for other groups to learn from. It is a duty for Jews and Christians to be open to groups that lack even more confidence and greater uncertainty over their identity, and possibly to serve as bridges for these communities. As 'The Parekh Report' identified, religions are in a position to help each other in a way that secular organisations cannot, and they should be able to respect an orthodox position before dismissing it as mere 'extremism'. There are indeed cases of one religious organisation providing a neutral meeting ground for two other religions to meet and discuss sensitive issues.

As in many societies today we can no longer speak of the dominance of one religion or tradition; the diversity of religions and ethnic groups allows room for new ground to be made. It is possible that Jewish-Christian relations as a modern discipline and activity expanded at a time (the first half of the twentieth century) when Christianity could still be perceived as the dominant force. The change in the balance in society and thereby the change in collective memory might provide the space for greater trust. We are all in the same diverse boat. And without a dominant Christian discourse (although this is not the case in every country), the question of the dangers of Christian teaching is minimized. Diversity of traditions is, therefore, probably more significant now than the question of bilateral relations. It is not possible to segregate one issue, however much we wish to, since questions of identity and the relationship to those around us have an influence, and our principles are shared cross-culturally. The real test for the future is how wide we spread our net.

Conclusions

I have spoken for the most part theoretically, but we often need to change the way we think in order to change the way we act. It has also been very much a western perspective, since in the limited time and in this setting that was all that was possible. Hopefully, some of the theoretical questions can be applied to other societies. The points made in this paper are related to the relationship between traditional Jewish-Christian relations and other communities, and the changing shape of identity in relation to each other.

Even if contemporary Jewish-Christian relations seems to be built on practical experience and to be the outcome of specific issues in life, as it was during the Second World War for instance, that is no reason not to consider the theoretical implications and to describe some of the theoretical possibilities. Such theory itself will, of course, draw upon the situations in our countries and communities, and thereby should not fall prey to mere idealism. Rather than working from a specific basis of debating whether, for example, our dialogue should include Muslims, a matter that has elicited much heated debate in recent years (not least here in Britain), we should analyse the principles on which our relations are founded, and from there we may reach a clearer vantage point to decide our present concerns and future goals. My first probings into the multicultural context of Jewish-Christian relations has been offered here; it is hoped that others will provide more detailed and more searching analyses in the future.

Since Jewish-Christian relations as a discourse participates in many fields and is influenced by them, both on the intellectual and the social levels, we should locate ourselves within the wider intellectual and social traditions. Hence, the work of Jewish-Christian relations should be co-ordinated with other activities that touch on similar issues. Its educational focus should first ensure that the participants are confident; a lack of confidence perhaps still pertaining today in Jewish-Christian relations. This self-confidence can be built up by a return to the positive elements of the tradition, and reading them as expressions of contemporary concern.

Reception and communication are key factors in Jewish-Christian relations. Concentration on details of the text can ignore wider issues of reception that can be shared by all religions. The problems of the force of a religion for hostility and division should comprise key focal points for discussion of reception history, and the message conveyed by Jewish-Christian relations in its present form can be both positive and negative.

A threat to Jewish-Christian relations is in fact the continually changing identity of each group within society, and the consequent changes of dominant discourse. This change should be taken as an opportunity to clarify the principles on which we work, and to open up to other religious traditions. The change in the relationship between the communities of the West mean that this opening up to others is inevitable, since the threat of destabilisation has changed. The danger coming to one community from another is no longer as it was. The identity and relationship of each has changed, and the influence of other communities and other religions must be taken into account.

Notes

1   On this secularisation see Owen Chadwick, *The Secularization of the European Mind in the Nineteenth Century* (Cambridge: Cambridge University Press, 1975).

2   Gerd Baumann, *The Multicultural Riddle: Rethinking National, Ethnic, and Religious Identities* (New York; London: Routledge, 1999).

3   M. Signer, 'One covenant or two: can we sing a new song?', in J.T. Pawlikowski and H.G. Perelmuter (eds), *Reinterpreting Revelation and Tradition: Jews and Christians in Conversation* (Franklin, Wis.: Sheed & Ward, 2000), 3–4.

4   *The Future of Multi-Ethnic Britain: Report of the Commission on the Future of Multi-Ethnic Britain*, [chaired by] Bhikhu Parekh (London: Profile, 2000).

5   See, for example, the recent contribution by Robert Bullock on the liturgy, in Carol Rittner & John K. Roth (eds), *"Good News" after Auschwitz? Christian Faith within a Post-Holocaust World* (Macon, Georgia: Mercer University Press, 2001).

6   A helpful survey of multicultural theory and some its critics is provided by James A. Banks, 'Multicultural education and its critics: Britain and the United States', in Sohan Modgil *et al.* (eds), *Multicultural Education: The Interminable Debate* (London: Falmer, 1986), pp. 221–31.

7   Ibid., 222.

8   E.g., Maureen Stone, *The Education of the Black Child in Britain: The Myth of the Multiracial Education* (Glasgow: Fontana, 1981).

9   It is a fear that *Dabru Emet* tried to assuage in its seventh statement, 'A new relationship between Jews and Christians will not weaken Jewish practice'.

10 Within fundamentalist Christianity one may also detect a certain insecurity, revealed through the lack of willingness to admit of change or error.

11 Mey, Jacob L., *Pragmatics: An Introduction* (Oxford/Cambridge, MA: Blackwell Publishers, 1993), 42.

12 Haugen, E., 'The Ecology of Language', in A.S. Dil (ed.), *The Ecology*

of Language. Essays by Einar Haugen (Stanford: Stanford University Press, 1972).

13 See, for example, Sugirtharajah, R.S. (ed.), *The Postcolonial Bible* (Sheffield: Sheffield Academic Press, 1998); id., *Asian Biblical Hermeneutics and Postcolonialism: Contesting the Interpretations* (Sheffield: Sheffield Academic Press, 1999). One should also be aware of the dangers of postcolonial theory when it has been applied to the detriment of the west. On this problem, see chapter 1 of Sugirtharajah, *Asian Biblical Hermeneutics*.

14 Archie C.C. Lee, 'Exile and return in the perspective of 1997', in Segovia, F.F. & Tolbert, M.A. (eds), *Reading from this Place. Volume 2: Social Location and Biblical Interpretation in Global Perspective* (Minneapolis, Minn.: Fortress Press, 1995), 97–108.

15 Archie C.C. Lee, 'Biblical Interpretation in Asian Perspective', *Asia Journal of Theology* 7 (1993), 35–39; cf. id., 'The Chinese Creation Myth of Nu Kua and the Biblical Narrative in Genesis 1–11', *Biblical Interpretation* 2 (1994), 312–324.

16 See the essays in Tod Linafelt, *Strange Fire: Reading the Bible after the Holocaust* (Sheffield: Sheffield Academic Press, 2000). Cf. Linafelt's own study, *Surviving Lamentations: The Afterlife of a Biblical Book* (Chicago: University of Chicago Press, 1999).

17 Gadamer, Hans-Georg, *Truth and Method*, 2nd edn., translation revised by Joel Weinsheimer & Donald G. Marshall (London: Sheed & Ward, 1989).

Jewish-Christian Relations in a Multicutural Setting: expanding the boundaries of dialogue

Judith Hershcopf Banki

James Aitken and I share central areas of agreement about the value of the Jewish-Christian dialogue and the need to expand its genuine, if still limited and uneven, achievements — increased understanding, prejudice-reduction, cooperation toward shared goals in the arena of social and civic life — into other areas of intergroup and interreligious activity, into the wider society as a whole. However, I suspect we come to this agreement starting from opposite ends of the spectrum, as it were, and reflecting vastly different experiences.

Aitken sets his thoughtful and perceptive remarks within the broad framework of a multicultural society, a somewhat secularized one at that, in which faith "is no longer the prime or sole formative element," although religion remains a powerful force. Philosophical questions regarding the limits of knowledge, plus the flourishing of new perspectives on history, the influence of anthropology, sociology, linguistics, politics and literary criticism impact on traditional understandings of both self and other, and add a host of complexities to the interfaith encounter.

To borrow from the film maker's vocabulary, Aitken pans across the panoramic landscape of a multi-ethnic, multicultural society and looks to the educational goals, exploring issues of promoting positive images of the other and combating prejudices, relating these goals to the area of Jewish-Christian relations.

Because of my personal experience, I approach the broader issues of a multicultural society from the opposite direction, focusing specifically on the dynamics and substantive issues of the Jewish-Christian encounter in the second half of the twentieth century, acknowledging its achievements and shortcomings, and then suggesting what we can learn from that encounter that may ease tensions and conflicts between other groups.

I am a child of that generation that awoke to the devastation and rubble of a post-World War II world, and discovered that six million of my co-religionists — one half the Jews of Europe and one third of the Jewish population in the world — had been murdered in the heart of Christian Europe, not only brutally, but deliberately and systematically, in an effort to wipe every Jew from the face of the earth. To this end the resources of advanced technology, the skills of engineers, chemists, doctors, lawyers and bureaucrats on every level were pressed into service. Entire cities were designed and created for the sole purpose of dehumanizing, starving, torturing and ultimately murdering human beings: gas chambers, crematoria, medical experimentation offices. Now, the passing of more than fifty years have somewhat dimmed the original shock and disbelief, but for those who encountered its reality, it is burned into our memories. Not only Jews who survived, but decent, conscientious Christians, asked themselves how this could have happened in a culture shaped and formed by Christian ideas. Moved by the writings of such visionaries as the French historian, Jules Isaac and the Anglican clergymen, James Parkes, among others, they came to believe that the roots of the poisonous antisemitism that had culminated in this frenzy of hatred could be found in certain traditions of Christian teaching and preaching about Jews and Judaism — i.e., the "teachings of contempt" — that depicted Jews as less than human, as the perpetual and mythological enemy, not just of Christianity, but of humanity itself. These conclusions were bolstered by the findings of self-studies of religion textbooks in the United States, Europe and Latin America, which revealed considerable hostility to Jews and Judaism even after the revelations of the Holocaust. No one, of course, claimed that the negative tradition of Christianity toward Judaism was sufficient to explain the Shoah. Racist ideologies and technology were enlisted in the cause. (Lucy Davidovich, author of the first book on the Holocaust, *The War Against the Jews*, defined Nazi antisemitism as "the bastard child of the union of Christian antisemitism and German nationalism") but the Christian roots of this ancient hatred could not be denied, and the need for Christians to confront and overcome this legacy became one of the starting points of the contemporary Jewish-Christian dialogue. However bogged down we may get in discussions over the fine points of recent Christian or Jewish documents or statements, or agonized by the pursuit of consensus on touchy issues, we should not forget the abyss which spurred our contemporary efforts at reconciliation. The initial successes of this movement have been considerable. Authoritative documents addressing the Christian roots of hostility to Jews and Judaism have been issued by major church groups, Roman Catholic and Protestant. Excellent papers (by Edward Kessler and John Pawlikowski) have examined and evaluated these documents. I would not tread over ground so well ploughed by others. But a few observations will help set my own remarks in context. I hope to address three questions: 1) The failure to fully implement or explore the implications of major church documents, cited elsewhere; 2) why it is that most organizations or programs devoted to Jewish-Christian relations have been reluctant to change their essential focus, or even to adapt their titles to make it easier to accommodate a broader interreligious outreach; (the International Council of Christians and Jews, for example, has established an Abrahamic Forum to sponsor tri-faith [i.e. Christian-Jewish-Muslim] programs but decided, after intensive discussion, to retain its title, which essentially defines its focus.) 3) What lessons can be learned from the very specificity of the Jewish-Christian encounter that may be useful in facing and alleviating the tensions and conflicts of other intergroup relationships.

The documents and their implementation

Kessler and Pawlikowski have summarized the major institutional documents, their accomplishments and their shortcomings. They have also provided some poignant examples of failures to fully implement even the best of these statements or to explore their implications. I would offer some others from my own experience. While a more positive attitude toward Jews and Judaism has been demonstrated in textbooks and teacher training materials, problems remain, particularly in liturgical practices, which are resistant to change, and scriptural texts, which cannot be treated trivially, altered or censored, particularly among communities which consider them divinely inspired. Christian friends and colleagues have reported, sometimes almost despairingly, that the sermons they hear in church during and after Holy Week still blame "the Jews" for the Crucifixion and death of Jesus, and that pastors or homilists have not absorbed the essence of even the most basic of the founding documents, *Nostra Aetate*. Reinforced by scriptural readings whose origins may be polemical, the preachers slip into comfortable categories of thinking and preaching. Despite all the scholarship, despite all the corrections, despite all the statements, in many a neighborhood church the Pharisees remain hypocrites and the Jews remain the villains of the drama. Aitken recognizes the persistence of the dilemma in his own paper: "The attempts to explain the social context of early Judaism, to explain what Jesus would have meant in the first-century, or to account for the polemics with which early Christian writers composed, are all futile in the face of an individual's capacity to read a text anew in their [*sic*] twenty-first century context." His conclusion — "we perhaps need to tackle the wider communicative function of our religious traditions within modern society" — is enticing, but he provides no leads as to how to proceed with the tackling.

Indeed, the power of a text — or more accurately, the story behind the text — is still awesome. In his classic study of Protestant religion textbooks, *Faith and Prejudice*,[1] Bernhard Olson repeats the story of 27 Bilaans hearing for the first time from Bishop Dia about the death of Jesus. They did not know anything about first century Judaism, they did not know the word or the meaning of "Jews," they did not know who the Romans were. But on hearing the story, they began muttering against the "crucifiers."

I wish I had a cheerful, optimistic solution for this dilemma. Christianity, at its best, teaches that the Christian himself is the crucifier, that his savior died for *his* sins and *because of his* failings. But the internalizing of responsibility is a complex theological process. How to communicate it to African tribesmen? Indeed, how communicate it to the Polish peasant who, when asked by Claude Lantzmann in the film *Shoah*, why this happened to the Jews, replied, "Because they killed Christ."

I do not wish to flog a dead horse. The Christ-killer charge is effectively gone from most Christian textbooks and classrooms, certainly in the United States, to the best of our knowledge. But not all. And it remains a potent image in popular culture, and in the context of Middle East tensions has been quite deliberately manipulated by antisemites as a political weapon against Jews and even against Israel.

There are other vestiges of the supercessionist mentality which, while not violent, certainly disparage Judaism. Let me give two examples from personal experience. After an ICCJ conference in Lille, France, in 1989, I was given a lift to the Belgian border by a priest/academic colleague from

Louvain. He stopped at a museum which displayed a precious painting, part of an altarpiece by a famous Flemish artist. "I want you to see this," he said, because this artist, unlike many painters of the period, acknowledged and honoured the Jewish background of Christianity. The Christ figure is in the center of the painting with a group of figures on each side. On one side, the apostles are depicted and on the other side, the patriarchs and prophets of the Hebrew Scriptures." Unable to find a parking placed, he waited in the car while I went in alone. It was a beautiful painting, Flemish in style, highly detailed and richly coloured. A group of schoolchildren were admiring it with their guide. They asked who were the figures on the right side of Christ. He replied, "the apostles." And who were the figures on the other side? He replied, "the disciples". So much for honouring the artistic intentions! The lesson had not penetrated.

The second example took place at an ICCJ consultation on religious education in Heppenheim in 1983. I met a high-level educational supervisor from Finland who informed me — I must admit to my surprise — that religious education was mandatory in Finland and that it included courses in comparative religion. "What religions do you teach?" I asked. "O different forms of Christianity, Hinduism, Buddhism, Islam…" "You teach about Judaism?" I enquired? "O no" he replied, " Judaism is subsumed under Christianity." It is not a new problem and it is not necessarily a harbinger of hatred or violence but the underlying conviction is that Judaism ceased to exist with the coming of Christianity, that it has no independent value or spiritual resources — in short, that its role was to prepare for the coming of Christianity — still finds widespread expression both in post Second Vatican Council documents and in mundane policy decisions about which religions deserve notice in world religion courses.

Moreover, the evangelical imperative, which is constant in some churches and re-asserts itself periodically in others, can also affect Jewish-Christian relations, particularly when Jews believe they are considered little more than "objects" for conversion, and that their religion is demeaned and caricatured to "prove" the superiority of Christianity. (Jews are generally civil libertarians, and have supported freedom of religion, including the right to try to convert by persuasion, so long as there is no coercion. But they do resent the defamation of their faith encountered in some evangelical initiatives.)

Why organizations devoted to Jewish-Christian relations have been reluctant to change their focus

It is an increasingly diverse world out there, and many of the countries in which we live have seen an influx of immigrants from cultures and religions neither Christian nor Jewish. Why not extend our dialogue from Jewish-Christian to "interfaith?" Why not stress shared universal values and seek common ground as a basis for cooperative actions, while preserving respect for differences?

Indeed, some organizations have changed their focus (in the United States, for example, the NCCJ is no longer the National Conference of Christians and Jews; it is the National Conference for Community and Justice). In Britain, the Three Faiths Forum was established to engage the Muslim community in interreligious dialogue. Who could oppose such an approach? And yet, there is a very specific Jewish-Christian agenda with unresolved issues particular to these two faith communities. There is a shared sacred literature, but it is understood and interpreted differently for Jews and Christians. There are historical issues, ancient and modern, that require further research and investigation. There is a need to look further into the parting of the ways between these religions, to understand their origins, their rootedness and their separateness. Many of these questions are particular to the Jewish-Christian relationship, and it is feared their relevance would be lost if that specificity is dissipated in broad, interfaith programs.

Aitken's reference to post colonial theory seems to me to underscore the particularity-universality dilemma. He notes that the application of postcolonialism to biblical studies mirrors biblical issues in Jewish-Christian relations and that misrepresentation of groups such as Arabs in New Testament commentaries is comparable to the portrayal of Jews through the writers on the New Testament and that the (ab)use of the Bible by colonialists has parallels to the application of the Bible to demonise Jews.

Of course, there is similarity in all situations where authoritative texts or traditions are invoked to justify discrimination and persecution against another group. In the US, pro-slavery apologists claimed that the curse on Noah's son, Kush, (the putative father of the Black races) justified slavery but the myth of the Jewish world conspiracy, originally built on

Christian antipathy to Jews, is a unique demonology.

As Christianity emerged out of the matrix of Judaism and defined itself in contrast to, and in conflict with Judaism, its founders were faced with a painful dilemma: how to explain that the religious leadership and most of the people from whom Jesus sprung rejected the messianic claims of his followers? The early Church fathers felt the need to lay this denial to inherent character defects of the Jewish people, and began the development of a systematic polemic against Jews and Judaism, full blown by the fourth century, C.E. It was during this same period that the fantasy of Jews as a brotherhood of evil was first conceived. As outlined and documented by historian Norman Cohn, this fantasy — "spawned as a weapon in the competition between Judaism and Christianity" — had developed into a "coherent and terrifying demonology" by the twelfth century, with accusations that Jews poisoned the wells, killed Christian children to use their blood in the making of Passover matzoth, and practiced various kinds of sorcery as disciples of Satan. [2]

Of course, many of the theologically-grounded myths about Jews fell by the wayside (although blood libels and the belief that Jews had horns persisted well into the twentieth century). Others, however, flourished in secular form. Abetted by the infamous forgery, *The Protocols of the Elders of Zion*, the myth of the Jewish World Conspiracy gained ground in many places at the very same time that its theological support system was losing credence. People who discounted the literal existence of sorcerers and Satan nevertheless found it eminently believable that there was a secret Jewish government aimed at domination of the entire world, and that all Jews were the instruments of this world conspiracy. About no other minority group have so many contrasting — indeed, contradictory — images been projected: Jews as both the founders and subverters of capitalism, as financiers and labor agitators, bankers and communists. What these shifting images share in common, at closer examination, are manipulation, deviousness and hidden power

I do believe that a demonology so specific, so enduring and so deadly is unique and requires a special and determined focus by religious leaders, scholars, teachers and activists to recognise, confront and overcome. American Indians, and South African Blacks have suffered from policies justified by appeals to Scripture but they have not been accused of running the world. It is worth remembering that *The Protocols of the Elders of Zion* is presently a bestseller in the Arab world.

This does not mean the Jewish-Christian dialogue cannot impact on the relationship between other groups, ethnic, national or religious. On the contrary, the successes and achievements of the Jewish-Christian dialogue provide a lesson and hold out hope for resolving other conflicts and tensions. Here are two faith communities with a history of persecution and violence from one side, and of resentment and mistrust from the other. (There were golden instances of coexistence and cooperation, but except for Spain — which ended tragically in the expulsion of the entire Jewish community in 1492 — these were few and far between.) The courageous initiatives of a few leaders, scholars and religious thinkers have allowed these communities to move from enmity and suspicion to an unprecedented level of mutual trust and co-operation, not by ignoring their differences but by accepting and trying to understand them. Jewish-Christian rapprochement has not been a search for unity. Faith is not a universal solvent to wash away distinctions. The differences may annoy but they are also precious. Both religions have learned from exploring them. The ground rules of the dialogue have protected and sustained both parties and even in times of anger and stress there is a commitment to continue the relationship.

Other groups have historic enmities and deep-rooted antagonism. Perhaps the lessons of the Jewish-Christian encounter are exportable in this regard. The importance of scholars who are willing to work together is inestimable. (There is little as counterproductive as an exchange of ignorances.) Facing differences is better than ignoring them. Respect and empathy for others can emerge from telling our stories but we must also listen to each other's stories. Neither the power of the state nor the power of the Church can be used to resolve theological issues between religious groups.

An observation by Aitken regarding compartmentalisation of areas of church activity is certainly true in the US and has an impact on Jewish-Christian relations, perhaps more so with Protestant denominations than the Roman Catholic Church (where policy making is more centralised). Protestants who engage in dialogue have come to understand the Jewish attachment to the Land of Israel as a central component of Jewish self-understanding but are not involved in drafting US Middle East Policy (which is sympathetic to the Arab position). Efforts by Christians whose opinions have been tempered by the Dialogue — or by Jewish organisational representatives — are often dismissed as 'special pleading.'

In addition, the fruits of the dialogue have not always penetrated the work of the liturgists or directors of education.

Clearly, more cross-fertilisation is necessary yet, despite the problems, Jews and Christians have achieved a measure of mutual respect and solidarity — imperfect though it is. They have done so in the face of permanent and irreconcilable differences, holding to their separate truths yet willing to work together for the healing of the world. If that is so, the ground rules which have allowed their dialogue to prosper should be transferable to other groups and other conflicts.

Notes

[1]   Bernhard Olson *Faith and Prejudice*, (Yale University Press, 1963, p 196).

[2]   See "The Myth of the Jewish World Conspiracy: A Case Study in Collective Psychology," *Commentary*, June 1966, pp. 35-42.

Conversation Seven

The Road Ahead:
The Next Generation Speaks

Reflections on the Goals and Nature of Jewish-Christian Relations

Melanie J. Wright

Introduction

Like the other contributions to this volume, this piece began life as a presentation at the Cross-Generational Conference in Cambridge, 2001.[1] During the conference, as I reflected on the title I'd been given — 'The Way Ahead: The Next Generation Speaks' — I found the task before me puzzling. As I write this, some unease persists, largely in relation to the terminology used and the assumptions it evokes.

Firstly, many dialogue practitioners (I think) aspire to speak primarily or only for themselves, and are less willing to claim to represent a movement, nor yet an entire generation. Moreover, although there can be dialogue between groups (2001 is the United Nations Year of Dialogue among Civilizations) it often seems that many participants in bi- or multi-lateral religious dialogue are not very representative of their traditions as a whole. For example, they may be adherents of traditions normatively suspicious of activities that challenge participants to re-assess their own self-understanding in the light of Others' experience and perception. There are also people who are interested in dialogue but have severed links with institutionalised religion, perhaps because they are affected by interfaith marriage or because their religiosity is highly individualised and integrative of resources drawn from a number of faith traditions. Awareness of these kinds of disjunctures is implicit in some contributions to this volume.

Secondly, the world of education, of which I have most experience (and which is the *locus* of much of the work necessary for future Jewish-Christian amity) has moved away from the view that one's chronological

JEWS AND CHRISTIANS IN CONVERSATION

age should be determinative of opportunity or status. Contemporary discourse emphasises 'lifelong learning,' the idea that interests and capabilities, rather than one's birth-date, decide one's place in the system at a given time. Yet the title, 'the next generation speaks,' implies that in Jewish-Christian conversation, generalisations based on chronological age are in some sense valid. Is this assumption accurate?

All this is a tortuous but necessary way of saying that the following should be read only as personal reflections arising from involvement in Jewish-Christian Relations in the past dozen years or so, and more immediately from the experience of the conference.

Different Voices: Turning the road less travelled into a well-worn path

So, which way/s now for Jews and Christians in conversation? Recent years have witnessed the appearance of volumes with assertive sounding titles — *The Future of Jewish-Christian Dialogue; Christian-Jewish Dialogue: The Next Steps* — but whose contents attest to a lack of consensus as to future direction.[2] Marcus Braybrooke speaks of a general sense that despite the achievements of the last fifty years, "Christian-Jewish dialogue has got stuck"; participants are oftentimes "treading water"[3] Alan Unterman goes further, disputing the presupposition behind much Jewish-Christian encounter, that is, the idea "that all religions exist on the same level, and that we inhabit a kind of mega-store of faiths". He argues that "the existence of unique, different, and incommensurate faiths is more in line with the existential reality of faith communities."[4] At our conference Judith Frischmann posed similarly pertinent questions, challenging whether Jews need conversation with Christians (other than as a pragmatic strategy) and if they do, whether it is meaningful to talk around the concept of shared textual tradition. There is a need to rethink both goals and rubric. Next century's dialogues cannot simply re-hearse the older agendas. They will need to re-theorise and re-conceptualise relations between communities (their nature and conduct). Holding diverse demands in creative tension will be a significant challenge for conversationalists in the future.

In this volume, a number of interfaith professionals offer their insights on the past conduct of Jewish-Christian relations and prophesy as to the

248

likely future course. Later, I will outline some suggestions about way/s ahead. But any ideas mooted here are made with humility; one thing Jewish-Christian conversation must do to ensure a viable, credible future is to attend to different voices.

It is common in dialogue circles to hear about the difficulties involved in translating the work done in committees and colloquia into actual bridge-building between ordinary Jews and Christians. One session in the Cross-Generational conference was titled, 'Presenting the Dialogue to the Public.' In another (on institutional documents) much discussion concerned the need for changes initiated at 'top-level' by the 'elite' to filter down to regional and local levels. Such discourse is predicated on hierarchical models of religious and community life, where (expressed simply) authority rests with a relatively small number of specialists, whose role is to disseminate authoritative teaching to the ordinary member. But these models may appear strangely out of date - even offensive - to religious adherents in the twenty-first century. Many denominations are changing their understandings of authority and leadership. For example, believing that religions must speak to the needs and in the idiom of contemporary members, Reconstructionist Judaism has tried to reconceptualise the rabbinical role. Rather than understanding the rabbi as an halakhic authority, preacher, or 'vicarious Jew' who models correct behaviour for the congregation, Reconstructionism trains rabbis to be teachers and facilitators. Alpert and Staub write, "The Reconstructionist rabbi wants to help Jews assume as many of the rabbis' functions as possible — by teaching as many people as are willing to learn to do the things that he or she has learned to do."[5] Of course, this is a somewhat idealised account, and Reconstructionism is a minority position within Judaism, but the goal of a community of empowered, engaged individuals is one that many Jewish and Christian groups would share. For this reason, efforts to broaden Jewish-Christian conversation need to take the experience of 'everyday' or 'typical' Jews and Christians more seriously than has sometimes happened in the past. Future discussions will need to be less about how to accelerate the 'trickle-down' of new theology and more about exploring the implications of a real commitment to inclusivity for our understandings of what dialogue is.

By way of illustration, the *modi operandi* of dialogue groups are socially conditioned, that is, they are patterned by culture, class and time. In Britain, a typical CCJ branch might regard the organisation of an annual series of speaker-meetings, punctuated by social events such as a cheese and wine party or a choral evening, as appropriate to the furtherance of its goals. The committee might, in the interests of inclusivity, attend to the provision of *kosher* refreshment at these events. But if the conversation between Jews and Christians is to broaden beyond the predominantly white, predominantly male, predominantly middle class circles with which it is associated today, there is also a need to discuss whether these types of events assume a particular set of cultural variables, thereby establishing barriers to dialogue — excluding those for whom attending a lecture, sampling cheese and wine, listening to European choral music, or leaving dependents at home in the evening would be uncomfortable, alien experiences.

Taking these questions seriously, perhaps drawing insights from the social sciences, could benefit Jewish-Christian relations in several ways. Broadening the ethnic, religious or socio-economic profile of participants can enliven the dialogue and promote wider ownership of concerns and developments. Equally, conversations about expanding participation can develop sensitivity to some of the factors that are crucial to actual reconciliation and community building between groups and individuals. They can highlight the barriers to change within exclusive cultures, or foster understandings of equal opportunities that move beyond 'treating everyone in the same way' towards cultural sensitivity, recognition of the effects of past discrimination, and treating people in ways that bring out the best in them.[6]

New Routes through the 'Old Agenda': Shoah and Israel

As suggested earlier, broadening participation will impact on the mode and focus of Jewish-Christian conversation. At present (from my European, Anglophone, perspective) it seems likely that the future agenda will combine both older and newer items.

In the post-war era Jewish-Christian encounter has been dominated by two historical events — the *Shoah* and the creation of the state of Israel. Most readers will be aware of their significance for the dialogue, which is also touched upon by other essayists. So I will only note here that the *Shoah* was a major impetus for Jewish-Christian dialogue, accelerating the creation of organisational frameworks for contact (the Council of

Christians and Jews was founded in Britain in 1942) and revision of Christian teaching on Jews and Judaism, already prefigured in the work of figures like R. Travers Herford and James Parkes in the 1920s and 30s. In less generalizable ways, Israel has also been a significant topic of conversation. For some Christians, as for some Jews, the creation and survival of the state indicates the continuing validity of God's covenant with Jews, and practical support for the state is an expression of Christian solidarity with the chosen people. Yet Israel can equally be a source of painful encounter, particularly if Christians seem to champion uncritically the Palestinian cause, or do not comprehend the notion of a religious tradition that regards one land as more holy than others.

The issues of the *Shoah* and Israel will continue to figure in Jewish-Christian conversation. For Christians, responsible ownership of their tradition must entail engagement with that tradition's history, including in many cases an awareness of its role in Jewish suffering in history and the fraught question of the interplay between Christian anti-Judaism and the conception and implementation of Nazi policy. Thinking through the issues will probably require repeated intra- and inter-religious dialogue. However, Jewish-Christian conversation conducted on the basis of any assumption (implicit or explicit) that Christian responsibility for the *Shoah* is inherited by generations increasingly distant from the events is likely to have more limited use-value as we move further into the twenty-first century. Perhaps on this issue it *is* meaningful to speak of inter-generational difference: participants who cannot access communicative memory of the *Shoah* will approach things differently. However, it is one of the more experienced figures in the dialogue, Norman Solomon, who has recently emphasised that no healthy relationship may be built on guilt.[7] New forms of discourse about and around the *Shoah* are needed, perhaps focusing on the problems of pain and suffering raised for both traditions by the events, or (as Michael Signer suggests elsewhere in this volume) exploring its implications for all our understandings of tradition and modernity.

Vis-à-vis Israel, too, new conversations are likely to recall but also modify older ones. If currently faltering bi- and multi-lateral negotiations succeed in resolving old conflicts and shaping a peaceful Middle East, this will clearly impact on Jewish-Christian conversation about the land. Rather in the way that the Peace Process has improved Israel's diplomatic standing in the international community, lingering reservations on the part of some Christians about Israel's right to exist could be expected to diminish.

Moreover, peaceable relations with the Muslim world would advance Jewish-Muslim dialogue in ways which are as yet unforeseen but which would affect Jewish self-understanding in relation to Christian tradition.

Praxis or Doxa?

In addition to new exchange on the *Shoah* and Israel, other significant topics of (or trends within) Jewish-Christian conversation are emerging. The first set of concerns I will touch on relate to a growing awareness of the limitations of the answers theology can offer to the questions raised by the realities of Jewish-Christian encounter. One session at the Conference was titled, 'What the Institutional Documents Have and Have not been telling us.' Read pedantically, what institutional documents do not tell us is about the attitudes and activities of people who do not produce institutional documents. These might be (for example) marginalized or disenfranchised members of document-producing groups, or people who belong to traditions that do not engage in these sorts of activities. Perhaps, as was suggested in one of the conference working groups, Jewish-Christian conversation needs to be reconceived not simply as verbal exchange, or as a primarily cerebral exercise, but as 'communication' or 'relation' in much broader terms. Students from the Cambridge Centre for Jewish-Christian relations this year reported that living together gave them experience of a more profound 'dialogue' with the Other than took place in some classroom sessions — it offered a genuine existential encounter. The quest for resolution of past problems in the form of a set of words in an institutional declaration or theological treatise will ultimately be fruitless. Although vitally important within some organisational structures, such things are always 'in process.' A new emphasis on encounter through event and lived experience is needed. (James Aitken develops related issues on communication in this volume.)

Further evidence that the answer to problems in Jewish-Christian relations is not exclusively (or primarily) a theological one may be found in studies of action during the *Shoah*. One family of churches not given to producing explicit theology, the Historic Peace Churches, exhibited significant diversity of behaviour under Nazism. Particularly interesting for the understanding of the dynamics of Jewish-Christian relations is the record of the German Mennonite community. Although core elements of Anabaptist theology — radical church-state separation; pacifism — should (*if* one assumes that having the 'right theology' leads to 'right action') have prevented them from participating in the Nazi project, German Mennonites abandoned their heritage in order to support Hitler. To understand this striking behaviour, one needs to turn not to theology, but to the socio-political realm. Many of the church's members were returnees from the Soviet Union (their ancestors had been invited there by Catherine the Great, to escape Prussian persecution) and consequently, in the context of the new ethnic politics, were keen to prove their identity as 'true Germans.' Failure to do this would have negative consequences for the Church.[8] In sociological terms, German Mennonites abandoned their goals in order to safeguard their institutional structures. Similarly, in a recent study drawing on survivor memoirs, Szczepinska has suggested that religious identification was relatively insignificant in determining the likelihood for inter- or intra-faith cooperation during the *Shoah*. What mattered was the ability of individuals to engage with the humanity of the Other.[9]

In short, there seems to be a growing recognition that fostering positive Jewish-Christian relations is as much about developing *praxis* or practice as it is about formulating right doctrine. Textual studies and philosophical underpinnings are important, but of equal (greater?) value are attempts to theorise and reconstruct the dynamics of inter-group and interpersonal behaviour.

Is the Medium the Message?

Another strand emerging in today's conversations relates to the significance of the media (especially print media and television journalism) in shaping popular perceptions of religion, and the ability of popular cultural forms such as literature and film to serve as *stimuli* for and vehicles of religious experience and theological reflection. Discussing recent debate surrounding the Jedwabne massacre, Konstanty Gebert's essay clearly illustrates how Jewish-Christian dialogue can be conducted through – and therefore constructed by – the media. There are also many examples of how literary and artistic forms are instrumental in Jewish-Christian exploration. In Britain, William Shakespeare's *The Merchant of Venice* is still a staple of both GCSE and A-level (secondary school) English Literature syllabi. Many schoolchildren (who are generally neither members of religious communities nor theologically literate) shape their perceptions of Jewish-Christian relations whilst studying Shylock and his treatment at the hands of the Venetian state. To cite another example, the making of Scorsese's *The Last Temptation of Christ* in 1988 provided an occasion for antisemitic activity against MCA chair Lew Wasserman.[10] Equally troubling from a Jewish-Christian relations perspective, the film itself (characterised by the anti-Wasserman lobby as a Jewish attack on Christian fundamentals) is — like most biblical films — visually indebted to the traditions of classical painting, including some deeply problematic pieces like Hieronymus Bosch's *Christ Carrying the Cross*, which depicts a crowd of grotesque faces about to submerge the irenic face of the suffering saviour.[11]

Few people would dispute the power of these images. The name 'Shylock' entered the English language as a synonym for a money-lender or loan-shark; there is a verb, 'to shylock,' meaning to lend money at exorbitant rates. Many readers will recall at least something of the *furore* surrounding *Temptation*. Yet despite this, Jewish-Christian relations (of the activist or academic kind) has barely engaged with the worlds of literature and the arts. In part, this is attributable to the history of Jewish-Christian discourse. The conversation has often been conducted between men (less frequently between women and men) whose training is in the fields of theology, religious studies, history or Jewish studies. These disciplines historically privileged the study of texts, or more particularly, certain kinds of texts.[12] Jewish-Christian relations, with its comparative neglect of artistic media and forms of popular cultural expression, has perpetuated these biases.

There is a need for Jewish-Christian conversation to embrace more warmly the worlds of literature, cinema, and fine art. This is partly because many practitioners in these fields lack knowledge of Judaism and Christianity, and their inter-action: According to one popular guide to *The Merchant of Venice* for A-level and undergraduate students, *Pesach* observance still entails animal sacrifice.[13] If Jews and Christians are concerned to advance understanding and combat ignorance, they need to care about how people in the literary world are constructing religious identity and meanings. But at the same time, attempts to comprehend the dynamics of Jewish-Christian relationship in the twenty-first century must recognise that literary texts and other cultural products — and their reception — do not simply reflect or document history, but actively constitute it. In order to make effective interventions, or to comprehend the encounter in a fuller sense than simply concentrating on the theological dimension can allow, it is necessary to understand the 'language' of these media — the rules, codes and strategies that come into play when they envision 'reality' for their audiences.

Jews, Christians, and Power

The final cluster of questions I want to raise relate to Jews, Christians and what I will loosely term, 'power.' Any introduction to Jewish-Christian relations will include an account of how Christian power has been exercised to the detriment of Jews. This is most clearly illustrated with reference to the medieval period in Western Europe, when convergence of church-state interests enabled the Fourth Lateran Synod to isolate Jews from 'normative' society by, for example, forcing them to wear special dress, and avoid travel during Holy Week. But there are contemporary examples, too. In Russia, Jews are amongst those affected by *Duma* legislation of the 1990s, whereby religious groups are relegated to a secondary status behind that of the Russian Orthodox Church (which is not legally established, but recognised by the state as having a special role in the formation of national spirituality and culture). Jewish activity is liable to suppression by the courts, if it is interpreted as a source of dissent from the religious or political hegemony, or viewed as a moral threat. Until 2000, Jews in Greece (like the rest of the country's non-Orthodox adherents) had their identification cards stamped with a special symbol indicating their non-normative affiliation. Much Jewish-Christian conversation has, therefore, rightly been about Christian acknowledgement of, and repentance for, the abuses inflicted by Christendom upon Jews. But in the years ahead, will it be profitable to conduct dialogue on the assumption of Christian power and Jewish powerlessness?

Tony Bayfield (the Chief Executive of the Reform Synagogues of Great Britain) has argued that Jewish-Christian relations today is characterised by asymmetries, one of these being an asymmetrical balance of power in favour of Jewish dialogue participants.[14] He notes that the Catholic Church has changed significantly since 1945, revising doctrines and opening itself to dialogue partners. Moreover, the Vatican has recognised Israel, and John Paul II has visited the Great Synagogue in

Rome. But in response, Catholics have been exposed to strong criticism, concerning the Church's decisions over canonization, its attitude towards past holders of papal office, and so on. At the same time, conversation with Christians has not generally required (or been held to require) of Jews equivalent soul-searching and self-criticism. Just as Solomon has argued against basing conversation on *Shoah*-guilt, so arguably the asymmetries inherent in current dialogue may not provide firm foundations for future cooperation. For Bayfield, "real dialogue pushes Jews into addressing some of the issues that we have hitherto only been insisting that Christians address."[15] Only when Jews explore such questions as the status of the New Testament text, or the implications for them of Jesus's Jewishness, will the relationship be one characterised not by inequalities, but by shared vulnerability and willingness to trust one another.

The suggestion that Jewish-Christian conversation should be at all theological remains controversial, despite the broad-based support given to this kind of position by signatories to *Dabru Emet*. For many Orthodox Jews in particular, doctrinal issues should not be discussed — indeed, they cannot be — Judaism and Christianity are unique faith orientations, each possessing their own languages and mental categories, "if the debate should revolve around matters of faith...then one of the participants will be impelled to avail himself of the language of his opponents. This in itself would mean surrender of individuality and distinctiveness."[16]

However, whether conversation focuses on matters theological, or on ethical problems such as war and peace, abortion, business ethics, or stewardship of the natural world, Jews and Christians in the future will, it seems, need to explore questions of power — not just in history, but also within their own, diverse encounters today.

In addition to considering the dynamics of power within interfaith encounter, it seems probable that Jews and Christians will be drawn into dialogue about (and with) the wider discussions on the nature of power and authority in contemporary society. Taking quite different approaches, the contributions of Jurgen Manemann and James Aitken to this volume both raise questions about religious commitment *vis-à-vis* contemporary polities. How do Judaism and Christianity — individually, and together — stand in relation to efforts to balance the demands of the modern economy (the quest for competitiveness on a regional or global basis), the need for social cohesion, and the liberty and freedom of the individual?

Questions about the role Christianity and Judaism should play in today's societies are far-reaching. In a British context, much discussion of the religion-state interface has tended to focus on whether the Churches of England and Scotland should follow the Church in Wales and be disestablished. In the USA, church establishment has been cultural rather than legal; that is, Christianity has long been identified with general social values and with the *mores* of the dominant classes. But many Christians feel themselves and their ideals to be increasingly peripheral in a largely consumerist society. Meanwhile, in Israel a central issue of controversy is the extent to which the country should manifest a Jewish *religious* identity. Nowhere is this more sharply disputed than in relation to personal status, over which (so far as Israeli Jews are concerned) Orthodox rabbis have jurisdiction. These examples show why discussions about the nature and desirability of power and authority deserve prominent place on the agenda for Jewish-Christian conversation.

In the post-Cold War era, the term 'civil society' has become something of a catch-phrase or mantra, around which much debate has coalesced. Discussions about civil society centre around how one might nurture and sustain societies of people who have rights, and accept obligations; societies which try to prevent exclusion, and are based on trust, voluntarism, and co-operation. They touch on issues of economics (especially the role or private initiatives and enterprise), politics (sovereignty and constitutionalism) and culture (including the interaction of the 'religious' with the 'secular' in society). These conversations have been particularly significant in the post-communist countries of East and Central Europe, where strong civil society is associated with the development of healthy democracy. However, more recently the concept of civil society has been discussed in Britain and North America, in response to social disintegration, disillusionment with unfeeling capitalism, and public fatigue with existing political systems.

What is unclear at present is the role of Jews and Christians *together* in shaping civil society. There are several strong reasons why Jewish and Christian conversationalists might feel a need to explore this in the future, and to clarify their responses. Firstly, although in ideal terms a civil society will act in ways that represent and serve the public good, the public good/ public interest is highly contested. (Studies have shown how even ostensibly consensus-oriented events, like public ceremonials and other celebrations of what is sometimes termed 'civil religion,' may in fact be occasions for conflict among varied interest groups.[17]) Jews and Christians may want to participate in the 'contest' to define the public good. If they do not, they may see society develop in ways that do not reflect, or even actively oppose, their traditions' ethical teachings or ritual practices. At the same time, Jews and Christians concerned about dialogue may have an interest in wider conversation about the creation of societies characterised by inclusivism and trust. For example, one aspect of the discussion of civic culture focuses on how far societies are able to embrace their own historic cultural particularisms without engendering hostility towards other particularisms, or alienation from the emerging global community.[18] These issues are profoundly relevant to interfaith dialogue, as are efforts within civic education programmes to raise consciousness about the nature and impact of stereotyping.

In addition to enhancing discussion about civil society, Jews and Christians can benefit from active participation in these debates. For example, ideas about fostering civil society as a means of social renewal may be useful for Jews and Christians rethinking the authority structures within their own denominations. The civil societarian's dream of an alliance of empowered, motivated people resonates with the ideals of religious adherents who seek to rejuvenate their own communities through the creation of more participative structures and practices. Finally, and perhaps more interesting, are the implications of the prominence of Central and Eastern European voices (and increasingly, African, Asian and Latin American voices) in the civil society debate. Too frequently, Jewish-Christian relations discourse still characterises these parts of Europe as places of, at best, comparative *stasis* or stagnation in comparison to the progressive 'west,' and at worst, as sites of Jewish suffering and danger (see also Konstanty Gebert's paper in this book). Incorporating the topic of civil society into Jewish-Christian relations would entail listening to and learning from Poles and Hungarians (or Argentinians and Yemenis) challenging (in particular) Anglophone assumptions, and thereby correct another of the asymmetries that blights our conversations today.

Conclusions

As I stressed earlier, the essay has been limited in scope and has been a personal statement on emerging trends and needs within the dialogue. I have tried to show that much has been achieved. But at the same time, the fact that Jewish-Christian conversation has attained a certain level of maturity necessitates re-assessment of its goals and nature — a questioning of the fundamentals underpinning our encounters. In prosaic terms, just as roles within an organisation typically become more differentiated as that organisation develops and grows over time, so individuals and institutions associated with Jewish-Christian dialogue can no longer try to cover all the bases. In discussing possible roads ahead, I deliberately chose to talk about diverse possibilities, as an indication of the scale and scope of the task ahead.

It seems to me that much current uncertainty as to our next steps together stems from a confusion of different kinds of Jewish-Christian conversation. Too frequently the roles of the academic practitioner and the activist practitioner are conflated. This can result in, for example, our defining as 'interfaith dialogue' activities (like the lecture–meeting or the colloquium) more accurately described as intellectual exercises. In consequence — as already suggested — our efforts may work against genuine existential encounter and reconciliation. Conversely, much 'scholarly research' in Jewish-Christian relations has not kept pace with developments in the wider academic context. I am speaking here both of work in history, psychology, politics and so on, and of the engagement with critical theory in other forms of inter-religious dialogue. Of course, an individual may adopt both activist and academic roles; usually interest in one is motivated by a prior involvement in the other. But for viable future growth to be possible, it is important to differentiate these roles; to be clear about what sort of conversation we are engaged in at a particular moment, and about the nature and 'standards' of that discourse. In this respect, I concur with Norman Solomon's call for increased professionalization of the dialogue. However, I do not think that the goal should be to establish Jewish-Christian relations as an 'academic discipline in its own right.'[20] The concept of a discipline normally implies a degree of consensus or uniformity as to presupposition, theory and method. It seems unlikely that this type of approach could tell us all we want or need to know about the relations between two families of traditions. Instead, Jewish-Christian relations needs to be established more firmly as a *field* of study, rather in the way that 'Holocaust studies' is accepted today as a field within which people use tools and insights from a range of different disciplines (either discretely or in combination) to tackle broadly related questions.

In short, if we can think seriously about the processes and dynamics of our conversation, then we can find new ways ahead for Jews and Christians together. I have tried to suggest that work is needed to think about what it might mean to undertake successfully the vital task of popularising the dialogue — not just its concerns and goals but also its mechanisms and processes. But equally, conversationalists who wish to don the 'academic' hat must not (as has occasionally happened in the past) believe that the worthiness and rightness of our desire to advance inter-religious understanding and respect excuses us from the normal tests and standards of scholarly credibility.

All this will not be easy – philosophically, practically, or personally. Many of us have gained much from our involvements in Jewish-Christian relations. Speaking personally, the friends I have kept in touch with since undergraduate days are those I met in dialogue groups; I have been privileged to attend conferences in interesting places; in blunt economic terms, I pay my mortgage and have food to eat in part because of my involvement in Jewish-Christian relations. Salaries, status and so on may all be at stake if we take seriously the task of critically evaluating and re-thinking the nature and scope of Jewish-Christian conversation. But at the same time, if we genuinely believe in the importance of positive Jewish-Christian relations, and want to share more openly the joy of this 'learning conversation,' then ultimately – regardless of age or generation – we must be willing to hazard those personal gains for the sake of greater, more beautiful ends.

Notes

1   I would like to thank the organisers for asking me to speak, and Lucia Faltin for commenting on a draft of this paper.

2   D. Cohn-Sherbok, ed., *The Future of Jewish-Christian Dialogue*, Lampeter: Edwin Mellen, 1999; M. Braybrooke, *Christian-Jewish Dialogue: The Next Steps*, London: SCM Press, 2000.

3   Braybrooke, *Christian-Jewish Dialogue*, p. 4.

4   A. Unterman, 'An Orthodox Perspective on the Future of Jewish-Christian Dialogue', in D. Cohn-Sherbok, ed., *The Future of Jewish-Christian Dialogue*, Lampeter: Edwin Mellen, 1999, p. 130.

5   R. T. Alpert and J. J. Staub, *Exploring Judaism: A Reconstructionist Approach*, Wyncote: Reconstructionist Press, 1997, p. 83.

6   See comparatively K. H. Ansari and J. Jackson, *Managing Cultural Diversity at Work*, London: Kogan Page, 1995.

7   N. Solomon, 'A Decade in Dialogue: reflections', in D. Cohn-Sherbok, ed., *The Future of Jewish-Christian Dialogue*, Lampeter: Edwin Mellen, 1999, p. 254.

8   See M. J. Wright, 'The Nature and Significance of Relations Between the Historic Peace Churches and Jews during and after the *Shoah*', in S. Porter and B. W. R. Pearson, eds, *Christian-Jewish Relations Through the Centuries*, Sheffield: Sheffield Academic Press, 2000, pp. 410-412.

9   U. Szczepinska, "Jews and Christians on the Side of the Oppressed during the Holocaust in Relation to God and to a Fellow Human", Thesis (MA), Cambridge: Centre for Jewish-Christian Relations, 2001.

10 W. B. Tatum, *Jesus at the Movies: A Guide to the First Hundred Years*, Santa Rosa: Polebridge Press, 1997, p. 163.

[11] D. Thompson; I. Christie, ed., *Scorsese on Scorsese*, London: Faber, 1996, pp. 140-141.

[12] This is no longer always the case, see the approaches of contributors to R. A. Rosenstone, ed., *Revisioning History: Film and the Construction of a New Past*, Princeton: Princeton University Press, 1995.

[13] M. and M. Alexander, *The Merchant of Venice – William Shakespeare* [York Notes Advanced] Harlow: Addison Wesley Longman, 1998, p. 84.

[14] Braybrooke, *Christian-Jewish Dialogue*, pp. 113-126.

[15] Braybrooke, *Christian-Jewish Dialogue*, p. 121.

[16] Summary of J. B. Soloveitchik's position, described in Unterman, 'An Orthodox Perspective on the Future of Jewish-Christian Dialogue', p. 127.

[17] For example, see J. Bodnar, *Remaking America: Public Memory, Commemoration, and Patriotism in the Twentieth Century*, Princeton: Princeton University Press, 1992.

[18] T. Bridges, *The Culture of Citizenship: Inventing Postmodern Civil Culture*, New York: SUNY Press, 1994.

[19] Solomon, 'A Decade in Dialogue', p. 262.

Women's Dialogue, Christology and Liturgy

Helen P. Fry

This volume of essays has clearly attested to the huge strides that have been made in Jewish-Christian relations in the last fifty years, on both the official level and through the personal encounter of individuals. Jews and Christians have travelled a long way along the road towards mutual recognition and reconciliation. The early pioneers have left a powerful legacy — they have transformed Jewish-Christian relations — and with it they have built foundations to ensure that there can be no turning back to the dark days of our history.

Those relations have moved from deep hostility, mutual contempt, the unspeakable tragedy that culminated in World War II, with the Shoah and the questions it raised, to a capacity to communicate, to reason together. The dialogue has achieved a depth of mutual understanding that makes possible the ability to confront the most painful issues with an openness and understanding.[1]

With such solid foundations, in this chapter I wish to focus on three particular areas which form significant challenges to Jewish-Christian relations for the future. The first is the need for women's dialogue, the second is theological and concerns Christology and salvation, and the third is in liturgy.

Transforming the dialogue: Women's Voices and Jewish-Christian Relations

Whilst women have been actively involved in the dialogue and in changing the face of Jewish-Christian relations, often their voices *as women* have not been heard. Much of the structures and theology of the dialogue have been centred on the male experience, and whilst this does not invalidate the enormous advances which have been made, particularly regarding Christian teaching on Judaism, it means that the journey is incomplete. First and foremost, only when *women speak from the women's experience* can they push the boundaries beyond the current plateau that seems to characterise contemporary Jewish-Christian relations. There are important questions to be addressed here: do women have a *distinctive* contribution to make to the Jewish-Christian dialogue? If so, what is that contribution? In what ways is the women's mode of dialogue different from that of the wider dialogue? Are the women who are engaged in this dialogue doing so from a feminist agenda or are they speaking from other experiences?

I will look first at the women's "way" of dialoguing. It is in this respect that women have a distinctive contribution to make to the wider Jewish-Christian dialogue. The genre of the women's dialogue is very different from the mixed groups in the use of story as the mode for sharing experiences. The very process itself of story-telling has affected the way in which women express their identity. It has been initiated solely from the *women's experience* and termed "situated knowledge." In dialogue with *the other*, women have been able to shape their own spirituality and affirm their identity within a new context; as Judith Plaskow, a Jewish feminist, has succinctly expressed, "through the telling of my story, I reach out to other women. Through their hearing, which both affirms my story and makes it possible, they reach out to me."[2]

The boundaries of the women's dialogue tend to be much more fluid and open. It is interesting to observe, as a woman and a participant in the dialogue, that women tend to speak much more from their personal experiences — they tell personal stories. Some of the reflections on the Bible or traditional religious beliefs could be termed a kind of 'midrash.' This is not to say that only women dialogue in this way, but it seems to be that very few men take up this model naturally. The process of 'storying' is important because, "when we tell stories we proclaim, or perform, our identity and make meanings of our experience. Our stories are powerful because they are necessarily particular....As we hear the others' story so our story is potentially transformed."[3]

It is important to encourage more women's participation because rather than diluting one's faith, the "storying" can affirm and enrich our faith experience as women.

It is particularly when we, as Jewish and Christian women, are struggling with issues, telling our stories and sharing our learning, that we are most deeply engaged in   dialogue. A very powerful stimulus for this dialogical sharing seems to be the biblical text, especially a narrative text, and this suggests the power of story in women's Jewish-Christian dialogue.[4]

I have been part of a group of Jewish and Christian women who have met regularly for five years now and it is interesting that there are some experiences which I am comfortable to share within that context and not within the wider dialogue.[5] I am thinking in particular about my perspectives as a Christian woman on messiahship and what it meant for me when I was bearing a child.[6]

A particularly successful area has been the joint study of biblical texts. Barbara Bowe in chapter 1 of this book has illustrated this point in the teaching of the New Testament, particularly John's Gospel, with a Jewish scholar. Such joint teaching and study enables us to deal with our inherently difficult texts. The voices of women have a crucial part to play in the ways in which they bring a different understanding of their textual traditions to the dialogue. One area of grave concern relates to the portrayal in Christian preaching and teaching of Jesus' attitude to women. The (unhistorical) assumption that Jesus was "a feminist" is finding its way into much popular Christian preaching. Not only that, but in anything relating to the status of women, Christianity is deemed superior and Judaism regarded as failing miserably. I cite here one example of such stereotyping from a letter written by a woman in support of the ordination of women, printed in a British provincial newspaper:

> The most popular argument (for non-ordination of women) is that Jesus did not have a woman disciple. First, it must be remembered that Jesus and his disciples were afoot in Palestine at a time when, if a woman even so much as thought about joining a bunch of itinerant preachers, she would probably have been stoned to death. Things in 21st century England are a little more liberated.[7]

Such "factual" material is not found in the Bible, so where does it come from? Christians are actually creating such stereotypes and it forms part of an overall traditional Christian perspective which sees everything in the New Testament as good and true in contrast to a patriarchal, misogynous, and oppressive Judaism. These anti-Jewish statements need to be challenged wherever they appear. The problem is that such anti-

Jewish stereotypes have already been transferred to the mind-set of the readers and are difficult to shift. I asked the people whom I was with at the time about this passage, but nothing struck them as particularly difficult about it and they had assumed that it was accurate. This is cause for concern because there is a tendency for Christians to feel an often unconscious superiority over Jewish faith that allows such statements to go unchecked.

The stereotyping of the status of women in Judaism (both the Judaism of today and the first century) needs to be fully addressed as a matter of urgency in our textbooks, clergy training, and in the universities and seminaries. It is here that the women's dialogue groups can make a significant contribution. I propose two dimensions to the women's joint study programme as a solution for addressing this form of anti-Judaism: first, that women study together the status of women in the Hebrew Bible and the Judaism of the first century C.E.; and second, that they conduct a study of Jesus' portrayal and treatment of women in his ministry.[8] Of course these studies are not, and should not be, limited to the women's dialogue groups, however the women's voices do have a particular contribution to make in how they look at those texts which marginalise women. An example of this is in the Mary Magdalene material in the New Testament where not only has her tradition been marginalised but it has also been neutralised.[9] Because much has already been written in Jewish and Christian circles on the position of women (including feminist writings), it is easy to assume that the work has been completed; but the numbers of Christians who read Jewish women's writings (whether feminist or otherwise) are extremely few and hence the importance argued here for bringing these two dimensions of study together within the context of Jewish-Christian studies.

There are a number of other areas where women's voices could fruitfully contribute to the Jewish-Christian dialogue, including some of the following:[10] prayer, education, tradition, family, Christology, redemption, the nature of God after the Shoah, the importance of symbols, the impact of secularism on religious observance, and liturgy. The area of joint textual study is a particularly enriching one. Such studies are often the most well-attended and popular in any wider joint Jewish-Christian dialogue meeting. Another area where the voices of women need to be heard is in the reshaping of theology after the Shoah.[11] What are their responses to the penetrating religious question: 'Where was God in Auschwitz?' Women survivors of the Shoah have given their testimonies and in this sense their voices have been heard; however on the wider scene few Jewish and Christian women have provided theological reflections on their belief in God after Auschwitz. Could this be because there is nothing new to be said theologically?[12] This is an inadequate assumption precisely because the women's way of storying is different and therefore may provide new insights into theology and spirituality after Auschwitz.

Turning now to the dialogue between feminists, I wish to make just a few brief comments because much more literature is available elsewhere. Since the early 1980s Jewish and Christian feminists have been in dialogue with each other, mainly in America and Germany and this dialogue has produced important results in terms of a recognition that anti-Judaism was developing in some aspects of Christian feminist theology.[13] It represents a significant move and one which may well not have emerged within the context of the wider Jewish-Christian dialogue where feminist issues are rarely, if ever, discussed. Many women who have participated in women-only groups would describe themselves as feminists and they often speak from a perspective where their faith has been shaped by feminist spirituality; however, that is not the case for all participants. Some do not speak directly out of the feminist experience and this is certainly true for some of the women in the Kent House Group, of which I am a part. It is vital to hear the voices of women who are not overtly feminist, whether from liberal, conservative, or orthodox backgrounds, because they too have an invaluable contribution to make to our understanding of faith and identity even though their religious expression may be radically different from our own. The voices of orthodox and conservative participants of both faiths are often sadly missing from the dialogue and this is one area of work for the future.

The challenges then from the voices of women have yet to begin to permeate the wider Jewish-Christian dialogue and the benefits of such a process will have far-reaching implications for the way in which we dialogue. As we move further into the twenty first century I believe that we will see a significant shift in the balance of participants to include groups from the Orthodox traditions,[14] and the voices from Latin America and Africa. The year 2001 marked an historic development for The International Council of Christians and Jews when it held its annual conference in Latin America, and this represented the largest Latin American participation in such a conference so far. The dialogue has rarely included the voices of those from Latin America, Africa, or Asia —participants who have virtually no experience or knowledge of the Shoah. Their theology for Jewish-Christian relations may develop differently because they are coming from a different cultural and historical background, not Shoah-based as in Europe. As the editors have suggested in the Introduction, the Shoah is clearly important for Jewish-Christian relations but the dialogue "cannot be built solely on responses to anti-semitism and Christian feelings of guilt....The sense of guilt is transient and does not pass to the next generation; moreover, it is unstable, inherently prone to sudden and drastic reversal."

Towards an Adequate Theology of the Other: Theological Challenges for Our Generation

Thus far the Churches have made huge advances towards building a theology of respect of Judaism, as reflected in the preceding chapters. Scholars who are engaged in Jewish-Christian relations would admit that there are still theological issues which need to be addressed. From a Christian perspective, our theologians need to look further at three key areas which are inextricably linked, where claims within one directly affect the others: these are mission, salvation, and christology. This is necessary for a coherent *summa theologia* (systematic theology) regarding Judaism because none of these areas can be addressed in isolation from the central tenets of Christian doctrine. Those of us engaged in the dialogue may understand the Churches' difficulty in dealing with these issues because they require a radical re-thinking of Church teaching, as Pawlikowski writes in chapter 5 in respect of the Roman Catholic Church: "the Vatican is well aware that formally to relinquish evangelical outreach to Jews has profound Christological implications that it is unwilling to confront at this time." These beliefs are the central backbone of Christian faith, developed over centuries, and yet if any part of those beliefs lead to anti-Judaism then we are bound to re-examine our faith. This re-examination cannot be done in isolation from our Jewish partners in the dialogue. We need their critical assessment, phrased *critical solidarity* by Clark Williamson, as a safe-guard to ensure that new forms of anti-Judaism are not lurking under the surface.[15]

Mission threatens to disrupt so much of the good work and trust which has been achieved by the pioneers in the field and can only be resolved when our theologians look at the issue of salvation. At the Conference (out of which these chapters have been produced) I remember sitting comfortably listening to, and enjoying immensely, the Jewish scholar Richard Rubenstein and hearing for the first time about his own personal journey in Jewish-Christian relations. Then I was jolted out of this relaxed atmosphere by two of his statements which I found surprising coming from someone who has been engaged in Jewish-Christian relations for so long, "nor do I believe that there is any way that the Christian Church can abandon its message that Jesus Christ has a unique and indispensable role in the salvation of humanity." And again, "Christianity must assert that Christ is indispensable to the salvation of humanity."

I wish to take issue with these statements and suggest that the Church can, and I believe will in the future, shift its understanding of salvation in relation to Jews — hopefully within my lifetime, although that may be over-optimistic. I am aware that because salvation is at the heart of the Christian faith, we have some tough dialogue ahead. I would appeal to the Jewish partners to stay in there because although some of what may be said in response to changes in our understanding of salvation could be explosive, we need to begin to work through this contentious material together. The Christian participants will need the stability and trust built so far to see them through this difficult task. The central question which Christians need now to ask is: *are Jews saved without reference to Christ?* If the Jewish covenant is still valid, as affirmed by so many of our Church statements, then surely it has within it (to use Christian language) the means for Jewish salvation? This for me is the pivotal problem within the whole mission debate. One's theology of mission (missiology) is determined by one's concept of salvation. If the covenant is still valid, then logically there is no need to missionise Jews or maintain a covert hope for their ultimate conversion. As Braybrooke writes in chapter 2: "to recognise that God's covenant with the Jews is still valid calls into question organised attempts to convert Jews." Is it possible to renounce exclusive concepts of salvation, *outside Christ no salvation*, and remain true to Christian identity and faith? I believe that it is and will provide a basic outline of such a framework.[16] As a Christian theologian involved in the dialogue, my motivation is to encourage discussions and hope that my comments may generate some theological dialogue as part of an intra-Christian and inter-faith debate.

In her book *Faith and Fratricide* Ruether disturbed the Christian world by claiming that the shadow side of Christology is anti-semitism. She argued that the ultimate disagreement between Jews and Christians over the messiahship of Jesus led to the denigration of Judaism. Christians believed that Jews had wilfully killed Christ, which meant that God had transferred all the promises of the Hebrew Scriptures to the new people of God, the Church. Ruether then argues that Christian anti-semitism was always forthwith focused on the Jewish rejection of Jesus and it was from this disagreement that the Church developed various myths about Jewish depravity. Christology and anti-Judaism had become so intertwined that now "it may seem impossible to pull up the weed without uprooting the seed of Christian faith as well."[17]

Ruether's linking of anti-Judaism with Christology may be part of the problem but it is not the whole picture. We need to look at the historical links between exclusivist concepts of salvation and the development of anti-Judaism in Christian teaching. In my Ph.D thesis, I have argued through a careful study of five (representative) Church Fathers that the difficulty lies not solely in a disagreement over Jesus but with traditional understandings of salvation. The Church has for centuries defended the idea that there can be no salvation apart from Christ. An ultimate disagreement arose between Jews and Christians over the nature of salvation, and according to certain strands of the Christian tradition (which became normative), Judaism had forfeited its right to be the people of God and no longer had the power of salvation. This in effect made the Jewish tradition worthless and dispensable. This disagreement over salvation led to the denigration of Jews because the very idea of *saving the other* means that *the other* has no separate validity and is deemed to be inferior. The Church Fathers developed a fulfilment christology linked to an exclusivist concept of salvation which fully expected the Jews to convert to Christianity. This exclusivist position necessarily led to an active mission to convert Jews and in making Christianity a viable option on the mission field it was necessary to view Judaism as sinful and to ultimately demonise and satanise it. Christian hostility often intensified when Jews refused to convert.[18] Historically, this linking of mission and salvation had severe consequences for Judaism, leading directly to periods of forced conversion, forced baptisms, legislation which restricted the legal rights of Jews, and the development of certain myths of Jewish depravity (including the myth of the wandering Jew, the mark of Cain, and charges of blood libel). Given this outlook it was always difficult for the Church to appreciate the value of the Jewish faith as a living faith which has not been rendered obsolete by the coming of Christ.[19]

It is possible to disagree with Jews over the significance of Jesus, but this in itself need not lead to anti-Judaism or the denigration of Jews. Jews and Christians can, and will, continue to disagree over the significance of Jesus — not necessarily the Jewish Jesus of history but the Christ of faith. This is an inevitable part of the boundaries of our faith. I believe that Christians can hold onto an absolutist view of Christ, namely that God's fullest revelation is found in the person of Christ, and still affirm that Judaism has the means of salvation for Jews by faithfulness to Torah. This may be holding onto the last bastions of Christian superiority, but it does not necessarily lead back into anti-Judaism. For myself, I would not claim so much. I would argue that it was through Jesus that the Gentile world came to know the Jewish God and we cannot know whether his life and ministry was the fullest revelation from God — that is an historically conditioned judgement that we can no longer make. However for me, the resurrection is central as God's endorsement of Jesus' selfless way of life and obedience, not as a matter of proof but of belief.[20] The Churches have already indicated that they are shifting by their affirmation that the Jewish covenant is still valid — a covenant that has not been made obsolete or superceded by the coming of Jesus. This position has led to a renunciation of any attempts at coercive proselytism or the setting up of organisations with the express aim of converting Jews. Daily, weekly, Christians recite the Apostles' Creed which states: *For us men and for our salvation he came down from heaven.* Can we understand salvation, then, as available through the death and resurrection of Jesus for those who confess it? It is an affirmation by a community of faith and is applicable to the people of that faith rather than a universally accepted truth which includes Jews.

Until the Churches affirm that the Jewish faith provides salvation for Jews without reference to Christ, the possibility of anti-Judaism remains. If Christianity wishes to root out anti-Judaism and develop an adequate Christian theology of Judaism it needs to re-examine its concepts of salvation. This in turn will provide a new framework for our understanding of mission, not in terms of a mission *to* Jews but a mission *with* Jews, in working together to build the Kingdom of God — a task which both faiths understand to be as yet unfulfilled.

Although the salvation debate does affect Christology, I wish to turn briefly to other Christological issues which I suggest are an important part of our theological journey in the future. Significant contributions have already been made in this respect, however there are central questions which our theologians need to examine further. The first area relates to the uniqueness of Jesus: must Jesus always be unique and contrasted with the Judaism of his day for Christianity to make sense?[21] In a sense this may seem a basic question and one which Christians will obviously answer as an unequivocal 'yes'. Those of us engaged in Jewish-Christian studies are keen to root Jesus firmly within the diversity of first century Judaism and therefore, whatever his life and ministry it must be a possibility within Judaism and not a radical departure from it. Must we claim uniqueness for Jesus? Must he be different from every other human being who has ever lived for Christianity to remain true to its inherited tradition? If Christians wish to claim uniqueness for Jesus, and that uniqueness lies in the Incarnation, then how can one affirm this in a way that does not invalidate the Jewish faith? And, what relevance does the *Jewishness* of Jesus have (if any) to the Christ of faith?

The second area in the debate concerns the messiahship of Jesus: if Jesus is not the Messiah of *Jewish* expectation, as confirmed by much New Testament scholarship and joint Jewish-Christian studies, wherein lies his significance? His Christological significance must be located elsewhere. Is it not time for Christianity to re-examine its claims for the messiahship of Jesus? I was amused when *The London Jewish News* reported that the recent Roman Catholic document written by Cardinal Ratzinger, *The Jewish People and the Holy Scriptures in the Christian Bible*, has "shocked scholars from both religions by claiming that the Jewish wait for the messiah is not in vain. According to the cardinal, both religions are waiting for the messiah, Jews for his first coming and Catholics for his second."[22] Hasn't it always been that way? Jews are waiting for the coming of the first messiah and Christians wait for his second coming.

My comments have been preoccupied with Christian concerns, however Christian theology does need the critical assessment of the Jewish partners in the dialogue because our theology can no longer be carried out in isolation from each other. The development of anti-Judaism in certain strands of Christian feminist theology has taught us that much. There may be radical changes ahead for Christian theology, but Jews too need to begin to work out a *Jewish theology of Christianity*, and likewise this cannot be done in isolation from the Christian partners in the dialogue. The recent statement *Dabru Emet* is a fine beginning and solid foundation for the task ahead. Its aims are succinctly defined by Sandmel in this volume, "it is now time for Jews to learn about Christianity in *our* terms, to hear how Christian belief sounds when it is taught in a Jewish language and vocabulary, and in categories that make sense from a Jewish perspective."

Tony Bayfield has issued a challenge to his co-religionists to push the boundaries of their understanding of Christianity in *Jewish terms* by asking two fundamental questions. The first concerns revelation, "is it possible for us, without betraying our own faith and the path we chose at the partings of the ways, to acknowledge that in the New Testament, in the life and death that it portrays, is revelation?"[23]

The second question pertains to the shared scriptures, which both faiths have inherited:

> ... for if we are siblings, born after the completion of the Hebrew Bible, then everything that precedes our birth - the story of Abraham and Sarah, the Torah, the Five Books of Moses, *our* Book of Revelation, the accounts of the journeys of the Children of Israel, the history..... our most cherished liturgy, the Book of Psalms – must be shared? Is that the implication of the partings of the ways?[24]

Christians will welcome such issues to be placed on the agenda on the road ahead, not because they expect this to lead to Jewish conversion to Christianity but as a move equated with the changes which the Churches have made within their own teaching. Many Christians involved in the dialogue would agree that it is no longer sufficient for Jews to see Christianity as an errant form of Judaism, even if that revelation is not applicable to Jews. They would welcome a clear acceptance within Jewish 'theology' that Christianity is a means of salvation for Christians through faithfulness to Christ and represents more than a fulfilment of the Noachide Covenant.[25] The Christian theological re-assessment of its relationship to Judaism needs also to be matched with an adequate Jewish understanding of Christianity if Jewish-Christian relations are to advance in the future.

Understanding Our Tradition: Christian Liturgy and Preaching

273

Attention to our liturgy and preaching is important, as aptly expressed in a working document for discussion within the Church of England:

> Christians' views of Judaism and Jewish people are both formed and reinforced by forms of prayer and biblical exposition as experienced in worship – not only the textual content of the liturgies as agreed centrally, but also the ways in which they are celebrated and interpreted at congregational level.[26]

Many of the Churches have made changes to their liturgy and lectionaries not least because the Jewish-Christian encounter has affected how we hear our liturgies and sermons in the presence of *the other*.[27] There are now an increasing number of occasions where Jews and Christians have reason to be present at the each other's services and this is affecting how we hear our own tradition in their presence.[28] It may be that Jews attend a Eucharist service or Mass because it forms part of a dialogue-weekend or Christians attend a Shabbat service and this forms an essential part of the encounter with the particularity of the tradition of the other. This is not the only liturgical encounter: new liturgies have been developed for commemoration of the Shoah; and also situations are arising where Jews and Christians are present at baptisms,[29] or funeral services.

In 1995, a close friend of mine died and during his final days and nights some of his closest Jewish and Christian friends were asked to sit with him. We shared in a profound way in his dying. I remember in the middle of his last night the local priest asked me questions about my Jewish practice and even though David could no longer communicate easily, a large smile transformed his face. In the quiet of his room at that time it did not seem appropriate to explain that I was not Jewish. We had travelled a long way on our journey together and worked closely through difficult issues which had arisen in our local Council of Christians and Jews; in particular an uncomfortable infiltration of evangelical missionary supporters of Messianic Jews. A week after David's death, his Roman Catholic funeral Mass took place in the local Anglican Church because his Church was too small to hold all the mourners. This raised some interesting dynamics because the Anglicans present along with other non-Catholics and Jews were all united in not being able to take the elements of bread and wine because they were not officially in communion with the Roman Catholic Church. The most difficult part of the service came with the readings which were tied to the liturgy for that week. It was just after Easter week and the reading was from John's Gospel — the story of 'doubting Thomas'. I can vividly remember my shock when the words of the first verse resounded throughout this quiet parish Church, heard in the presence of most of the local Jewish community, "on the evening of that day, the first day of the week, the doors being shut where the disciples were, for fear of the Jews, Jesus came and stood among them."[30]

Shortly after this, the president of the local synagogue gave the eulogy. Nothing was said, of course, about the reading but this experience highlights just how difficult it can be to hear our tradition in the presence of *the other* — the one who has also come (on this occasion) to express grief at the loss of a friend. It has raised a number of questions for me, questions which are still part of the ongoing debate in Jewish-Christian relations and should continue to be part of our dialogue. Should we omit those parts of our traditions which are difficult? On the occasion of this funeral, should the words *for fear of the Jews* not have been read? Could the reading have started at the next verse instead? Do we omit the hard sayings of our traditions and choose another reading or do we confront the challenges which the text poses? Philip Cunningham has published an excellent volume with a preface to each of the biblical texts that are used in Sunday worship in the common lectionary.[31] Each of the texts can be prefaced with an explanation in the light of the new Jewish-Christian understanding. In the context of a funeral, it may not be appropriate to preface the reading with a commentary and so in these circumstances, the challenge of difficult texts remains. In my tradition, the United Reformed Church, the minister or preacher chooses the theme of the service for that week and therefore also chooses the reading.[32] The opportunity is there not to preach on particular texts — *ever*, if the minister so chooses. However, this may be dangerous for Jewish-Christian relations because if we do not read some of our difficult texts in community, or in the presence of the other, the opportunity to deal with them in a constructive way passes us by.

This incident is just one example where the encounter with *the other* forces us to grapple with those parts of our tradition which have led to the isolation and hostility between Jews and Christians for two millenia. When we are present at each other's liturgies or hear the sermons, our faith is not the same again because something changes within us and in our understanding of faith.

Concluding comments

In this chapter, I have focused on three main areas which I see as an essential part of the future dialogue. There have been ground-breaking advances in Jewish-Christian relations, changes which the next generation are proud to inherit. The last fifty years have taught us that through the encounter, both Jews and Christians cannot remain unaffected by their shared experiences. The *encounter* has been the transformative power in Jewish-Christian relations – the meeting with people of a living faith other than our own as well as a realisation of the legacy of anti-semitism in the culmination of the events of the Shoah. It has not always been an easy journey and one which has sometimes been tense and unstable; however solid foundations have been built for the future.

On a personal level, for me, the encounter with Judaism has shaped my faith and profoundly affected the way in which I understand my own tradition. There have been some experiences which have touched the depths of my soul and transformed my understanding of life and death. The following quotation from the Chief Rabbi, Jonathan Sacks, is a poignant reminder of the depth of the Jewish-Christian friendship, "those whose faith is deepest reach the point where, transcending boundaries, soul speaks to soul. Out of that conversation true peace is born."[33]

Notes

[1] John T. Pawlikowski & Hayim Goren Perelmuter (ed.) *Reinterpreting Revelation and Tradition: Jews and Christians in Conversation* (Sheed & Ward: 2000), p.vii.

[2] Judith Plaskow, 'The Coming of Lilith' in *Womenspirit Rising*, (ed.) Carol Christ & Judith Plaskow (Harper Collins: 1990), p.199.

[3] Lynne Scholefield, 'The Importance of Story in Women's Jewish-Christian Dialogue', in *Feminist Theology*, no 23, January 2000, p.70.

[4] Lynne Scholefield, 'The Importance of Story in Women's Jewish-Christian Dialogue', in *Feminist Theology*, no 23, January 2000, p.78.

[5] In Britain, there is currently only one such active group which has met regularly since 1997 to discuss topics such as prayer, messiah, feminist experience, pilgrimage, eucharist, biblical text study, the Shoah and education, and tradition.

[6] I speak more about this in a chapter in a forthcoming book entitled *Women's Voices: New Perspectives for the Christian-Jewish Dialogue* (ed.) Helen Fry, Lynne Scholefield and Rachel Montagu.

[7] *North Devon Journal*, 13th December 2001, p.44, letter entitled "What is so wrong with women clergy?"

[8] This is where the Flexible Learning Network, mentioned by Edward Kessler, can play a vital role in the re-education programme. Such material can be incorporated into courses on Jewish-Christian relations at all levels, whether in short introductory courses, diplomas, or undergraduate and postgraduate degrees.

[9] See Lynne Scholefield, 'Mary Magdalene' in *Women's Voices: New Perspectives for the Christian-Jewish Dialogue* (ed.) Helen Fry, Lynne Scholefield and Rachel Montagu, publication forthcoming.

[10] See also Helen Fry, 'The Future of Christian-Jewish Relations' in Dan Cohn-Sherbok (ed.) *The Future of Jewish-Christian Dialogue* (Lewiston: Edwin Mellen Press, 1999), p.81-96.

[11] For a discussion of the Shoah and Jewish feminism, see Melissa Raphael, 'When God Beheld God', in *Feminist Theology*, vol. 21, 1999.

[12] Have most human responses been developed in this respect - from the death of God theology of Richard Rubenstein to the suffering God imagery of Marcus Braybrooke and Elie Wiesel?

[13] Christian feminists were challenged to recognise that whatever Jesus view of women, it was an option within first century Judaism rather than a radical departure from it. See Judith Plaskow, 'Feminist Anti-Judaism and the Christian God', in *Journal of Feminist Studies in Religion*, vol.7, no.2, Fall 1991, p.105. Also of relevance here is the work of Katharina von Kellenbach, *Anti-Judaism in Feminist Religious Writings* (Atlanta: Scholars Press, 1994).

[14] There are now a small number of Orthodox Christians who have participated in the dialogue and contributed to conferences on Jewish-Christian relations, but these are as yet a small minority. There are major challenges still facing the Orthodox Churches as they seek to address the anti-semitism in their tradition, liturgy and teaching, however there have been small but significant beginnings on the road to reconciliation.

[15] The dialogue between Jewish and Christian feminists have taught us that much when Jewish feminists challenged the anti-Judaism which was developing in much Christian feminist theology.

[16] A more detailed study and rigorous argument can be found in my Ph.D thesis, *Converting Jews? From a Mission to Jews to a Mission With Jews* (University of Exeter: 1996, unpublished).

[17] Rosemary Radford Ruether, *Faith and Fratricide* (Seabury: 1974), p.226).

[18] This was particularly so in the writings of Martin Luther. The young Luther had high hopes that the Jews would see the errors of Catholicism and convert to Protestantism. When they failed to convert, his writings became violently anti-Jewish and can be seen as a bedrock for the later developments in anti-semitism. Compare his early writings, *That Jesus was a Jew* with his later work *On the Jews and their Lies*.

[19] Neither is the continued existence of Judaism to be understood as a preparation for the ultimate conversion of the Gentiles (followed by the conversion of Jews), as expounded in much evangelical millennial theology.

[20] Here I would develop my theology and Christology along the lines of Braybrooke, *Christian-Jewish Dialogue: The Next Steps* (SCM: 2000),

p.74ff.

[21] This question was initially raised by Judith Plaskow in 'Feminist Anti-Judaism and the Christian God', in *Journal of Feminist Studies in Religion*, vol.7, no.2, Fall 1991.

[22] *London Jewish News*, 26th January 2002.

[23] Tony Bayfield, "Response" in Marcus Braybrooke, *Christian-Jewish Dialogue: The Next Steps* (SCM: 2000), p. 124.

[24] Bayfield, *ibid*, p.125.

[25] There are already foundations to build upon; see for example Franz Rosenzweig's *The Star of Redemption*, Samuel Sandmel's *We Jews and Jesus*, and Walter Jacob's *Christianity Through Jewish Eyes*.

[26] *Sharing One Hope? The Church of England and Christian-Jewish Relations: A Contribution to a Continuing Debate* (Church House: 2001), p.29.

[27] A helpful overview of the changes in Roman catholic liturgy can be found in Eugene Fisher, 'The Roman Liturgy and Catholic-Jewish Relations since the Second Vatican Council', in *Twenty Years of Jewish-Catholic Relations* (ed. Eugene Fisher, A. James Rudin & Marc H. Tanenbaum (Paulist Press: 1986).

[28] There is also an awareness on the part of Christians of the Jewish roots of Christian liturgy. See Eugene Fisher (ed.), *The Jewish Roots of Christian Liturgy* (Paulist Press: 1990).

[29] As in the case of my three sons when in 1998 and 1999 some of our Jewish friends attended their Dedication Service (similar to a Christening Service).

[30] John 20. v.19-29.

[31] Philip A. Cunningham, *Proclaiming Shalom: Lectionary Introductions to Foster the Catholic and Jewish Relationship* (The Liturgical Press: 1995).

[32] The readings would reflect parts of the Christian liturgical year, such as Easter, Christmas, Pentecost and so forth, but for some Churches these readings are not necessarily fixed to particular weeks but a matter of choice.

[33] The Chief Rabbi Jonathan Sacks writing about Cardinal Basil Hume in *Celebrating Life: Finding Happiness in Unexpected Places* (Fount: 2000), p.167.

Postlude

Postlude

Martin Forward

I find myself irritated that I could not attend the conference from which these papers are taken. If they are a sure indication of quality, then it must have been the place to be for anyone fascinated by Jewish-Christian relations.

Since there is an excellent introduction that summarizes the content of each contribution, I am free from the need to précis the papers. Instead, I would like to pick out a number of themes that emerge from this collection, and ruminate upon them. In the course of doing so, I will occasionally consider whether some issue might form the basis for some useful further conversation and research. Finally, I will inquire whether there are significant differences in the ways younger scholars interpret the dialogue between Jews and Christians from older ones.

Theme 1: A Brave New World?

The first theme to mention is the context within which our present dialogue is done. Much appears gloomy. The conference took place before the events of September 11, 2001. In its light, Michael Signer's words about the attitude of Haredi Jews towards the contemporary world seem almost prophetic: 'People who have profound suspicions about the modern world and reject its fluidity or pluralistic framework are ready to exploit its technology towards their own ends.' So, within Islam, Osama bin Laden and the Taleban form one strand of the 'fundamentalist' interpretation of religion that is only able to flourish because of modern knowledge and expertise, yet affects to despise much of what it uses or, arguably, mis-uses. Signer's following words may help us to see the difference between such obscurantist fanatics and those who engage in more appropriate religious responses: 'Many of us also exploit that technology but we do not consider the modern world evil, but something that can be transformed by a more nuanced and complex model of its past.'

Au contraire, fundamentalists hardly ever teach and live the fundamentals of life as most religions teach them: where is the fundamentalist passion for social justice beyond their own kind, for compassion, for an inclusive vision that embraces transcendent and mundane reality? Rather, such doctrinaire and blinkered extremists should be called reactionaries, reacting as they do to certain changes in the modern world by focusing upon a shriveled and illusory obsession with their religion, interpreted in an exclusive and intolerant fashion.

Pluralism is surely here to stay, however difficult it is to deal with, whether by governments, factions or individuals. A number of papers in this book witness to this reality, not least that of Jurgen Manemann. By affirming the permanence of pluralism, I mean that diversity is built into the contemporary world in such a way that it cannot be eradicated, though many have tried to do so and will continue to. Religion can easily be used to justify, for example, Afghan culture as Islamic, though tell that to an Arab or a Nigerian or an American Muslim, and she will laugh at the thought. Still, Jews and Christians are equally guilty of purveying essentialist views of religion, as if Judaism and Christianity were monolithic phenomena; or, which is worse, that the particular individual's interpretation of his (it usually is a he, in my observation) religion is the only possible and authentic one to hold. Upholders of a simplistic notion of their own good religion and others' bad faith go against the grain of common sense and easily observable reality, but their pious certainties, however implausible, can cause immeasurable pain and anguish in the world, and effect suffering and even murder in the name of God.

Signer's observations about technology, like all good prophecy, is based on a discerning insight into the signs of the times. Technology, after all, although much vaunted by many unthinking secularist supporters, was put to dreadful purposes in the twentieth century, as the history of the Holocaust shows. It is unlikely to be better utilized in the future, unless we can provide an ethic for inter-religious behavior.

The cynicism of Huxley's brave, new world could easily be held to be a desirable quality for our own circumstances. For the globalization of the postmodern world has not thrown up enough ethically trained religious gurus who can help us to make choices amid its bewildering range of choices the many ambiguous moral state of affairs we often encounter and for which we have no easy solutions. Proponents of the need for a global ethic clearly have a point, though much of their work has the appearance of over-simplicity and betrays a western cultural blinkeredness. Konstanty Gebert's powerful piece about 'Catholics, Jews and Jedwabne' illustrates the need for à penetrating moral vision so that we do not re-enact pride, prejudice and power-games that ought to be things of the past in Jewish-Christian relations.

Theme 2: The Need for Dialogue

The introduction to this book makes a good case for the necessity of dialogue. Indeed, the papers as a whole either explicitly or implicitly witness to its powerful transformative effect upon Jewish-Christian relations. That a dialogical encounter requires a respectful attention to the religiously 'other' should go without saying.

Still, dialogue is a tough word, not a sentimental one. In this regard, it's worth recording the reference to dialogue in the New Testament book, *The Acts of the Apostles*. According to Acts 19, about the late summer of 52, Paul made his way to Ephesus, in west Asia Minor; today, on the Turkish coast, south of Smyrna. The book of Acts records this as a time of great opportunity for Paul, but also when he faced many adversaries. Upon his arrival he found about twelve 'disciples,' possibly followers of John the Baptist, whom he baptised in the name of Jesus. He then entered the synagogue, where for three months he spoke about the kingdom of God. Then he removed to the lecture-hall of one Tyrannus where, for a period of two years, perhaps from about 11am to 4pm each day, he held public debate there. (This is the record of the western text of Acts, different at points from the version in the New Testament, but certainly a credible account of this incident.) Apparently, Paul healed people, and converted numbers of those who had practised magic arts. Just as he resolved to leave the city, Paul fell foul of the president of the guild of silversmiths, Demetrius by name. According to Acts, the guild made a lot of money out of fashioning miniature images of the goddess Artemis. Paul's success at persuading some of her erstwhile worshippers to join the Jesus movement led to a riot stirred up by Demetrius. The silversmiths and others raised the cry, 'Great is Artemis of the Ephesians,' artfully linking the goddess to a sense of civic identity. They manhandled two of Paul's associates; Paul himself had to be persuaded not to go and try to appease the crowd. A certain Alexander seems to have tried to defend his people, the Jews, to the crowd, by dissociating them from the apostle's work but they saw he was a Jew, like Paul, and continued crying out the more. Eventually, the town clerk quieted the crowd, arguing that matters should be resolved with due process of law; he would have been mindful of his responsibility to the Roman colonial authorities for the maintenance of public order. Thereafter, Paul soon left Ephesus.

At first glance, Paul's visit to Ephesus hardly looks like either a success-story or the triumph of dialogue over more violent religious stances. But aspects of the story merit careful attention for practitioners of dialogue, and to those we now turn.

It is intriguing that Paul lasted for three months in the synagogue, arguing his case there. The words used in Acts 19:8 about his teaching method are often translated along the lines of him 'lecturing' and 'persuading' Jews about the kingdom of God. The first Greek word used, transliterated, is '*dialogomenos*'; close to our word dialogue. It could be argued that it is a relaxed or *au contraire* an over-stated view of how language functions to deduce from this that Paul was involved in dialogue in the synagogue. But there are grounds for thinking that he must have been. If he had merely preached, or spoken and not listened, he would surely not have lasted two hours, let alone two months. In fact, all Jews would have believed in God's kingdom. There would have been much common ground between all people at the synagogue and Paul, though most Jews would have drawn the line at his presentation of Jesus as the Messiah who brought in God's kingly rule. So it is very likely that Jews were happy to hear Paul's claims about Jesus, though eventually most wished to reject them, eject him and get on with their religious lives. Even so, according to Acts, it was not the synagogue authorities but some unidentified individuals who 'were stubborn and disbelieved, speaking evil of the Way before the congregation' (19:8; RSV version). Furthermore, when Paul moved his centre of activity to the hall of Tyrannus, he no doubt employed the debating methods of Greek philosophers to attract and interest new Gentile recruits, as well as to edify older followers, just as he had done at the Areopagus in Athens on a one-off occasion (Acts 17:22-34). So there is reason to believe that Paul conformed his method of presenting his good news to the style his different audiences were used to; but also, that he listened and pondered as well as urged and challenged.

Clearly, Paul was not apologetic about his message. With some pardonable exaggeration, the author of Acts wrote that Paul's methods in Ephesus ensured that all residents of Asia (by which the writer meant, roughly, modern Turkey) heard the word of the Lord, whether Jew or Gentile. Yet Paul trusted enough in his own faith not to shout down another's, and he believed that his message built upon his hearers' authentic prior encounters with God. No doubt, he believed that the message of God's dealing with his human children in Jesus should transform the knowledge of God or the gods that his audience had already experienced; yet his good news was no bolt from the blue to people who otherwise would have known nothing of the demands of transcendence upon their lives.

The violent end to Paul's stay in Ephesus does not negate its witness to Paul as a dialogician. Certainly, that uprising helps to underline the fact that the practice of dialogue is no sentimental swapping of insights that have no real value or consequence for people. Paul was a troubler for the sake of truth, as he understood it; he died for his vision. Like many dialogicians, Paul has been a much misunderstood man. His aims and motives have been trivialised. His willingness to listen and learn has been downplayed. He has been claimed by some as a villain, a betrayer; by others, as a proclaimer of exclusive certainties who would brook no other point of view than his own; by yet more, as a misogynist, and the muddier of the clear teaching of Jesus the Galilean preacher that he unnecessarily complicated. Paul was a much more complicated and interesting person than his opponents or even many of his supporters have supposed.

So, dialogue is not simply respect and tolerance (though without it few will get far in their inter-religious relations). Since religious people have some sort of commitment to truth, dialogue with 'other' religious people will reveal clear differences as well as (sometimes, surprising) agreements. My wandering into the world of Paul is meant to illustrate this fact. Just occasionally, the fine papers in this book draw back from an acute analysis of some of the almost impossibly difficult issues that thwart intra- as well as inter-faith dialogue: one such issue is theological and territorial Israel, and how to handle that dialogically in the contemporary world. Another example is found in Marcus Braybrooke's contribution. His recognition that 'in Britain, CCJ [the Council of Christians and Jews] has rejected that

option [of incorporating Muslims into a bilateral dialogue], so besides
CCJ we have the Three Faiths Forum', doesn't quite convey the
exasperation, bitterness and even betrayal that many CCJ members and
others have felt about that process. Even so, this doyen of dialogue has
produced a characteristically wise piece. His comment that when he was
director of CCJ, theological dialogue was *verboten* reminds us that dialogue,
however painful, changes the circumstances within which people handle
relations and even how they manage them. In my opinion, the British
CCJ still officially finds theological dialogue difficult to handle, but provides
individuals with the space and setting where they can raise anything they
wish to, include matters about our knowledge of God, and God's of us.

Theme 3: The Scope of Dialogue

I came to Jewish-Christian relations somewhat late in the day, after a greater
expertise in dialogue between Christians and Muslims. Let no-one argue
that Christian-Muslim dialogue is a non-starter. The sterling work of the
World Council of Churches proves otherwise, as does that of organizations
like the Henry Martyn Institute in Hyderabad, India; and the Christian
Study Centre in Rawalpindi, Pakistan; and extraordinary stories of Muslims
and Christians working with others in South Africa's freedom struggle
against white minority and oppressive rule.

Still, there is nothing comparable to the results in Christian-Jewish
relations, in the dialogue between Christians and Muslims. Quite why this
should be so, is interesting to debate. It may well be that, despite the
flawed history between Christians and Muslims, there was nothing
comparable to the Holocaust to galvanize Christians into repentance and
action, and Jews into better understanding the worlds of dominant
Christian cultures within which they live. A number of contributors to
this book have rightly pointed out that the Holocaust cannot remain the
defining event or the arena within which Jewish-Christian relations operate.
True; but it was the terrible impetus to a sustained, notable, brave, educative
and transforming process of relationship and knowledge between the
two faiths. It isn't easy for a Christian like me to write these words (but, as
I've indicated, how can honest dialogue ever be easy?), given the ease with
which I could be held to be a polemicist, but the willingness of many
moderate and humane Muslims to connive at reactionary, essentialist and

trivial interpretations of the history of Islam has undermined much Christian-Muslim dialogue. Many such Muslims are genuinely scared of what speaking the truth may earn them from noisy, fundamentalist co-religionists. Although Osama bin Laden and his like-minded confreres have attacked western secularized Christianity, international Jewry, and other targets in a simplistic way that seems to glory in spurning self-criticism, they have kept some from noticing the absolutely dreadful governance of many Islamic countries by their Muslim leaders that has also gotten in the way of decent and humane dialogue. Moreover, the sheer poverty of many Muslims calls into question the somewhat wordy and cerebral stance taken by many dialogicians: Christian-Muslim dialogue (and Jewish-Muslim dialogue?) may require a greater dose of social activism than much Jewish-Christian dialogue has needed to engage in. Of course, Christian equivocation about how to dialogue with Muslims in a post-Imperial world hasn't helped improve relations between members of the world's two largest religions, either.

For all that, the achievements of Jewish-Christian relations have much to teach others involved in dialogue. Let me list some of them, in no particular order of importance, all of which could be illustrated from papers in this book:

- Get religious leaders on your side, whether popes, chief rabbis, bureaucrats or whomever.
- Make education of both clergy and laity (or their equivalents) a primary goal. To know and own the past is the first step in the process of changing the present into a better future.
- Recognize that what starts out as a pragmatic or even idealistic stance is likely to be modified by the friendships you make, so that dialogue will come to be done not as a reactive process but often as a proactive one.
- Read the scriptures together and prepare to have your eyes opened, your heart and mind transformed, and your passion for truth and justice summoned forth.
- Learn how to disagree with your fellow dialogician, respectfully and even affectionately.
- Religions have contexts, histories, and are lived on Planet Reality by actual people. They are not confined to the process of mental gymnastics. Dialogicians have to be truth-seekers and problem-

289

solvers, of many kinds.

Well, other things could be added to this list, but this gives the flavor of the considerable achievements that have resulted from about half a century of Jewish-Christian dialogue.

What about incorporating Jewish-Christian relations into multilateral dialogue? Marcus Braybrooke observes that there is a place for bilateral, trilateral and multilateral dialogue. I believe him to be right, but his tantalizing observation could do with some penetrating further thought. (Perhaps this might be done by him in a forthcoming book?) I find some of the arguments for privileging Jewish-Christian dialogue from outside participation to be less than compelling. Perhaps the most persuasive reason for the future of that bilateral dialogue is the somewhat functional attitude: if it's not broke, don't fix it! So much good and creative thought and action comes from Jewish-Christian dialogue that it would seem foolish to pour it into a larger interfaith mould without seriously compelling reasons for doing so. Still, as it continues, it behoves its participants to take Muslim and other interests very seriously indeed, and to ask what can and needs to be done on a broader map of partners.

Theme 4: How to Deal with Texts, Ancient and Modern

A number of contributors point to the importance of dealing sensitively yet faithfully with difficult texts. Although I've gently criticized the somewhat wordy nature of much Jewish-Christian dialogue (and so warm greatly to Melanie Wright's very shrewd paper), one cannot get away from texts. Barbara Bowe's contribution shows how very difficult scripture is to interpret and live by, in the modern world. But also, she makes it seem exciting: a worthwhile wrestling with the particularity and prejudice of documents the faithful believe, somehow, to be holy writ, and which, for many, despite their problems, continue to mediate transcendence to mundaneness. Liam Tracey's and Marc Saperstein's thought-provoking pieces suggest that the liturgy may not be the most fitting place to encounter and appropriate certain anti-Jewish Christian texts, a point with which I am inclined to agree, and which needs further careful elucidation. Edward Kessler's reference to the MA programme of the Centre for Jewish Christian relations could, if he had had more space at his disposal, have waxed eloquent about the struggles students have with scripture, to make inclusive and humane sense of it in their lives.

Incidentally, if I may refer back to Christian-Muslim dialogue, how wonderful it would be if we could honestly sit down and face the difficulties of the Quranic text without having to privilege it from any critical discussion. To be sure, Muslims like Fazlur Rahman, who died in 1978, have begun to help Muslims see the mundane-ness as well as the transcendence of the text, but Christians and Muslims are very far away from the work done by Jews and Christians with their scripture.

Both Kessler and Pawlikowski have fascinating things to say about church documents since the war, as they have touched and transformed Jewish-Christian relations. It is worthwhile pointing out that they have also been uncomfortable for people to deal with. It is certainly true that many Christians (and no doubt Jews) either remain in ignorance of such texts or else ignore their teaching. Still, when I was a church bureaucrat from 1988 to 1995, wandering around Methodist churches in the UK talking about interfaith relations, I took a perverse pleasure in responding to the prejudiced by saying: 'You may very well believe that. The church doesn't, however, teach it. You will have to accept your view as contradictory to the church's interpretation of the meaning of good news, and square that with your conscience as best you can.' By such means, I raised many a laugh from the (relatively) pure in heart at the expense of people who had clearly annoyed them for ages by their doctrinaire prejudices. A more measured comment than the one I have just given would simply note that if anti-Jewishness has been a sad fact of Christian belief and practice for well over a millennium, it will no doubt take well over a decade or two to eradicate it. The cluelessness and even malevolence of some, including those who should know better, ought not to draw attention away from the extraordinary rapprochements that have occurred between Jews and Christians in the last few years.

Theme 5. Is Choice Possible, or even Desirable?

Jewish experience in the twentieth century illustrates how unimportant personal religious choice can be. The Third Reich's racial laws sent people to the gas-chambers as Jews, who were unobservant, wholly secularized or who had converted to Christianity. It is commonplace to hear it affirmed that being Christian is a matter of personal choice, whereas a more complicated web of history and relationships creates a Jew. Still, I think that routine observation to be fundamentally flawed, betraying a culturally parochial western view of religion that Wilfred Smith and others have so effectively challenged. Richard Rubenstein's moving autobiographical reflections, revealing his inability to eradicate his Jewishness by becoming Christian causes me to reflect that something of his insight can be paralleled in Christian experiences.

I offer an example from within the world of Christian-Muslim relations. Once, I had to talk with a very unhappy woman. She had been a practicing Christian in Britain, then met and married a Pakistani Muslim. She converted to Islam, moved with him to Rawalpindi, and they brought their boys up as Muslims, which Muslim Law presently insists upon. When I met her, she had no regrets about her marriage, nor anything but respect for her husband's and sons' religion. But she had come to feel it wasn't for her. Intriguingly, she felt that her identity was bound up with her Christian roots. I concluded that she wasn't fooling herself about the state of her marriage, or about her willingness to live in a far country. She had bravely and discerningly located the major and nagging problem in her life.

Foolish, of course, is the person who would deduce from a story like this that conversion shouldn't happen. People in significant numbers do cross boundaries of religious identity: Jews become Christians, Christians become Jews, and so on; no doubt, sometimes for good reasons, sometimes not. My point is the more limited one that matters of birth, upbringing and early, often tacit allegiances matter to many, perhaps most people. Christian (and Muslim and some Buddhist and other) mythology often fails to wrestle with these deep matters of identity in its sometimes facile missionary zeal. I think that much work could be done in the psychology of conversion that could affect how Christians interpret missionary strategies and goals in the contemporary world. Maybe I should come clean and admit that I have no interest in the conversion of others. On those occasions when I've been drawn into people's debates about whether to remain within one religion or transfer to another, I have wanted to adjust the prophet Isaiah's response to God's call to: 'Here am I. Send someone else.' Still, Christian-Jewish relations need to recognize the strong missionary strand in the younger religion, and ask how it can appropriately be interpreted and operated in our times.

Theme 6. A Future for Theology?

Rubenstein's courteous words about Karl Barth cause me to wonder what is the future for Jewish and Christian theology. Barth (this is my spin), great thinker as he was, did seem to live inside his head much of the time. Although some recent Christian theologians have attempted to rescue and build upon what he said about other religions, it seems an attempt doomed to the failure of irrelevance and, frankly, ignorance. Maybe Rubenstein's and Aitken's enlightening papers indicate that philosophy rather than theology provides a better way forward for Jewish-Christian relations. We have already noted Marcus Braybrooke's admission of what a hot potato theology has been in British CCJ circles.

Still, David Sandmel's excellent piece on *Dabru Emet*, with its suggestion that Jews may now be able to begin articulating a Jewish theology of Christianity, excites me. I doubt whether aspects of such a theology would make many Christians comfortable, but I've already alluded to the discomforts of dialogue. Jews and Christians ought now to have reached a point where we can amicably disagree about central issues. (I am reminded of many exhilarating and lively conversations with a particular Muslim friend who always likes the last word, invariably one of disagreement, yet disarms me by concluding 'but God knows best'!)

Can Christians and Jews do theology together? Despite the reservations of many, it's hard for them not to, given one definition of theology as 'God-talk.' Theology is fundamentally about what sort of God, God is; and, maybe, what sort of people, people are who hold particular beliefs about God. Admittedly the field of religious studies is strewn with the corpses of those aspiring scholars who assume that religious people are all interested in God. Not so: Buddhists fundamentally are not; nor are Confucianists and a pile of other religious people. Not so often admitted is that traditionally theistic religions like Judaism, Christianity and even Islam produce people for whom God is low on their list of dialogical topics of conversation. Still, many Jews and perhaps most Christians are involved in dialogue because of their convictions about God. The church documents about Christian relations with Jews often arise from the conviction that bad church theory and practice about Judaism and Jews fundamentally betrays the sort of God, God is. It would be pleasing to see Jews and Christians work towards Wilfred Smith's vision of a world theology. He did not mean to uphold a totalitarian universal religion. Rather, he maintained that it is not wise to do our theology in ghettos, but together. Only such a joint enterprise is fitting for a global village. I guess that Smith, who died in 2001, may not so much reflect current practice, as prove to be a prophet of the medium-term future. Maybe one of our tasks in Jewish-Christian dialogue is to ponder how we might attain that future, and then translate our ruminations into actions.

Finale: A Generation Gap?

Do the contributions to this book show any significant differences between younger and older scholars? If so, I am hard put to discover them. One or two older scholars are inclined to reminisce, helpfully; a natural reflex of increasing age, as I am beginning to discover. One or two younger scholars are concerned with new initiatives and with distancing Jewish-Christian relations from the Holocaust, as is equally natural. I have the impression (but this may simply be projecting my prejudices upon the evidence before you) that some younger scholars delight in the opportunities of postmodernism, whereas one or two older ones feel wearily and even cynically, like the Preacher in the book of Ecclesiastes, that there is nothing New under the sun.

A great deal is shared in common by all these writers, whatever their age and the differences between them. Not least is a vision that the improvement in Jewish-Christian relations has transformed the disciplines they work in, and continues to be a liberating, if sometimes bumpy, experience. Am I right to think that the younger scholars are impressed and inspired by the achievements and continuing commitment of older intellectuals? And am I also correct to suspect that older academics have been rejuvenated in their work by the dedication and insights of younger scholars? I would like to think so.